Structured Meanings

⌐┐ Bradford Books

Jon Barwise and John Perry. SITUATIONS AND ATTITUDES. 1983.
Norbert Hornstein. LOGIC AS GRAMMAR. 1984.
Ruth Garrett Millikan. LANGUAGE, THOUGHT, AND OTHER BIOLOGICAL
    CATEGORIES. 1984.
William G. Lycan. LOGICAL FORM IN NATURAL LANGUAGE. 1984.
Rachel Reichman. GETTING COMPUTERS TO TALK LIKE YOU AND ME. 1985.
Gilles Fauconnier. MENTAL SPACES. 1985.
M. J. Cresswell. STRUCTURED MEANINGS. 1985.

Structured Meanings:

The Semantics of Propositional Attitudes

M. J. Cresswell

A Bradford Book
The MIT Press
Cambridge, Massachusetts
London, England

This book was set in Palatino by Village Typographers, Inc., and
printed and bound by The Murray Printing Company in the
United States of America.

Library of Congress Cataloging in Publication Data

Cresswell, M. J.
    Structured meanings.

    "A Bradford book."
    Bibliography: p.
    Includes index.
    1. Semantics (Philosophy) I. Title. II. Title:
Semantics of propositional attitudes.
B840.C74   1985   160   84-21810
ISBN 0-262-03108-6

To George Hughes, Professor of Philosophy at the Victoria
University of Wellington from 1951 to 1983

Contents

Preface   ix

Introduction   3

PART I
Sense and Reference

Chapter 1
Compositional Semantics: An Arithmetical Analogy   9

Chapter 2
De Re Attitudes   17

Chapter 3
Structured Meanings   25

Chapter 4
Structural Ambiguity   33

Chapter 5
Attitudes *De Expressione*   41

PART II
What Meanings Are

Chapter 6
Why Meanings Are Not Internal Representations   53

Chapter 7
Possible Worlds   61

Chapter 8
A System of Intensions   69

Chapter 9
Structured Meanings Again   77

Chapter 10
Iterated Attitudes   85

PART III
Formal Semantics

Chapter 11
λ-Categorial Languages   95

Chapter 12
Indirect Discourse (I)   105

Chapter 13
Indirect Discourse (II)   113

Chapter 14
Discourse *De Se*   121

Chapter 15
Semantics in the Picture   131

Bibliographical Commentary   137

Bibliography   187

Index   197

Preface

In his book *Formal Logic*, Arthur Prior describes the study of expressions like 'it is said by the ancients that', as providing an embarrassment of riches for the logician. It was with such heady thoughts that I went to Manchester as a graduate student in 1961, to study with Prior and solve the problem of propositional attitudes. Although my work, since those far-off days, has not been exclusively concerned with propositional attitudes, that problem has never been far from my thoughts. In this book I try to set out and defend what I now believe to be the correct solution, a solution that makes essential use of structured meanings.

In order to make for easier reading, I have concentrated on presenting a positive thesis. Almost all discussion of the literature has therefore been put into a bibliographical commentary. This occupies a more substantial part of the book than would normally be filled by notes and is designed to be read as a sustained commentary. There are no numbered references in the main text.

A number of people read and commented on the first draft of this book. They include Emmon Bach, Andrew Brennan, Bill Lycan (who suggested the title), Barbara Partee, Neil Tennant, and Robert Wall. In addition, five weeks at the University of Konstanz, at the invitation of Arnim von Stechow (with support from the German Science Foundation), forced me to put my thoughts into a form suitable for seminar presentation. For the hospitality and ideas of all these people, and others unnamed, my thanks are due. For her ability to transform my manuscripts into a linear ordering of legible sentences, my thanks go also to Helen Fleming.

The end of 1983 marks the retirement of George Hughes after thirty-three years as Professor of Philosophy here in Wellington. For the aim of trying to make whatever I write say exactly what I mean, and say it as simply as possible, and for his constant professional and personal example since my first philosophy lecture as an undergraduate in March 1957, I owe him a far greater debt than can be repaid. To him this book is dedicated.

M.J.C.
Wellington, New Zealand

Structured Meanings

Introduction

What is meaning? The meaning of a sentence, wrote Wittgenstein in the *Tractatus*, is the conditions under which it is true. What he had in mind might be illustrated as follows: Whether you speak English or not, you presumably know the difference between the following two situations:

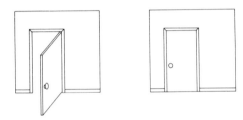

In the leftmost situation the door is open; in the rightmost it is not. If you are a speaker of English, you know something more. You know that the sentence

(1)   The door is open

is true in the leftmost situation and false in the rightmost. This is the kind of knowledge that distinguishes one who knows the meaning of (1) from one who does not. And truth-conditional semantics is based on the idea that the meaning of (1) can be identified with the (actual or possible) situations in which (1) is true.

Undoubtedly there is more to meaning than that, and even truth-conditional theories of meaning are more elaborate than that. This book addresses what I take to be the most serious problem facing truth-conditional semantics—namely, the problem of the semantics of propositional attitudes, which I shall describe in a moment. I shall attack it by showing two things: first, that it is a problem for a very wide class of semantic theories, not just truth-conditional ones, and second, that it has a solution within truth-conditional semantics.

The version of semantics I propose to defend is possible-worlds semantics. A possible world (of which the actual world is one) is just a complete possible situation. (I shall say more about this in chapter 7.) The meaning of a sentence in possible-worlds semantics is just the set of worlds in which that sentence is true.

The problem of propositional attitudes arises in the following way. If the meaning of a sentence is just the set of worlds in which the sentence is true, then any two sentences that are true in exactly the same set of worlds must have the same meaning, or in other words must express the same proposition. Therefore, if a person takes any attitude (for instance, belief) to the proposition expressed by one of those sentences, then that person must take the same attitude to the proposition expressed by the other.

Yet it seems very easy to have sentences about believing, and about other attitudes, in which replacement of sentences that are true in exactly the same worlds turns a truth into a falsehood. A very nice example of this comes from John Bigelow. Consider the following two sentences:

(2) Robin will win.

(3) Everyone who does not compete, or loses, will have done something Robin will not have done.

If you work it out, you will see that every possible world in which (2) is true is also a world in which (3) is true, and *vice versa*. On the truth-conditional view of meaning, then, (2) and (3) have the same meaning. Now consider the following two sentences:

(4) Marian believes that Robin will win.

(5) Marian believes that everyone who does not compete, or loses, will have done something Robin will not have done.

If (2) and (3) have the same meaning, then it seems that what Marian believes must in each case be the same. That would give (4) and (5) the same meaning. But (4) and (5) do not have the same meaning. It is not at all difficult to imagine a possible world in which (4) is true but (5) is not; Marian may not have realized that (2) and (3) are true in just the same worlds.

The solution I will defend is that the meanings of propositional attitude words like 'believes' are sensitive not solely to the proposition expressed by a whole sentence but also to the meanings of its separate parts. Sentence (3) has a much more complex structure than (2), and so the meanings of its parts fit together in a much more complex manner. In (4) and (5) the meaning of 'believes' is sensitive to this fact.

Such a solution stated at that level of generality is not particularly original or surprising. For that I am grateful. Most solutions I have come across that claim to be new turn out to be inadequate or to reduce to one of a small number. What is more important is the detailed working out of the solution and the demonstration that it is the right one. This is what I have tried to provide in this book.

In this area an idea that looks good when stated in general terms often turns out to have hidden snags when expressed in detail. For this reason I consider it vital to show how the proposed solution can be incorporated into a formal semantical theory. But formal semantical theories can be formidable things and can often obscure the essential features of a solution to a problem. I have therefore deferred the formal semantics until part III, and in parts I and II I have tried to set out the essence of the solution in a relatively informal and, I hope, easily understandable way. I have tried to make this part of the book available to readers without any knowledge of logic or formal semantics.

I have assumed in this book that a language is an abstract system whose sentences exist even when no tokens of them are uttered, and that the very same word or expression that in fact has one meaning could well have had a different meaning. These assumptions are not uncontentious, but I do not propose to defend them here.

I further assume that there are such things as propositional attitude sentences and that they do have truth conditions. Although this last assumption may seem truistic in the face of examples like (4) or (5), it has been questioned in recent philosophical work. For instance, if Donald Davidson's account of indirect discourse is applied to all propositional attitudes, then there are no such things as propositional attitude sentences. If this were right, it would certainly make possible-worlds semantics much simpler and much more plausible than many have thought. But it seems to me about as certain as anything can be in semantics that there are sentences like (4) and (5) and that their meanings do depend on the meanings of sentences like (2) and (3).

In actually using a language, in many cases we do not say exactly what we mean or do not mean what we literally say; often, even, there is no exact thing that we mean. Formal theories of meaning idealize from this messy state of affairs. They assume that words have precise and definite meanings and that sentences are understood literally. The hope, of course, is that beginning with a theory of meaning of this idealized kind, one can then use it as the basis of a model of actual language use.

In part I I use the language of arithmetic as an illustration of what a semantic framework might look like. The principal conclusion of this part is that whatever kind of entity the meaning of a sentence is held to be, there are occasions on which an attitude verb must be sensitive to the parts of the sentence that follows it. I show that this is needed in order to explain a range of diverse phenomena. One important argument in this part is that propositional attitude sentences are structurally ambiguous. I provide evidence as well that the ambiguity should show up in the that-clause rather than the attitude verb.

Once it is shown that attitude verbs can be sensitive in varying degrees to the structure of the sentences that follow them, the way is open to develop a system of meanings based on the idea that propositions are sets of possible worlds (actually sets of pairs of worlds and times). I develop and defend such a system in part II.

The aim of part III is to show that the solution set out in parts I and II really is capable of occurring as part of a formal semantical theory. To that end I have chosen to use the framework of λ-categorial languages. In such languages one can get very close to natural languages, and yet their syntax and semantics are very simple. Almost any truth-conditional semantics can probably be translated into this framework, and as the literature attests, an enormous range of linguistic phenomena has been given such treatment. A framework of such power seems to me to provide the necessary and sufficient conditions for testing the adequacy of the view expounded earlier in the book. After an introduction to λ-categorial languages I undertake a detailed consideration of the semantics of indirect discourse in such a framework.

The problem of propositional attitudes has intrigued me for over twenty years. At one time or another I have probably espoused virtually every solution available. In this book I try to say why I think that the structured-meaning approach, if carefully spelled out, is the correct one.

PART I

Sense and Reference

Chapter 1
Compositional Semantics:
An Arithmetical Analogy

Expressions in a language, whether words, phrases, or sentences, have meanings. So it seems reasonable to suppose that there are meanings that expressions have. Of course, it is fashionable in some philosophical circles to deny this. One could say that although expressions have meanings, this no more warrants concluding that there are meanings that they have than the fact that the average family has 2.4 children shows that there are 2.4 children that the average family has.

One concern of philosophers is ontological. One might hold that the question is whether, in some sense, meanings really exist, and if they do, in what sense they do. These will not be my questions, if indeed such questions make sense. Suppose the answer to the ontological question about meanings is no, that they do not exist. Then, assuming that expressions do have meanings, some analysis of this fact is owed. If the analysis is such that anything I want to say about meanings, as if they were existent things, can equally be said in the "true" theory of what is going on, then I will be satisfied. If it cannot, then the dispute will turn on who is right about the particular things that I want to say. And these issues should be faced as they come up.

But not only do expressions have meanings. It is also a fact that the meaning of an expression could have been different. One of the striking features of language is its conventionality. The meaning of a word is something that has to be *learned*. This means that it must be possible, at least in one's linguistic theorizing, to identify a word or an expression without knowing its meaning. Therefore, if a theory talks about expressions and about meanings, these must be mutually independent things (whatever their nature), which, in a given language, happen to be correlated in some particular way. A semantic theory, thus conceived, will therefore include a class of linguistic entities (the expressions of the language) specified without reference to semantics, a class of "meanings" specified without reference to the language being studied, and an account of which meanings are correlated with which expressions.

I will not pretend that what I have said so far is universally accepted. But it is hardly new. Nor is the next feature of language to which I shall allude: namely, *compositionality*, a long-recognized feature of many linguistic theories. Very roughly, to say that meaning is compositional is to say that the meaning of a complex expression is determined by the meaning of the words in the expression and the way they are combined. By contrast, the meanings of the words themselves are not compositional; that is, they are independently learned. This picture is rough, and it is not my intention at this stage to refine it. In part III I shall introduce a semantics for a formal model of language in which these vague notions will have precise counterparts, but at the moment it is better to leave things vague.

The reason for compositionality is simply that complex expressions are just too many and too varied for us to learn their meanings one by one. Most sentences we hear or read are new to us. We have not met them before. Yet we can understand them, because we work their meanings out from their structure and the meanings of their individual words.

The subject of this book is the semantics of sentences about propositional attitudes. This is frequently portrayed as a problem for certain views about what kinds of things meanings are. In this chapter I shall argue that the problem of propositional attitudes involves compositionality and is independent of what sorts of things meanings are.

What form might a compositional theory of meaning take? To answer this question would be to produce a particular semantical theory, and this I want to postpone for a little. Instead, since the statements of arithmetic are compositional in a way that should be familiar to everyone and can therefore be used to illustrate my point with the minimum of preparation, I shall offer an arithmetical analogy.

We have all surely experienced trying to add columns of numbers, with varying degrees of success. Today, of course, we are just as likely to get our pocket calculator to do it for us. But what goes on is the same in each case. Suppose we want to add 5 and 7. As Kant realized, the correct answer to this problem is 12. If we do it with a calculator, we press the button for 5, the button for 7, and the button for +, and in a (very) short time the answer 12 appears. Or at least 12 appears if the calculator is functioning correctly. If we do it ourselves, the same thing happens. We might first count five on our fingers and then seven more and read off twelve. For a more complicated example we might use pencil and paper, but still the same thing happens.

We begin with certain numbers, perform an operation on them, and end up with a certain result. And in all cases the same moral can be drawn. *It must be logically possible to get it wrong.* I stress this point because, to me at least, it seems obvious that the fact that we can get it wrong does not in any way depend on the kind of entities we are dealing with. One could imagine a rather complicated code involving letters that had similar possibilities of error. The reason that we can get it wrong is simply that we do not learn the answer as a whole but have to work it out from the meaning of its parts. And that is why I claim that the problem of propositional attitudes is connected with compositionality rather than with the nature of meanings.

But we must sharpen the question a little. In adding 5 and 7 there seem to be at least four things involved: the number 5, the number 7, the operation of addition, and the result of performing that operation on 5 and 7. First consider the operation of addition. This may be performed in a variety of ways, depending on whether the performer is an electronic calculator or a human brain, aided perhaps by pencil and paper. It is therefore important to be aware that the particular way the operation is to be performed should not be part of what is involved in describing the task. But how then can we describe the operation? In fact, there seems to be only one plausible candidate, the one that can be described in set theory by the notion of a function. The function simply states what would count, in each case, as the correct carrying out of the task. A function is nothing more than a correlation—a sort of infinite list. To the left, arrayed in two columns, are all the pairs of numbers, and to the right is the number that is their sum. One row in this list would be

5   7   12,

and the condition of functionality would require that there be no row in which 5, 7 is associated with any number except 12.

With this in mind we can let the operation + simply *be* this infinite list. In set-theoretical terms it would be the class of all ordered triples of numbers in which the third number is the sum of the first two. Then, when we write '5 + 7', we simply mean the number associated with 5 and 7 in the + list. Any other arithmetical operation can be described in the same way.

Now the arithmetical expression '5 + 7' is a different expression from the numeral '12', and this difference can cause a certain ambiguity. For we might look at the meaning of '5 + 7' as having three parts: '5', '7', and '+'. Indeed, in describing someone as trying to calculate 5 + 7 or as wondering what 5 + 7 is, we seem to be making essential reference to those three parts. I shall argue that the key to solving the problem of propositional attitudes lies in recognizing this ambiguity in the expression '5 + 7': it sometimes refers to the two "input" numbers 5 and 7 together with the operation to be performed on them, and it sometimes refers to the result of performing that operation. One way of making the distinction is to let the triple consisting of 5, 7 (the numbers—not the numerals), and the function + (the infinite list just described—not the symbol '+') represent one of the meanings of '5 + 7' and the number 12 represent the result (for 12 is what we get when we carry out the operation correctly). So far there is nothing wrong, and from many points of view this is perfectly adequate. The problem arises because by '5 + 7' we may want to refer sometimes to the "input" structure (which is the triple 5, 7, and +) and sometimes to the output structure 5 + 7 (i.e., 12). In a case typical of this kind (which I shall discuss further in chapter 4), Yvonne tells Zane that the map indicates that it is 5 + 7 kilometers from Motueka to Upper Moutere, her map being one that shows 5 kilometers from Motueka to Lower Moutere and 7 kilometers from Lower Moutere to Upper Moutere. Zane might choose to report this by saying,

(1)   The map indicates that it is 12 kilometers to Upper Moutere.

Here the use of the expression '5 + 7' is just another way of talking about the number 12—understandable because of the way the map is being read.

Since this ambiguity in the way we can treat an expression like '5 + 7' will prove crucial, something more should be said about the meaning of sentences describing arithmetical operations.

Consider the sentence

(2)   Xavier has calculated what 5 + 7 is.

As yet I shall leave its meaning undetermined but shall try to say what would have to go on to make it true. It is clear that the phrase '5 + 7', whatever its syntactical properties, must refer to the triple of 5, 7, and +. We can see this by paraphrasing (2) as

(3)   Xavier has taken the two numbers 5 and 7 and performed on them the operation of addition.

In fact, what Xavier has probably done, is to take a numeral, say '5', which represents 5, and another numeral, say '7', which represents 7, and then use some algorithm for producing the numeral '12'. Of course, Xavier may not have used '5' and '7'; instead, he may have used 'v' and 'vii'. Or, if Xavier is a Turing machine, it would have converted the string *||||||*|||||||||* into the string *|||||||||||||||* by passing through the series of configurations that its input together with its table dictates (and different machines could do it differently).

By contrast, if we say

(4)   Xavier put 5 + 7 roses into the bowl,

we just mean that he put 12 roses in, though perhaps we have chosen a rather perverse way of saying it.

Crucial to this particular analysis of what goes on to make (2) true is the fact that Xavier represented the numbers to himself in some way. This fact has led some authors to claim, or at least to appear to claim, that meanings actually are internal representations. I shall try later to show why this view is wrong, although I shall not deny that, maybe, the only way we can understand meanings is by representing them in some way.

Actually, we can see already why the representations are not the meaning. For neither '5', 'v', nor *||||||* is crucial to the fact that Xavier is operating on the number 5. What is crucial is that he is operating on a representation *of that number*. For suppose we also have

(5)   Wendy has calculated 5 + 7.

I claim that (5) in at least one of its senses implies that Wendy has calculated the same thing that Xavier has—and this even if the way Wendy represents 5, 7, and + is different from the way Xavier does. So the *meaning* of '5 + 7' in these sentences must be those *numbers* and that operation, *not* the way those numbers are represented. As noted, I shall enlarge on this theme later.

Sentences like (2) and (5) refer to activities of calculating and seem quite clearly to involve performing an operation on 5 and 7 to get 5 + 7. But it is also plausible to think that the same thing is happening in a sentence like

(6)   Yvonne knows what 5 + 7 is.

This sentence presumably does not report that Yvonne knows what 12 is. (Though I suppose it could mean that—for instance, in a situation in which I am reading a map and am aware that it is 5 + 7 kilometers from Motueka to Upper Moutere and Yvonne is a child and I wonder whether she realizes how far that it. Yes, she does, her mother tells me, Yvonne knows what 5 + 7 is.) (6) seems paraphrasable as something like

(7)   Yvonne knows what the result would be of taking
      the numbers 5 and 7 and (correctly) applying to them the
      operation of addition.

Knowledge of this kind is of course logical knowledge, and yet it is
knowledge a person may not have. Certainly that is so in more complicated examples. It is not trivial knowledge because it takes calculation to get it. And there is always the logical possibility of an error
if the calculator is an actual physical person or thing.

I shall be returning to this arithmetical example from time to time.
This is because it illustrates, in what I hope is a reasonably ap-
proachable form, various important features that an adequate semantical system should possess. In part III I shall set out a formal
theory of language that will make clear how the points made in the
earlier parts fit in precisely.

In the rest of part I I shall use the arithmetical example in two ways.
First, I shall be using sentences from the language of arithmetic, specifically those made up from numerals using '+' and '=', as the complement sentences of propositional attitude sentences. For example:

(8)   Xenia told me that $8 + 3 = 15$.

This sentence has as its subject the name of a person and as its object
a that-clause followed by a sentence of arithmetic. (The sentence following 'that' is often called the *complement sentence*. When I talk
about the that-clause itself, I mean the complement sentence pre-
ceded by 'that'.) The sentence of arithmetic will be in arithmetical
notation. The verb (or verb expression such as 'told me' in (8)) will be
a verb of propositional attitude. By this I mean no more than that it
takes a that-clause as its object. One of my principal concerns is to
give a unified semantic framework for all such sentences. In parts II
and III I shall consider a much wider variety of propositional attitude
sentences, and even in part I I shall sometimes use sentences in
which the arithmetical expression is only a part of the complement
sentence, but when I do I shall only be interested in the meaning of
the arithmetical part.

This is because the semantics of such arithmetical expressions
seems to me completely clear. Numerals denote numbers—that is, '5'
(or 'v' or *||||||*) denotes the number 5 (whatever that is; though, as
I have said, that kind of question doesn't worry me much). '7' denotes 7 and '5 + 7' denotes the result when the meaning of '+' operates on the numbers 5 and 7. The meaning of '+' is just the infinite
list (function) described earlier, and the way it operates is that the

meaning of the whole expression is the number associated with the pair of numbers that are its parts.

Second, I shall use the arithmetical example as an analogy for a complete semantic theory, where numbers correspond to the meanings of certain kinds of expressions and the meanings of other kinds are functions in the way that the meaning of '+' is. Throughout part I I want to have to say as little as possible about what meanings are, so I shall illustrate as much as I can by means of this analogy.

In fact, we can already see how certain features are emerging. For instance, although the meaning of the expression '5 + 7' seems to be just the number '12', yet one can often fail to know this. But the important point seems to me to be that the example generalizes to *any compositional semantical system*. No matter what the entities and operations are, it seems that we can have failure of logical omniscience. If I am right about this, then the problem of the semantics of propositional attitudes has nothing to do with questions about the nature of propositions, but is solely a consequence of the compositional nature of semantics. As the book progresses, I shall draw on this argument in more specific areas in a way that I hope will both show the argument at work and add to its persuasiveness.

An easy reply might be to say, so much the worse for compositionality. But such a drastic cure would almost certainly kill the patient. We must try to find a better way.

Chapter 2

De Re Attitudes

Consider the paraphrase given in chapter 1 of

(1) Xavier has calculated what 5 + 7 is,

namely, 'Xavier has taken the two numbers 5 and 7 and performed on them the operation of addition'. This paraphrase makes it clear that Xavier has done something with 5 and 7, namely, he has added them together. A similar analysis could be given of the sentence

(2) Zane knows what 5 + 7 is.

If it is the case that the only plausible models of the mental life are computational ones, as Jerry Fodor among others has suggested, then (2) would seem to be paraphrasable in some way similar to (1) or perhaps by saying that Zane has the ability to do something like calculating 5 + 7. But what about a sentence like (3)?

(3) Zane believes that 5 + 7 is 11.

Presumably this would be represented by saying that Zane has added 5 and 7 together and come up with 11. Of course, he has not "really" added them, if by real addition we mean to imply that he has got the right answer. But it is obvious that people often get calculations wrong and so it is clear that, whatever analysis is to be given of it, one must be able to talk about something as being a computation of 5 + 7 but being a mistaken one.

I do not at this stage want to suggest that a paraphrase such as

(4) Zane has computed 5 + 7 and obtained 11

really does capture the meaning of (3). In fact, I do not have, in this book, any particularly good answer to the question of what belief is. I only want to motivate the suggestion that the proper analysis of (3) should involve taking 5, 7, and + and doing something with them, like obtaining 12, or 11, or whatever.

The semantics suggested for (4) relates Zane to the numbers 5, 7, and 11 and the operation of addition. If this is plausible for (4), then it seems equally plausible to claim that the semantics of sentences like (3) should also relate persons to numbers and operations. Following the style of analysis argued for in Cresswell and von Stechow (1982), one could claim that the semantics of

(5)   Veronica believes that $5 + 7 = 12$

should make it true iff Veronica believes of the pair of numbers 5 and 7 that, added together, they make 12. Just exactly how the latter statement is to be analyzed is, of course, a problem in itself; here I shall note only that it is what has come to be called in the philosophical literature a *de re* belief about the numbers 5 and 7, to the effect that they have a certain property, *viz* the property of summing to 12.

It is important to contrast this analysis with another one, because otherwise the account just offered of (5) might seem almost truistic. On one view the meaning of '$5 + 7 = 12$' is said to be a *proposition,* the proposition that $5 + 7 = 12$, and (5) is true iff Veronica stands in the belief relation to the proposition that $5 + 7 = 12$. This account is a very attractive one. The sentence '$5 + 7 = 12$' is assigned a proposition as its meaning, or rather the meanings assigned to 5, +, 7, 12, and = together with certain rules of functional composition (as described in chapter 1) determine the proposition that is to be the meaning of the sentence '$5 + 7 = 12$'. The meanings of 'believes' and 'Veronica' will then in their turn give a proposition that is the meaning of (5) from which the truth of (5) may be determined.

I shall call this account the *propositional account* of belief, and I want to show why it is not the same as the *de re* account. Consider more closely the sentence '$5 + 7 = 12$'. If its meaning is determined functionally, then at some stage we must determine the meaning of '$5 + 7$'. Let us suppose that the meanings of '5', '7', and '12' are the numbers 5, 7, and 12, respectively. What is the meaning of '+'? As noted in chapter 1, that meaning would seem to have to be the function (list) that gives the number $n + m$ for the input numbers n and m. Further, the value of '$n + m$' will just be the output number. This means that the meaning of '$5 + 7$' is just the number 12. The proposition that $5 + 7 = 12$ is therefore just the proposition that 12 is 12. But in (5) this cannot be its meaning, because it seems at least logically possible that (5) could be false while

(6)   Veronica believes that $12 = 12$

is true.

This is not really a problem about numbers, nor is it really a problem about the nature of propositions. It is a particular manifestation of the general problem of identity in sentences about propositional attitudes. But before we discuss this problem more generally, let us consider why the *de re* semantics solves it, and therefore why the *de re* semantics is not the same as the propositional semantics.

On the propositional account (5) is true iff Veronica stands in the appropriate relation (the believing relation) to the proposition that $5 + 7 = 12$. Since $5 + 7$ is the same number as 12, then the proposition that $5 + 7 = 12$ is the same as the proposition that $12 = 12$, so Veronica, on this account, believes that $5 + 7 = 12$ iff she believes that $12 = 12$. On the *de re* account (5) is true, when it is true, not because Veronica stands in a certain relation to a proposition but rather because Veronica stands in a slightly more complicated relation to a more complicated group of entities. Specifically, she stands in the relation to the (ordered) pair 5 and 7 of believing them to sum to 12. In this solution there is no proposition that $5 + 7 = 12$; thus, the question whether it is the same proposition as the proposition that $12 = 12$ just does not arise. Obviously, the belief about 5 and 7 that they sum to 12 is different from the belief about 12 that it is identical to 12. Moreover, there is no suggestion that the meaning of '5', '7', and '5 + 7' need be anything other than what the statements of ordinary arithmetic require.

As noted, the problem about $5 + 7$ and 12, as it appears in the propositional solution, is a problem about identity. The *de re* solution avoids the problem of choosing not to analyze '5 + 7' as a constituent of the belief that $5 + 7 = 12$. Problems regarding identity arise not only in mathematical belief but also in belief in contexts where definite descriptions are involved. Suppose that the most beautiful building in Wellington is also the biggest wooden building in the southern hemisphere. Presumably this fact is contingent, so that although it is in fact the case, it might not have been. Yet it is not too hard to state a paradox involving this building that appears to be the same in structure as the one involving Veronica and $5 + 7 = 12$:

(7) The most beautiful building in Wellington = the biggest wooden building in the southern hemisphere.

(8) William believes that the biggest wooden building in the southern hemisphere is a greater fire risk than an earthquake risk.

Now suppose that William is under the impression that the most beautiful building in Wellington is the Hunter building at the university and quite correctly realizes that *this* building is not a greater fire risk than an earthquake risk. In fact, the following is false:

(9)   William believes that the most beautiful building in
      Wellington is a greater fire risk than an earthquake risk.

Yet it seems that (9) can be obtained from (8) by the principle of the substitutivity of identity. Failure of such inferences is often taken to imply that the substitutivity of identicals does not hold in belief contexts. If so, then it might seem that the argument given above against the propositional construal of (5) might be dealt with in the same way, in that although '5 + 7' and '12' might indeed be terms that designate the same number, yet replacing one by the other in a belief context is no more warranted than replacing 'the biggest wooden bulding in the southern hemisphere' by 'the most beautiful building in Wellington'. But although it may seem at first sight that the situations are the same, a closer look reveals an important difference: What William believes is that there is a building that is the most beautiful building in Wellington and that it is more an earthquake risk than a fire risk. That is, his belief is a belief about quite a different building. It is not a belief about the most beautiful building in Wellington at all. To be sure, it is about a building that he thinks is the most beautiful building in Wellington, but it is not a belief about the building in that town that *is* the most beautiful.

In this book I shall have very little to say about how this is to be analyzed. Suffice it to say at the moment that I support a roughly Russellian account. For present purposes all that is needed is the observation that this cannot be what is going on in (5): Veronica's belief that 5 + 7 = 12 cannot be about some different number than 5 + 7. (Of course, on the *de re* solution it is not about 5 + 7 at all but about 5 and 7 and what they sum to.) The situation is more like the Phosphorus and Hesperus example. If Phosphorus = Hesperus and Ursula believes that Phosphorus is Phosphorus, then does Ursula have to believe that Phosphorus is Hesperus? Presumably not. But if Ursula's belief is about anything, surely it is about Phosphorus? There does not seem any more possibility of there being another planet involved. It is not like William's case where there were two buildings. In the Phosphorus and Hesperus case it seems plausible to suppose that the belief is really in some sense a belief about what certain names refer to. For what Ursula may not know is that the two names are used to refer to the same planet.

But Veronica's case is not quite like Ursula's either. For Veronica's belief is *not* that the phrases '5 + 7' and '12' denote the same number. Suppose that Trevor believes that '5' actually refers to the number 3 (and that '3' refers to 5) but that his arithmetical beliefs are normal. If we were to construe

(10)   Trevor believes that $7 + 5 = 12$

as

(11)   Trevor believes that '7 + 5' and '12' denote the same number,

then (11) would be true, for we have said that Trevor's arithmetical beliefs are normal. But (11) is false, because Trevor believes that '7 + 5' denotes 10 because he believes that '5' denotes 3. Yet Trevor has no false arithmetical beliefs; he is as good at arithmetic as we are. In particular, he believes that $7 + 5 = 12$, though he would not express it in that way. (But then neither would a Greek or a Roman.) In order for (10) to represent Trevor's belief, '7' must denote 7 and '5' must denote 5 (and '+' must mean + and so on). In fact, any representation that has this property will do, and that is just what the *de re* solution amounts to.

What is *de re* belief? In a very well known paper Quine (1956) envisages a person, Ralph, glimpsing a man in a brown coat on one occasion and in a grey coat on another. Unknown to Ralph, it is the same man, Bernard J. Ortcutt. On the first occasion Ralph says 'I think he is a spy'. On the second occasion he is sure that the man he glimpses is not a spy. So he believes of Ortcutt both that he is and that he is not a spy. The problem arises because the proposition that Ortcutt is a spy is logically incompatible with the proposition that Ortcutt is not a spy. Of course, people can have logically inconsistent beliefs—one of the aims of this book is to show how that can be so. But Ralph's beliefs are not. He is simply factually mistaken about the man he has glimpsed. So one thing at least can be said: the object of Ralph's belief is not the proposition that Ortcutt is a spy (or the proposition that he is not). The *de re* solution says that Ralph has two beliefs about Ortcutt, one that he is a spy and the other that he is not; that is, he ascribes two properties to Ortcutt, the property of being a spy and the property of not being a spy. To be sure, these properties are incompatible; they cannot logically both apply to one thing, and we can suppose Ralph to be clear-headed enough to know this. The problem is that he is unaware of the *res* to which he is ascribing the property. In other words, he is unaware of certain important properties it has, *viz* that the *res* glimpsed on one occasion is the same as the *res* glimpsed on another occasion.

There are two propositions that might directly be said to be the object of his belief:

(i)   The proposition that the man in the brown coat is a spy.

(ii) The proposition that the man in the grey coat is not a spy.

These are the ways that Ralph represents his beliefs to himself. (i) and (ii) of course are not logically incompatible. The problem for the semantics of propositional attitudes, on the propositional account, is how to recover (i) and (ii) from the sentences

(iii) Ralph believes that Ortcutt is a spy

and

(iv) Ralph believes that Ortcutt is not a spy.

The *de re* solution goes something like this:

(iii′) There is a way of picking out Ortcutt (*viz* being the man in the brown coat) such that Ralph believes the proposition that whoever is so picked out is a spy.

(iv′) There is a way of picking out Ortcutt (*viz* being the man in the grey coat) such that Ralph believes the proposition that whoever is so picked out is not a spy.

In (iii′) and (iv′) of course the parenthetical *viz* is no part of the analysis. All that is needed is a way of picking out Ortcutt that is available to Ralph. Not any old way will do. It must put Ralph in the right sort of cognitive contact with Ortcutt. (Quine's story suggests that glimpsing someone wearing a certain kind of clothing is sufficient.)

(iii′) and (iv′) make essential use of splitting the belief up into the reference to Ortcutt and the property of being a spy (or not being a spy). In this we have a link between *de re* belief and the examples involving arithmetical calculation considered earlier in this chapter and in chapter 1. It is much more difficult to see how the propositional approach can deal with the Ortcutt case. One would have to argue that (i) puts Ralph in cognitive contact with the proposition that Ortcutt is a spy, and it is not at all easy to see what the analogue of (iii′) would have to be that would do this. (Similar remarks apply to (ii) and (iv).) I suppose it would have to be something like

(v)   There is an appropriate way of picking out the proposition that Ortcutt is a spy such that Ralph believes that whatever proposition is so picked out is true.

This certainly releases Ralph from contradictory beliefs (assuming a suitable account of appropriateness can be given), but at the very least it seems to take a fairly simple account (being in the right sort of contact with a thing) and make it more complicated. Actually, though, I think it can be shown to be inadequate. Note first that on any reasonable account of propositions, the proposition that Ortcutt loves himself ought to be the same as the proposition that Ortcutt loves Ortcutt. Now consider Ralph, who has observed the way the man in the brown coat behaves toward himself. Ralph, who by now does know Ortcutt, but does not know that he is the man in the brown coat, therefore has a *de re* belief about Ortcutt that he loves himself; that is, when Ortcutt is pointed out to Ralph and Ralph is asked whether that man loves himself, he says 'yes'. Therefore,

(12)   Ralph believes that Ortcutt loves himself

is true if taken as a *de re* report. But if Ralph is asked whether that man loves Ortcutt, he replies 'no', not realizing that that man is Ortcutt. Therefore,

(13)   Ralph believes that Ortcutt loves Ortcutt

is false when construed as

(14)   Ralph believes of Ortcutt that he loves Ortcutt.

But if (12) is analyzed as putting Ralph in contact with the proposition that Ortcutt loves himself, then (12) and (13) would have to have the same truth value. For these reasons I shall assume an analysis of *de re* attitudes along the lines of (iii') and (iv').

Chapter 3
Structured Meanings

In chapter 1 I stated that a theory of meaning should be *compositional.* That is, the meaning of any complex expression should be determined by the meanings of its simple expressions together with the structure of the expression. Usually the expression will be built up in several stages, with successively more complex expressions being embedded in even more complex ones until the level of the sentence itself is reached. But the theory of meaning envisaged so far has been not merely compositional but what might be called *functionally* compositional. Consider the example of 5 + 7. The idea was that the meaning of the expression '5 + 7' is the number associated in the list that is the meaning of + with the pair of numbers 5 and 7. Put more formally, the meaning of '5 + 7' is the result of letting the function that is the meaning of '+' (i.e., the operation of addition) operate on the two numbers 5 and 7 and deliver their sum. The sum is of course the number 12, and it is this number that is the meaning of '5 + 7'.

The problem with sentences about propositional attitudes is that the attitude verb seems sensitive to more than the meaning (in this sense of meaning) of the complement sentence. The *de re* solution claims that the attitude is sensitive to the meaning of the parts of the sentence, together with its structure. In the propositional solution, the attitude verb operates just on the meaning that results from the functional application of the parts.

The problem of propositional attitudes arises because, in a functionally compositional theory of meaning, distinct structures can turn out to have the same meaning. In this case '5 + 7' has the same meaning as '6 + 6', *viz* they both mean the number 12. The *de re* solution consists in having the propositional attitude relate, not to the meaning of '5 + 7' taken as a whole, but to the meaning of its parts taken separately. This is opposed to the propositional solution, in which the attitude relates to the meaning of '5 + 7' taken as a whole.

One attempt to amalgamate these approaches is to take the meaning of '5 + 7' to be not the number 12 (i.e., not the result of +

operating on 5 and 7) but rather the initially given structure $\langle 5,7,+\rangle$ and to say that that *structure* is involved in the object of the attitude. Presumably the object of a belief that $5 + 7 = 12$ would be the structure $\langle\langle 5,7,+\rangle,12,=\rangle$ or some such thing. From one point of view this is just a way of rewriting the *de re* analysis so that it has the form of the propositional analysis. However, there are some hidden snags.

The main problem is where 12 fits into all this. For if the meaning of '5 + 7' is just $\langle 5,7,+\rangle$, how is that supposed to be equal to 12? Obviously, that structure is not 12. There are two rather different kinds of solution here. The first is to take '=' not as having identity as its meaning but rather as being a predicate that relates structures in such a way that '$s_1 = s_2$' is true iff the results of evaluating s_1 out according to its functional structure (e.g., by letting + operate on 5 and 7 to get 12) and of evaluating s_2 out according to *its* structure are the same.

The second type of solution is to say that 12 is not strictly the *meaning* of '7 + 5'; rather, it is the number denoted by or referred to by that expression. Using a terminology derived from the views of Frege, we could say that the structure $\langle 5,7,+\rangle$ is the *sense* of the expression '5 + 7', whereas the number 12 is its *reference*. In fact, the *de re* solution has much in common with the Fregean solution, though it is importantly different in ways I shall describe later. First, however, I want to show why the first kind of solution, in which the meaning of '=' is taken to be not identity but instead something laxer, will not do. As a way into the difficulties here, let us consider '+' rather than '=' and let us begin with the expression '(5 + 7) + 2'. If the meaning of '5 + 7' is just the number 12, then there is no problem. We recall from chapter 1 that the meaning of '+' may be represented by an infinite list of triples of numbers in which the number in the third column is the sum of the numbers in the first two columns. To find the meaning of '(5 + 7) + 2', we first look up the number associated with 5 and 7 in this list. It is 12. We then look up the number associated with 12 and 2 in the same list and find that it is 14. No problem.

But suppose that the meaning of '5 + 7' is not the number 12 but is the triple $\langle 5,7,+\rangle$. Remember that we are considering a solution in which the meaning of an expression $\alpha + \beta$ is obtained by using the meaning of '+' to operate on the meanings of α and β, and the meaning of '+' is an infinite list of triples that associates the meaning of $\alpha + \beta$ with the meanings of α and β. But the meaning of '5 + 7' is now the triple $\langle 5,7,+\rangle$. And this means that one of the members of the list that is + must be the list that is +. And one of *its* members must be that list. And so on. On this view it would seem that + never could have a definite meaning.

Of course, all this has depended on the assumption that the compositionality is functional; for instance, we have assumed that the meaning of '(5 + 7) + 2' has been obtained by the meaning of '+' (in the form of the infinite list) "operating" on the structure ⟨5,7,+⟩, which has meant looking it up in the list. But what if we let the meaning of '(5 + 7) + 2' simply be the structure ⟨⟨5,7,+⟩,2,+⟩? Then the problem is that it is no longer clear what the meaning of '+' should be. Since we have abandoned the requirement that the compositionality be functional, there is no reason why it should be the kind of infinite list described above, or any other list. The reason for making that particular list the meaning of '+' was that, among other things, when applied to 5 and 7, it delivers 12. But on the present, nonfunctional, view of meaning, the number 12 is not the meaning of ⟨5,7,+⟩. Rather, it is the reference. And here we have a curious phenomenon. If we look at '(5 + 7) + 2', we see that the *reference* of this whole expression is determined from the references of '5', '7', and '2' by the function +. In this process the structure ⟨⟨5,7,+⟩,2,+⟩ plays no role at all. In other words, the choice of + in a *non*functional account of meaning is motivated because of its role in a functional account of reference. Otherwise, there is no motivation for the choice of meaning for '+' or even for '5' and '7'. The argument for compositionality in the case of the arithmetical language has proceeded on the assumption that there is an intimate connection between meaning and reference. On Frege's view, the reference of a numerical expression like '5 + 7' would be a number, in this case 12, and the reference of an arithmetical sentence would be a truth value: T in the case of 5 + 7 = 12 and F in the case of 5 + 7 = 11.

In the introduction I argued for a very intimate connection between truth and meaning. Specifically, I argued that a crucial element in knowing the meaning of a sentence is knowing the difference between conditions under which the sentence would be true and conditions under which it would be false. Explaining this knowledge seems to me the most important single goal of a semantic theory, and I for one have not seen any semantic theory that explains this knowledge that is not functionally compositional.

Nonfunctional but compositional theories of meaning have certainly been advocated. One of the best known is that defended by Jerrold Katz. But Katz takes truth and reference to have no part in a semantic theory and so, whatever enterprise he is engaged in, it is not a semantical one as I understand the term. As far as I can understand it, Katz has in mind the construction of a formal language underlying English in which there are no ambiguous sentences and no semantically anomalous sentences and in which entailment relations between sentences are somehow syntactically displayed. (It is rather like the state modal logic was in before the work of Kripke.)

To say that compositionality must be functional does not of course mean that reference in general has to be as simple as it is in the arithmetical case. In particular, it is certainly not plausible to identify the meaning of an empirical sentence simply with a truth value. Obviously, knowing the meaning of a sentence is not the same as knowing whether it is true. In part II I shall deal with what the analogue of reference should be in such cases. In the rest of part I I shall still use the arithmetical example. In the case of this language the notion of reference does seem reasonably clear.

The situation then seems to be that truth-conditional semantics (applied to the arithmetical language) requires functional compositionality at the level of reference. And if we have functional compositionality at the level of reference, then it seems we do not need a separate level of meaning. But the point is that functional compositionality at the level of reference fails in the case of propositional attitudes. That is, the truth or falsity of a propositional attitude sentence depends on more than the reference of its complement sentence. It must, in addition, take note of the references of the parts of the complement sentence. Recall, too, that functional compositionality fails in the case of propositional attitude sentences *whatever* kinds of entities are the meanings of the complex expressions, provided only that distinct structures sometimes evaluate to the same meanings.

Our problem is the meaning of propositional attitude sentences. And one might say it is the problem of the *reference* of propositional attitude sentences. For even the truth value of a propositional attitude sentence can be affected by substituting an expression with the same reference. The examples in chapters 1 and 2 make exactly this point. Veronica's belief that $5 + 7 = 12$ is not a belief that $12 = 12$. In other words, the truth of a sentence reporting it is affected by replacing '$5 + 7$' with '12'. Consider, then, how we might analyze the sentence

(1)   Helen believes that $5 + 7 = 12$.

If the above remarks are correct, an adequate account even of the reference of this sentence may relate Helen to what was called previously the *sense* of '$5 + 7 = 12$', that is, to the structure $\langle\langle 5,7,+\rangle,12,=\rangle$, in which 5, 7, and 12 are numbers, $+$ is the addition function, and $=$ is the identity predicate. (For the moment we do not know precisely what its values are except that $\ulcorner x = y \urcorner$ is to be true iff x and y are identical.) In fact, that is just another way of putting the points made in chapters 1 and 2 about *de re* attitudes. What is required if functional compositionality is to be preserved, therefore, is a device for converting the *sense* of the complement sentence into the *reference* of the complement taken as a whole. The easiest way to do this in English seems to be to take seriously the role of the word 'that'. Of course, 'that' is often omitted, particularly in colloquial spoken English, and an equivalent word may not exist in all languages. Nevertheless, if the claims I am making are right, there will have to be some mechanism for achieving the result that English achieves by the use of 'that', and I would hope that the structure of this mechanism will be sufficiently indicated in what follows.

The first point I want to make is a syntactic one—namely, that the verb 'believes' in (1) is just an ordinary two-place predicate of the same syntactic category, whatever that is, as 'kicks', 'types', or 'frightens'. To be sure, there are semantic differences. The kinds of things that it makes sense to speak of as being kicked or frightened are not the same kinds of things that can be believed, but there seems little syntactic distinction between the following pairs:

(2) a. Vladimir types what he has been told to type.
    b. Vladimir believes what he has been told to believe.

(3) a. Helen kicks the winning goal.
    b. Helen believes the winning answer.

(4) a. Imogen kicks something.
    b. Imogen believes something.

Since this is so, then the role of the word 'that' seems to be to turn a sentence into what is often called a *noun phrase* (or what I called in Cresswell (1973a) a *nominal*)—that is, into an expression of the same syntactic category as 'something', or 'the winning answer', or 'what he has been told to believe'. This feature of 'that' explains how we can deal with inferences of the following type:

(5) Rob told Bill on Monday that Derek was out of the Cabinet
    Bill believed what Rob told him
    Bill believed that Derek was out of the Cabinet.

An important goal of part III will be to show how to provide a formal semantical theory within which these inferences will be valid.

Among phrases like 'something' or 'the winning answer' are those like 'Humpty Dumpty' or 'Carthage' that are just names. Although we will see in chapter 5 that the issue is actually more complicated than that, yet, for many purposes, the semantic function of a name can be regarded as being simply to refer to something. Its reference, therefore, is just the thing it names. For the present, it seems plausible to regard that-clauses as names, and, at least in the case of complement sentences in the language of arithmetic, there even seems a possibility of saying what their references might be.

The analogy with '+' might suggest that the meaning of 'that' is the function that operates on the reference of '5 + 7 = 12' to get the reference of 'that 5 + 7 = 12'. However, the reference of '5 + 7 = 12' is the same as that of '12 = 12', and we know that the truth (reference) of (1) is affected by a change from '5 + 7' to '12'. So the meaning of 'that' will have to work rather differently.

Recall that the *de re* solution takes Helen's belief to be about the numbers 5 and 7 and how they are related to 12. If this belief has an object, then it does seem to be the structure $\langle\langle 5,7,+\rangle,12,=\rangle$. So the function that is the meaning of 'believe', by contrast with the meaning of + or =, *should* take as arguments complex structures. This is where 'that' comes in. We want the *reference* of the clause 'that 5 + 7 = 12' to be the structure $\langle\langle 5,7,+\rangle,12,=\rangle$. So we want the reference of the word 'that' to be a function that operates on the references of the parts of the complement sentence that follows it, and operates on them in such a way as to produce the structure $\langle\langle 5,7,+\rangle,12,=\rangle$ as a value. If we call this latter structure the *sense* of '5 + 7 = 12', then we have a rather Fregean account in which the reference of the that-clause is the sense of the sentence that follows it. Of course, Frege's own theory did not identify sense with structure, as has been done here, but such an identification makes a plausible link with the *de re* account of propositional attitudes.

Thus, we let the meaning of 'that' be a function (infinite list) that operates, not on the sentence that follows it as a whole, but on its parts. Consider the following example:

(6)   that 12 = 12.

On the *de re* solution a belief, say, that 12 = 12, could be a belief about 12 and 12 to the effect that they are identical. If the meaning of 'that' is a function, then it would be a set of quadruples, the first two terms of each quadruple being numbers, the third being a function from numbers to numbers, and the fourth being just the triple consisting of the first three columns of that row. In this case, the first two columns would be 12 and 12, the third column would be = (= would be the list of pairs $\langle x,x\rangle$ for every number x), and the fourth column would be $\langle 12,12,=\rangle$.

This solution makes the *reference* of 'that 12 = 12' the same as the *sense* of '12 = 12'. But notice, strangely enough, that it does so without actually using the notion of sense. For the meaning of 'that', as described, operates on the *references* of '12', '12', and '='. To be sure, it does not operate on the reference of '12 = 12' taken as a single sentence, and it has the effect of operating on what we have called the *sense* of that expression, but it does so in the unified functional way in which the meanings of all the other expressions work.

But one gets nothing for nothing, and there is a price to be paid. One price is that the sentence following 'that' is no longer a constituent of the that-clause. The constituents are the symbols taken separately. This immediately causes a rift between surface syntax and logical form. But such a rift may be inevitable. For if, as I argued in chapter 2, the objects of *de re* beliefs are not single propositions, but structures, then at some point this will have to be indicated. So at some point there will have to be a rift between surface syntax and logical form.

In what I have just said about 'that', I have assumed that the reference of a that-clause is the whole sense of the complement sentence. But the example involving the map in chapter 1 suggests that sometimes the that-clause may be sensitive not to the whole sense of '5 + 7' but only to its reference. Indeed, the example was intended to suggest that the sentence is ambiguous. In the next chapter I shall argue for two things: first, that sentences of propositional attitude are ambiguous, and second, that the ambiguity is to be located in the word 'that' (or in whatever mechanism plays the equivalent structural role) and not in either the attitude verb or any part of the complement sentence.

Chapter 4
Structural Ambiguity

We have seen how the *de re* solution to the problem of propositional attitudes may be incorporated into a functionally compositional semantics. The idea is that the reference of a that-clause can sometimes be the structure that is the sense of the sentence that follows it. The sense of a sentence is just the structure composed out of the references of its parts. In the case of our arithmetical language, the references of the numerals are just the numbers they conventionally denote, the meaning of '+' is a function (in the sense of an infinite list), and the meaning of other arithmetical operation signs is analogous. The other kind of symbol is a predicate like '='. What sort of thing is its meaning? Presumably the meaning of '=' is a function from x and y to the proposition that $x = y$. But what is this proposition? Propositions have often been held to be the objects of propositional attitudes. Why else indeed were the latter so called? Presumably not because of their size. But one of the claims of chapter 2 was that things are a little more complicated. For the present I would like to postpone the question of the nature of propositions. It will form the principal topic of part II. All I want to note here is the intimate connection between propositions (whatever they are) and truth and falsity. For I hold the most certain principle of semantics to be that any two sentences that differ in truth value differ also in the proposition they express.

In chapter 1 I suggested that propositional attitude sentences are ambiguous. Here I want to amplify the arguments for this ambiguity, in a way that will support and extend the treatment of that-clauses outlined in chapter 3.

In order to show this, I propose to consider the semantics of a variety of propositional attitude words. This will show that the problem is not really, as many philosophers have supposed, a problem about the nature of belief, but a rather more general one. Two important constraints will guide the discussion. I will insist that the kind of analysis offered for one attitude should be applicable to all. That is, the only difference allowed in the semantics of

(1) $x \phi$ that p

for different choices of ϕ will be that which arises from the meaning of ϕ. The other constraint is that ϕ be unambiguous. This constraint is linked with the first, in that an ambiguity postulated for one ϕ would have to be systematically repeated for every ϕ and therefore should be represented not by an ambiguity in ϕ, but rather by an ambiguity in its complement. Part of the evidence for putting the ambiguity in the that-clause comes from the fact that parallel ambiguities appear in a variety of attitude verbs and it is undesirable to postulate a parallel system of ambiguities in a large range of words and phrases (particularly when a possible infinity of verb phrases may be involved) when one will do. What I want to do now is to develop further the examples from chapter 1 involving the verb 'indicates'.

Suppose that I am reading a map in which sectional distances are given along a route my wife and I propose to travel. The map might look like this:

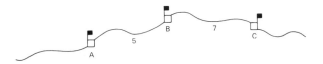

It is clear to me that the map indicates that it is 12 kilometers from A to C. Suppose now that my wife is driving and asks me how far it is from A to C. It seems to me that I might equally well give any of the following answers:

(2)   Well, the map indicates that it is 12 kilometers from A to C.

(3)   Well, the map indicates that it is 5 + 7 kilometers from A to C.

(4)   Well, the map indicates that it is 7 + 5 kilometers from A to C.

I might utter (2) if I had done the addition; I might utter (3) if I had been reading the map from left to right; and I might utter (4) if I had been reading the map, against the direction of travel, from right to left. But the point is that they could all be equally true reports about what the map indicates. (I would argue that this is a case in which only the reference and not the sense of '5 + 7' and '7 + 5' is involved.)

Contrast this with a situation in which I am putting the map to a different kind of use. My wife wants to know whether the long stretch or the short stretch comes first, so she asks me to tell her what the map indicates about distances in the order in which we are driving. I again utter (3):

(3)   Well, the map indicates that it is 5 + 7 kilometers from A to C.

In this situation I claim that (3) is true but (4) is false:

(4)   Well, the map indicates that it is 7 + 5 kilometers from A to C.

The interpretation of (4) in which the relative order of 7 and 5 is important can be clinched by adding 'in that order':

(5)   Well, the map indicates that it is 7 + 5 kilometers from A to C, in that order.

From these examples we can conclude, then, that (4) is ambiguous. We have to decide where the ambiguity should be located. Given the principle that we should not postulate an ambiguity in the attitude verb, in this case 'indicates' (there would seem to be no question of an ambiguity in the phrase 'the map'), the ambiguity must therefore be in the that-clause. How might that be? I suggest that the answer is found in the discussion of *de re* attitudes in chapters 1 and 2, which made it clear that there is no ambiguity in the complement sentence itself. Rather, ambiguity is in whether that sentence is evaluated as a whole unit, or whether the references of its parts are taken separately.

What has been said so far about *de re* attitudes suggests that, at the level of logical form, a variety of distinct symbols might underlie the one surface 'that', depending on how the complement sentence is to be evaluated. This means that (3) and (4) have different syntactic structures at the level of logical representation. An alternative solution would be to say that 'that' is a context-sensitive symbol, and that it is the duty of one of the contextual indices to tell it how to apply to the sentence that follows it. I do not myself find the latter alternative very plausible, but I do not think much turns on whether or not it is adopted. Either the structure of the sentence says 'Sometimes operate on the references of the parts and sometimes on the whole' or the context says to do this. (Even the first alternative will require principles of some kind to say which structure should be chosen to represent the sentence involved in some particular speech event. But they would not be strictly semantic principles in this case.)

In the formal language to be introduced in part III the ambiguity will be accommodated by postulating a range of distinct lexical items underlying the one surface word 'that'. This seems to be the most appropriate device for the formal framework adopted there, but, details aside, the key feature is simply that the ambiguity in propositional attitude sentences should be located in the that-clause but not in the complement sentence.

In locating the ambiguity in propositional attitude sentences in the that-clause rather than in the attitude verb, I do not of course want to suggest that each verb operates in the same way. Some verbs, like 'say' and (even more strikingly) 'giggle' and 'holler', seem to be sensitive even to the form of the complement sentence and to operate in a partly quotational manner. Some, at the other extreme, seem sensitive to nothing more than the reference of the embedded sentence. (Recall that I am using the term 'reference' to mean the proposition that is the semantic value of the complement sentence obtained in a function-and-argument way from the references of the words in the sentence. In part II I shall mention a pair of rather different notions of sense and reference. In the arithmetical language the reference can be identified with a truth value, but that is because of a peculiarity of that language.)

A verb expression that seems least sensitive to sense is the phrase 'is true'. (I shall treat this as a single phrase, though the fact that it is constructed using the adjective 'true' would eventually have to be accounted for along with the various uses of that adjective.) The phrase 'is true' can take not only that-clauses but also direct quotations as its arguments:

(6) '5 + 7 = 12' is true.

(7) That 5 + 7 = 12 is true.

The latter is often phrased as

(8) It is true that 5 + 7 = 12.

I am taking (8) to be a more elaborate version of (7) (presumably derived from it by extraposition).

Surprisingly, this very simple case causes problems. The problems arise because of our assumption that the attitude verbs are univocal. Applied to this case, it means that the phrase 'is true' in (6) and (7) must be the same. Unfortunately, it is known that the phrase 'is true' in (6) (via its negation 'is false') leads to semantic paradox in a language with the richness of English. Since this book is not about the semantic paradoxes, I shall say little more than that I favor some sort of levels of language theory in order to solve them. I will come back to this point later. At the moment note only that there will be problems in identifying 'is true' in (6) and (7) (because of the problems in the case of (6)).

What about (7) on its own? If we consider only a sentence like (7), there need be no problem, because 'is true' in (7) need operate only on the reference of the complement sentence. Remember that ambiguities in propositional attitude sentences are indicated by the meaning of 'that'. In the case of (7) we can take the meaning of 'that' to be simply the identity function, the function that operates on the reference of the complement sentence to give, as its value, the very same thing. This function is just the two-column list in which the same thing appears (in each row) in both columns. The "things" now are propositions, things whose nature we have as yet not specified. So the reference of a that-clause is just the same as the reference of the sentence that follows it. However, syntax prevents a that-clause from being a sentence. We need a predicate to turn it into one. One such predicate is 'is true', the predicate whose meaning is also the identity function, the very same list as the meaning of 'that'. As a result, (7) has the same reference as '5 + 7 = 12'. And in general 'it is true that α' has the same reference as α. The fact that 'it is true that α' means no more than α has led to what is called the *redundancy* of truth. It can be seen why this view is false. The word 'that' is independently needed because of other predicates besides 'is true', and the predicate 'is true' is needed because of other complement phrases, as in

(9)   What Helen said is true.

It is only their combination that leads to redundancy.

A sentence like (9) is interesting because it does not seem to be clear whether the phrase 'is true' is the paradox-generating predicate of sentences or the innocuous predicate of propositions. Perhaps in this case we can (as I think most philosophers have supposed) just assume that until we know which 'is true' is involved, the meaning of (9) is just unclear.

But the situation is actually worse than that when we consider a that-clause that is sensitive to the parts of the embedded sentence. Let us call the 'that' in (7) 'that$_0$'. The meaning of 'that$_0$' is just the identity function operating on the reference of '5 + 7 = 12'. Now consider a 'that' of the kind discussed in chapter 3 that makes the reference of 'that 5 + 7 = 12' the structure $\langle\langle 5,7,+\rangle,12,=\rangle$, which is the sense of '5 + 7 = 12'. Call this 'that$_s$'. What happens if we try to predicate 'is true' of 'that$_s$ 5 + 7 = 12'? In this case the meaning of 'is true' cannot be the identity function, because $\langle\langle 5,7,+\rangle,12,=\rangle$ is not a proposition. What it should be is a function that in the case of this

structure gives the proposition obtained by allowing + to operate on
5 and 7, and = to operate on the result and 12. In other words the
reference of

(10)   That$_s$ 5 + 7 = 12 is true

ought to be the very same proposition as the reference of '5 + 7 = 12'.
Which of these functions should be the meaning of 'is true'? Two
answers are possible, and unfortunately both lead to difficulties. One
is that 'is true' is defined only to operate on propositions (i.e., defined only to operate on the references of complement sentences) and
its meaning is then the identity function. (The predicate of sentences
would then be a different 'is true'.) The other is to allow the meaning
of 'is true' to be defined for all structures, but for its value to be the
result of evaluating out those structures. Thus, for example, it would
operate on $\langle \langle 5,7,+ \rangle,12,= \rangle$ to get the proposition that is the reference
of '5 + 7 = 12'. With sentences like (7) these two approaches seem to
give equivalent results. On the first approach the surface sentence

(7)   That 5 + 7 = 12 is true

would only have a meaning when interpreted as

(11)   That$_0$ 5 + 7 = 12 is true.

On the second approach (7) could have the underlying form of either
(10) or (11), but the semantics for 'is true' would give the same result
in each case.

The problem with the first approach comes when 'is true' is applied to something when it is not a that-clause. Suppose that

(12)   Mary said that$_s$ 5 + 7 = 12

is true but that

(13)   Mary said that$_0$ 5 + 7 = 12

is not. This could easily happen because (13) is equivalent to

(14)   Mary said that$_0$ 12 = 12,

and (14) could certainly be false while (12) is true. But if 'is true' only
operates on that$_0$-clauses, then the following sentence would have to
be false:

(15)   Mary said something which is true.

This is because the only thing that Mary said is 'That$_s$ 7 + 5 = 12',
and this is not even in the domain of the predicate 'is true' when

construed as only applying to references. Yet it seems obvious that (15) ought to be true, because Mary did say something true. On this approach we would have to postulate not merely an ambiguity between 'is true' as a predicate of sentences and 'is true' as a predicate of that-clauses but also an ambiguity between 'is true' as a predicate of various kinds of that-clauses.

The second approach, in which 'is true' is a predicate of structures but in which the meaning of the whole phrase 'it is true that α' is just that of α, irrespective of what kind of 'that' is involved, has difficulties of a rather different kind. These difficulties have been raised by Richmond Thomason as an objection to the whole idea of structured meanings, and they involve an application of Gödel's theorem on the incompleteness of arithmetic. Because I am trying to keep things as simple as I can at this stage, I will do little more than outline Thomason's proof. Yet it must be discussed because, if Thomason is right, it poses very serious questions for the views I have been advocating.

The difficulties arise in any language that is capable of expressing the truths of arithmetic. The language discussed so far is one of these. We also need to assume that such a language has been disambiguated and that there is an effective one-to-one correspondence between sentences and what I have called their *senses*. Further, since we may effectively number the sentences of arithmetic, there is an effective one-to-one correspondence between numbers and senses. By the techniques used in Gödel's theorem, this means that there is an expression *in the language* that may be read 'the sense with gödel number —'. This expression becomes the name of a sense when its argument place is supplied with a number.

Now suppose the language contains a predicate 'is true' when applied to all senses. This means that we can define a predicate T of numbers in the following way:

$T(n) =_{df}$ 'the sense with the gödel number n is true'.

(Strictly, we must distinguish between the number n and the numeral that represents it. The latter is usually written $\bar{n}$.)

Now, given any sentence α, we may suppose that its sense is the nth. This means that quite generally, where n is the gödel number of the sense of α,

(16) $T(n)$ iff α

is a truth of our semantical theory.

Using the techniques of Gödel's theorem, Thomason is able to show that there exists a sentence α that has two properties:

(i) The gödel number of the sense of α is n.

(ii) α is the sentence 'not $T(n)$'.

This means that from (16) we have the following as a truth of the semantical theory:

(17) $T(n)$ iff not $T(n)$.

And this of course means that the theory is inconsistent.

What are we to make of this? The question is whether these problems lie in the nature of semantics itself or are the consequences of an erroneous theory. My opinion is that they lie in the nature of semantics itself. In the first place I think, and have tried to show, that there are occasions when we refer to senses, though perhaps there are no occasions on which we want to refer to all senses. In the second place I think that there are arguments for identifying the semantic truth predicate and the indirect discourse truth predicate. These are arguments from the existence of sentences of the following kind:

(18) Jeremy believed that the sentence Miriam uttered and what Mary hinted were equally true.

If sentences like (18) are possible, then we are stuck with a paradox-generating truth predicate in any case and must take some steps to deal with it.

Thomason concedes that the inconsistency of such a truth predicate may not bother those who advocate a semantical view of the kind he is attacking. He is more worried by the fact that (following Montague's adaptation of Tarski) the same argument can be carried out for the predicate 'knows' when its second argument is a structured meaning. The paradox arises provided the phrase 'a knows' obeys certain principles used in Hintikka's epistemic logic. Now Hintikka's epistemic logic only applies in a community of logically omniscient beings, and Thomason takes himself to have shown that such a community cannot exist if knowledge is taken that way. However, the real moral seems to me to be that in a community of logically omniscient beings every that-clause following a verb of knowing only involves a 'that$_0$' and therefore the second argument is just the reference of the embedded sentence. Hintikka's semantics shows what this reference might be and shows as well that no inconsistency arises.

Chapter 5
Attitudes *De Expressione*

One popular solution to the problem of propositional attitudes is simply to say that they involve attitudes to sentences. For then, it is suggested, the reference to the structure is already automatically included, because of the structure of the complement sentence. The attitude verb for which this account is most plausible seems to me the verb 'say', which will be the focus of a large part of this chapter.

Certainly there are cases in which a person is reported as being related to a sentence:

(1) Lyell says 'Robins are red'.

I shall take it that (1) is true iff Lyell utters a token of the sentence 'Robins are red', and I shall ignore the possibility that saying may require in addition a certain level of understanding or any intention to communicate. Uttering is, presumably, a relatively unproblematic notion, though even here the question of just what counts as the uttering of a token of a sentence, or even just what a sentence is, could well be debated at length.

Now suppose that (1) is offered as an account of

(2) Lyell says that robins are red.

The reason why this analysis will not do is that (2) makes no claim that

(3) Robins are red

is the sentence that Lyell uttered. Any one of a variety might do, for instance,

(4) The robin is a red bird

or even

(5) Rotkehlchen sind rot.

What about (6)?

(6)   Lyell uttered a sentence synonymous with 'Robins are red'.

The first comment about this analysis is that whereas in (1) 'say' just means 'utter', in (6) it means 'utter a sentence synonymous with'. It may be that we should simply tolerate an ambiguity in 'say' between its meaning in direct discourse and its meaning in indirect discourse. However, as in the case of 'is true' in chapter 4, the ambiguity would require distinguishing not only between direct and indirect discourse but also between various levels of structural sensitivity. For example, consider the sentence

(7)   Melissa says that it is 7 + 5 kilometers from Motueka to Upper Moutere.

In chapter 4 I argued that such sentences are ambiguous depending on whether the sense or the reference of '7 + 5' is involved. If (7) is to be analyzed as

(8)   Melissa utters a sentence that is synonymous with 'It is 7 + 5 kilometers from Motueka to Upper Moutere',

we would be obliged to disambiguate two synonymy relations: one that is sensitive to the sense of '7 + 5' and one that is sensitive merely to its reference. This has the consequence that where 'say' means 'utters a sentence that is synonymous with', there are as many different meanings of 'say' as there are levels of sensitivity to structure. This directly contradicts the requirement that the ambiguity not be located in the attitude verb.

But the sentential analysis just described is in fact open to an even more serious objection. This is because whether two sentences are or are not synonymous depends on the meanings of those sentences. In the case of (3), for instance, Peter Geach has told me that the word 'robin' has a different meaning in British English from the meaning it has in American English, though I confess I don't know what these meanings are.

The assumption underlying this book is that a language is a syntactically specified system of symbols to which can be added a semantical interpretation. The semantical interpretation consists of an assignment of values or meanings to the words from which may be determined a meaning for each complex expression. This has already been illustrated for the language of arithmetic and will be specified precisely in part III. If we call the syntactically specified language $\mathscr{L}$ and the meaning assignment V, then $\langle \mathscr{L}, V \rangle$ can denote a semantically interpreted language. Obviously, whether or not two sentences

α and β, belonging to the same or different $\mathscr{L}$'s, are synonymous depends upon the particular V. A sentence α of $\langle \mathscr{L}_1, V_1 \rangle$ will be synonymous with a sentence β of $\langle \mathscr{L}_2, V_2 \rangle$ iff $V_1(\alpha) = V_2(\beta)$. (This ignores for the present the problem discussed a few paragraphs back posed by the existence of a variety of distinct synonymy relations corresponding to differing levels of sensitivity to the structure of the complement sentence. The present problems would still arise even if that extra difficulty did not.)

How then should (6) be analyzed? Presumably somewhat as follows:

(9)   There is a sentence α in a language $\langle \mathscr{L}_2, V_2 \rangle$ such that Lyell is using $\langle \mathscr{L}_2, V_2 \rangle$ and utters α and $V_2(\alpha) = V_1$ (Robins are red).

In (9) V_1 is understood to be the language in which (2) is being reported, which is not necessarily the same as the language $\langle \mathscr{L}_2, V_2 \rangle$ that Lyell is using. It should be clear from (9) that Lyell is reported as standing in a certain relation to a *meaning*, and only derivatively to a sentence. This can be seen as follows. In (9) let m be the meaning, whatever it is, of 'Robins are red' in $\langle \mathscr{L}_1, V_1 \rangle$. Then (9) can be rephrased as

(10)   There is a sentence α in a language $\langle \mathscr{L}_2, V_2 \rangle$ such that Lyell is using $\langle \mathscr{L}_2, V_2 \rangle$ and utters α and $V_2(\alpha) = m$.

I have little quarrel with (10) as an analysis of (2). Indeed, the formal semantics for 'say' that I shall propose in chapters 12 and 13 is in effect along these very lines. But the point about (10) is that the reference to the sentence 'Robins are red' has now dropped out of the meaning of (10). That sentence only enters in because, when we report what Lyell says, we do so by a sentence of our own, and in this sentence the content of what he said is specified by a that-clause that operates, with varying degrees of sensitivity to the structure, on the complement sentence. In (10) the meaning of 'say' is in no way quotational, because it would have operated in the same way on any sentence in any language that means m.

By contrast, a purely quotational sentence such as (1) relates Lyell only to the syntactically specified form. Unfortunately, there exist cases in which both the syntactically specified sentence and its meaning appear to be involved. The best examples I have seen are due to Barbara Partee:

(11)   She giggled that she would feel just too, too liberated if she drank another of those naughty Martinis.

In a case like (11) the meaning of the that-clause would seem to have to be something like the pair consisting of the sentence itself, or at least certain parts of it, and its meaning. And of course 'meaning' here might be sense or reference.

To 'say' a pair $\langle \alpha, m \rangle$ in which α is a sentence and m a meaning presumably consists in uttering α, where α is a sentence in the language $\langle \mathscr{L}, V \rangle$ of the utterer such that $V(\alpha) = m$. That at any rate is the style of analysis I shall present in chapter 13. If m is a structured meaning, then the analysis requires refining in a way I shall take up there.

One particularly troublesome kind of case that seems to be a partly quotational one, at least at first sight, is the case of identity statements involving proper names. Recall from chapter 2 the example of Ursula, who does not know that Hesperus is Phosphorus. Suppose Quentin tells her.

(12)   Quentin says that Hesperus is Phosphorus.

It is easy to see that (12) is not a purely quotational case, for the following will not do as an analysis of it:

(13)   Quentin says 'Phosphorus is Hesperus'.

This will not do because (12) makes no claim that 'Phosphorus is Hesperus' was the sentence Quentin uttered. He might have said

(14)   Phosphorus and Hesperus are the same thing

or even

(15)   You may not realize it, but Phosphorus and Hesperus are really one and the same planet.

But if (12) is not quotational, and if the meanings of names like 'Phosphorus' and 'Hesperus' are just the things the names name, then, on the assumption that 'Hesperus' and 'Phosphorus' name the same thing, they would have the same meaning and therefore (12) would mean the same as

(16)   Quentin says that Phosphorus is Phosphorus.

Some authors have taken the hard line at this point and have simply said that (12) and (16) are synonymous. For such authors the problem that I am discussing simply does not arise; if they are right, then my task in the rest of this book would be very much easier. However, it does seem to many authors, including myself, that (12) can be used as a report of a situation in which Quentin is telling Ursula something she did not already know, and I shall proceed on the assumption that it has a meaning different from that of (16). On the other hand, I will not deny that (12) may *also* have a meaning in which it *is* synonymous with (16). In fact, I think that much of what has been said about names relies on the fact that sentences like (12) are ambiguous.

Is (12) then one of the mixed cases like (11)? Under the analysis suggested for the mixed cases, (12) could then be paraphrased as

(17)   Where $\langle \mathscr{L},V \rangle$ is the language Quentin is using, Quentin uttered a sentence 'Phosphorus is Hesperus' of $\mathscr{L}$ such that where a is the planet Venus, V(Phosphorus) = a and V(Hesperus) = a and V(is) is the identity relation.

In (17) the meaning of 'Phosphorus is Hesperus' has been decomposed into parts so that the essential connection with the planet can be recovered. The analysis given in (17) is certainly an improvement on either the purely quotational or the purely nonquotational account. However, it does not seem to me to be entirely satisfactory for a number of reasons, the principal one being that it is open to the same objection as the objection to (13), that it does not allow sentences like (14) or (15) to be what Quentin said.

A more plausible analysis is to construe Quentin as giving Ursula information about the use of the names 'Phosphorus' and 'Hesperus'. Thus, (12) becomes

(18)   Quentin says of Phosphorus that 'Phosphorus' and 'Hesperus' are names for it.

The first occurrence of the name 'Phosphorus' in (18) (the occurrence in which it is used rather than mentioned) is a genuine *de re* occurrence; the word could be replaced by another name of the same planet ('Hesperus' or 'Venus'). We could even use a definite description, provided we agreed that it should have wide scope.

Of course, (18) does make it look as though Quentin is giving Ursula some information about linguistic usage. No doubt such information is empirical, but it is surely not the kind of information Ursula lacks, because she may have been present at the ceremonies when the names 'Phosphorus' and 'Hesperus' were bestowed, or, if the idea of such a ceremony is a little too fanciful, she may be well aware that the star seen in the morning is called 'Phosphorus' and the star seen in the evening is called 'Hesperus'. It is knowledge of astronomy she lacks, not knowledge of linguistic convention. But I do not think (18) has to be taken as reporting the imparting of linguistic knowledge. Imagine that last night you hit a hedgehog. When we go out and look at it this morning, we wonder whether the one we see really is the same one. Previously we had given a saucer of milk to a hedgehog and named it 'Chatterbox'. Suppose I say to you this morning

(19)   The hedgehog before us might not have been named 'Chatterbox'.

One reason why (19) could be true is that we might have given the hedgehog a different name. But (19) could also be true because even if the hedgehog before us *is* the one we named 'Chatterbox', it could have been that a different hedgehog had crept up in the night and replaced the one that was there. Perhaps the reason why we do not so readily think of this second way of taking (19) is that we construe (19) as saying

(20)   The hedgehog before us, although it is named 'Chatterbox', might not have been.

For pragmatic reasons, (20) makes it unlikely that we could consider the possibility of a switch, and leaves as its natural reading the assertion that naming conventions are contingent.

With this in mind, we can go back to (18). Although (18) could be used to inform someone about the linguistic habits of language users, in this case it is not. Quentin is informing Ursula that there is only one thing that is named 'Phosphorus' and 'Hesperus' and furthermore is telling her which thing it is.

Arnim von Stechow has called attitudes of the kind reported in (11) attitudes *de expressione*. The idea is this. In sentence (12) Quentin is not merely held to be saying something about the *res* Phosphorus (or Hesperus, or Venus—anyway, about that planet); in addition, (12) reports how Quentin's attitude to the *res* is expressed.

Attitudes *de expressione* should be distinguished from attitudes *de dicto* (the meaning of the Latin terms must not be taken too seriously). William's beliefs about buildings in Wellington discussed in chapter 2 are *de dicto*. *De dicto* beliefs in this sense involve the scope of definite descriptions and are not strictly beliefs about a dictum at all. Sentences about *de expressione* attitudes like (11) must be distinguished from purely *de re* attitudes on the one hand, in which the reporting sentence does not claim to specify how the subject represents the *res* (this was Ralph's situation with respect to Ortcutt in chapter 2), and from quotational attitudes on the other, in which a relation is claimed to hold between a subject and a particular sentence.

The analysis presented in (18) solves the problem with (12) by suggesting that in some cases at least a name like 'Phosphorus' can be replaced by a definite description such as 'the planet called "Phos-phorus" '. In fact, such an analysis has been advocated in a number of places, and it does seem to have advantages over approaches like the mixed quotational account offered in (17) or the hard-line ac-count. I will call any theory that says that a name is synonymous with an equivalent definite description a *description theory* of names. Not all description theories need hold that the description should have the form 'is called—', and even in the case of those that do, such phrases allow a great deal of flexibility in interpretation. The phrase 'the planet called "Phosphorus" ' is capable of a variety of interpre-tations depending on who is supposed to be doing the calling and on what precisely are the limits to the name 'Phosphorus', since it no doubt takes different forms in different languages. Of course, it may be that a name like 'Phosphorus' has the meaning of a quite different kind of definite description, say 'the star that appears in the morn-ing'. This kind of description might have to be invoked if we want to say that it was the Babylonians who first discovered that Phosphorus was Hesperus. I have no specific suggestions as to what kind of de-scriptions names might be synonymous with.

The description theory of names is not uncontroversial—quite the reverse—but I do not plan here to discuss all the objections to it. In fact, I shall address myself only to what I shall call the *modal objection.* Stated most simply, it says that 'Phosphorus' cannot mean the same as 'the planet called "Phosphorus" ' because, although

(21)　The planet called 'Phosphorus' is the planet called 'Phosphorus'

is a necessary truth, yet

(22)　Phosphorus is the planet called 'Phosphorus'

is not.

But what is the evidence for the contingency of (22)? Presumably it is that Phosphorus might not have borne that name. In other words,

(23)　Phosphorus might not have been the planet called 'Phosphorus'.

But equally

(24)　The planet called 'Phosphorus' might not have been the planet called 'Phosphorus'.

According to Russell's theory of descriptions, (24) is possible be-cause the description 'the planet called "Phosphorus" ' can occur outside the scope of the modal operator. And this allows us to speak about the thing that is in fact called 'Phosphorus' and ask what would happen to it, even in situations in which it is not called 'Phosphorus'.

Some people are not convinced by this reply. David Kaplan is one. His objection amounts to pointing out that in (22) there is no modal operator and therefore no way of letting the description refer "rigidly" to whatever it is that is in fact named 'Phosphorus'. Strictly speaking, Kaplan's complaint here need not be worrying because in a propositional attitude sentence like (12) we always *can* give the description wide scope and have it refer rigidly. And in fact the account of *de re* attitudes proposed in chapter 2 allows the objects of *de re* attitudes to be picked out by a wide-scope description. Nevertheless, one could accommodate Kaplan's concerns in either of two ways. One is to make a distinction between a rigid and a nonrigid interpretation of the description. Rigidly interpreted, the description singles out whatever it is that is *in fact* named 'Phosphorus' and continues to refer to it even in situations in which it is not so named. Nonrigidly interpreted, it picks out whatever, in any situation, is named 'Phosphorus' in that situation. The second way in which the description theory can be modified is just to say that although in most contexts names do nothing but denote, they can on occasion be used as descriptions.

If any one of these accounts is correct, then we have the possibility of an ambiguity occurring in sentences involving names depending on whether those sentences are interpreted in a *de re* manner or a *de expressione* manner. In the remainder of this chapter I shall argue that such an ambiguity does indeed exist.

A sentence like (12) is not a good example for this because the purely *de re* interpretation is not a plausible one. What is needed is a use of a name like 'Phosphorus' or 'Hesperus' in which it is not clear whether the information conveyed is information about which object it is that is Phosphorus or Hesperus or about some properties of the known object. The sentence I want to focus on is

(25)   Prunella has just learned that Venus is uninhabitable.

I have used the name 'Venus' in this example because that is now the way we regularly refer to the planet. If I had used 'Phosphorus', the fact that this is unusual might have made it difficult to accept that (25) could be a purely *de re* sentence. Now let us imagine that Prunella lives in a community of scientists who use the name 'Phosphorus' to refer to Venus and that Prunella has never heard the name 'Venus'. These scientists, however, have sent their own rockets to Venus and have obtained information about its atmosphere. They have just learned that it is uninhabitable. So (25) is true. But the following sentence is false:

(26)   Prunella has just learned that the thing of which 'Venus' is a name is uninhabitable.

Or rather (26) is false if the description 'the thing of which "Venus" is the name' has narrow scope with respect to 'Prunella has just learned that'. This shows that there must be a purely *de re* reading of (26) that is not in any sense *de expressione*.

Now consider (25) used in rather different circumstances. Prunella's community of scientists is many years ahead of our own and (25), taken in a *de re* sense, is false. Many years later they come across writings that describe a planet called 'Venus', but it is unclear from these writings whether 'Venus' refers to the planet Prunella's community calls 'Phosphorus' or the planet they call 'Earth'. Prunella is charged with the task of studying these writings carefully to try to decide this issue. These writings date from a time when our science has advanced enough for us also to discover that the atmosphere of Venus will not support life, and at last comes the day when Prunella, from her study of the documents, learns that Venus is uninhabitable and is able to resolve the problem about which planet the documents refer to.

So (25) is true. But this means that (25) is ambiguous since, taken in the *de re* way, it is false, because Prunella, along with the rest of her scientific community, had the result of the rocket's expedition many years before and has certainly not just learned it.

In chapter 2 I suggested that mathematical beliefs are not quotational, by the example of imagining that Trevor uses the numeral '5' to refer to the number 3 and the numeral '3' to refer to 5. But perhaps Trevor's belief could be *de expressione*. If so, it might enable us to dispense with structured meanings. But in fact it is just as easy to show that Trevor's mathematical beliefs are *de re* as it was to show that Prunella could have a *de re* belief about Venus. Let us suppose that the interchangeability of '5' and '3' occurs also in their role as digits, and let us suppose that the community of scientists and mathematicians that Prunella and Trevor inhabit is one in which some mathematicians have interchanged the digits and some have not. This state of affairs is potentially confusing and so those who have interchanged the digits wear a red badge on their lapels, while those who have not wear a green badge. Now Trevor has the habit of studying a new prime number every day, though he only began this a fortnight ago when he thought a lot about the evenness of two and how unique a prime it was. Yesterday he studied 13. Unfortunately, we do not know whether he wears a red badge or a green badge, so we have no idea whether he uses the numeral '13' or '15'. However, we do know that the following is true:

(27)   Trevor is now able to prove that 13 is prime.

This surely has to be so for the following reason. We are the Mathematical Studies Board that is required to select mathematicians for further training. The nature of the community is such that there is no hope of reforming the nonuniform nomenclature in the numeral system. Nevertheless, the community is able to operate this system, with the aid of the badges, perfectly well. It is, though, very important to be able to prove that certain numbers are prime and so, faced with both red and green badges, we ask ourselves

(28)   Which of the candidates is able to prove that 13 is prime?

and we get the answer (27), that Trevor is.

I do not want to suggest that there may not *also* be a *de expressione* sense of (27) as there was in Prunella's case (though we do not, I think, say that Trevor has just learned that 7 = vii). But I do want to suggest that there is a genuinely *de re* sense, and further that mathematical beliefs often involve that sense. Nor of course do I wish to deny that an essential part of what goes on when Trevor has the belief he does is that he uses a numeral or some other representation of the number 13. The point is that the semantics of (27) makes no reference to what this representation is. It is necessary that it be a representation of 13. If the representation of 13 had represented something different, then (27) would no longer be true. And it is sufficient that it be a representation of 13. If anything else had represented 13, that something else would do. This is the whole purpose of the example. I hope these points are obvious, and maybe they are; but I shall have to belabor them a little more because there is a very strong tradition in cognitive science that at least appears to claim that meanings are representations. It is often conceded that the external public sentences that state the content of the attitudes will not do, but it is claimed that *internal* representations will. What has been explicitly claimed is that internal representations are the "objects" of propositional attitudes. In the next chapter I shall show that if this is taken to mean that the meanings of the embedded sentences in sentences reporting propositional attitudes are internal representations, then it is false.

PART II
What Meanings Are

Chapter 6
Why Meanings Are Not
Internal Representations

Actually this chapter is about why meanings cannot be representations of *any* sort.

It comes at this point in the book because in part I nothing was said about what kind of things meanings are. All I have said so far is that meanings form a compositional system and that meaning has a connection with truth. In the next few chapters I shall give an account of a collection of entities that will do the job that meanings need to do.

In chapter 1 I stated briefly why meanings are not representations. Perhaps that statement ought to suffice. However, in cognitive psychology, linguistics, and artificial intelligence there is a strong tradition that appears to claim that they are. To be specific, there is a strong tradition that appears to claim that the meanings of expressions in the overt public language that we use to communicate with each other are expressions in a "language of thought" in which we think. I say that this tradition "appears" to claim this because the claims are usually expressed a little differently. What is usually claimed is that the "objects" of propositional attitudes are expressions in a system of internal representations, the characteristic propositional attitude being taken to be belief. I shall show that this way of putting the question masks a confusion between two quite different tasks, and that the concentration on belief obscures the relative importance of the semantical task.

One of the most explicit defenses of the view that the objects of propositional attitudes are internal representations is found in Jerry Fodor's *Propositional Attitudes* (Fodor (1981, 177–203)). Fodor tells us on p. 177 that he is going to put forward considerations that "pretty clearly demand a treatment of PA's as relations between organisms and internal representations." First note that Fodor's way of putting the question can be taken in two ways. To show this, I will choose 'say' (as used in indirect discourse) as my example of a propositional attitude verb. (Although Fodor is careful to make his points about propositional attitudes in general, he does seem to have in mind the more mental ones like belief; so he may not have seen that there are two quite distinct questions.) Consider

(1)   Ambrose says that it will rain.

Let us call Ambrose the subject of (1). The attitude is that of saying: What is the object? One way of taking this question is to ask what the meaning of the that-clause is. That is the way of taking it that this book is all about. But there is another way, for one might well ask what makes (1) true. The answer will be that (1) is true because Ambrose utters a certain sentence. In this way of taking the question, the object of the attitude will be the sentence that Ambrose actually produces. Perhaps it is the sentence 'It will rain', but perhaps it is not. What does seem to be true is that it is a sentence which *represents* that it will rain. There is of course a problem about what it is for a sentence to represent something and about what it is that is represented. In fact, that is the problem of this book. However, it can perhaps be seen why the object (in this sense) of the attitude is called a representation. But notice that the object of the attitude reported in (1) cannot be the meaning of the that-clause. This can be seen even if we do not have much idea of what the meaning of a that-clause actually is; for we can use and understand (1) without knowing what sentence Ambrose actually uttered. Indeed, if (1) is false, there will be no appropriate sentence that Ambrose uttered. Yet none of this prevents (1) from being used and its meaning from being known.

When Fodor speaks about the object of belief being an internal representation, he must be taken as understanding 'object' not in the semantic way as the meaning of a that-clause but rather in a way in which the objects of indirect discourse are the sentences that are uttered when these reports are true. Taken in the semantic way, Fodor's claim is wrong. But there is clearly a sense in which Fodor's claim is at least partly right in the case of saying. For when (1) is true there is a relation, that of uttering, possibly with additional conditions involving sincerity or at least comprehension, that holds between an organism and a representation. In this case the representation is not an internal but an external one—a sentence in a public language—but it is certainly there. In fact, it is fairly clear that Fodor's concerns—the place of propositional attitudes in psychological explanation—are not the semanticist's. In the case of saying, Fodor's concerns would be paralleled by those of the speech-act theorist engaged in giving an analysis of what goes on during the activity of discourse. Fodor is particularly interested in the belief/desire explanation of behavior. His views have been disputed (by Paul

Churchland (1981), for instance), but the important thing here is to see that these concerns are not the concerns of the semanticist.

In (1) the empirical concerns involve Ambrose and what he does. The theorist for whom these concerns are paramount wants to give an account of what goes on when Ambrose utters a sentence and how it is related with the rest of his behavior. The semanticist's concerns are rather different. To be sure, sentence (1) is about Ambrose, and it is what Ambrose does with his sentence that makes (1) true, if it is true; but in investigating what its meaning is, it is not what Ambrose does or what goes on in Ambrose's mind that is relevant. If anyone's mind is relevant, it would have to be the mind of the user of sentence (1). But that is not plausible either, because we want the meaning of (1) to be independent of who is using it.

This means that a detailed account of how the subject represents the object of the attitude may actually confuse the semantical question, however valuable such an account may be in understanding what goes on when an organism has a certain attitude. It is convenient at this stage to introduce two technical terms. In a sentence like (1) I shall call the *object* of the attitude the sentence that Ambrose uttered. I shall call the *content* of the attitude the meaning of the that-clause that reports the attitude (in (1) it is the meaning of 'that it will rain'). This book is about contents; Fodor is concerned with objects. (At times Fodor seems to realize this, but, if he does realize it, he gives little indication that the semantic problem has not been solved by anything he says.)

One reason why the distinction between objects and contents (in the sense just introduced) becomes important is that, although the objects of different propositional attitudes are often different things, the contents are always the same. In (1) the object is a sentence of a public language; in fact, it is a public token of such a sentence. In the case of a belief sentence, if Fodor is right, it is a sentence in the believer's language of thought. Yet to make sense of a sentence like

(2)   Beatrice believed what Callum said,

we have to assume that the contents of sayings and believings are the same.

Fodor is interested in the causal role that beliefs and desires play in behavior, and a large part of his work is designed to articulate and defend the view that this is best understood in terms of the manipulation, by the subject of the attitude, of formulae in a mental code. As I have said, I do not wish to dispute any of this. (Nor of course am I competent to defend it, either. Patricia Churchland (1980) has pointed out that this view of things may do little justice to behavior at the semiconscious or unconscious level.) But I do want to elaborate what I have just said by looking at why the entities required in the causal explanation of behavior cannot be the meanings of that-clauses.

Consider the sentence

(3)   Fodor believes that meanings are in the head.

Suppose that meanings are internal representations. How does this help with the semantics of (3)? (3) is a sentence that might be uttered by various people on various occasions. And it is being assumed that it can have the same meaning on these various occasions. (If an assumption like this is not made, then the problem of propositional attitudes can hardly arise in the first place, for that problem is to say just how the meaning of (3) depends on, among other things, the meaning of the embedded sentence.) Suppose that I assert (3) to you. The problem is how you are to understand its meaning. Presumably you have to work it out by working out the meanings of its parts, among them the meaning of the embedded sentence

(4)   Meanings are in the head.

And now comes the problem. (3) is *my* sentence. So if the meanings of it and its parts are representations in anyone's head, they must surely be in *my* head. This means that when, by uttering (3), I tell you what Fodor believes, then the object of Fodor's belief is something that is in my head. But then it is obscure (to say the least) how it could play *any* causal role (except perhaps accidentally) in *Fodor's* behavior. Fodor, in Boston, is hardly likely to be causally affected by what goes on in my head when I utter a sentence in Wellington.

But you may say that this is unfair. The object of Fodor's belief is indeed in his head. What is in yours is the report of what Fodor believes. I reply that this will not help. For if (3) really is a true report about what Fodor believes, then the belief I attribute to him will have to be the very same belief as the belief he has.

The answer is surely this. What is important for the semantics of (3) is not the particular way that Fodor or I represent the proposition that meanings are in the head. It is rather the fact that what is in both our heads represents the same proposition. If you like, the meaning is a common property of all representations that represent the same thing. When I utter (3), then, I am attributing to Fodor a representation that shares with mine the property of representing that meanings are in the head.

This I think is right. But it shows that for semantics the invoking of internal representations is idle. If the meaning is now a property of representations, why not cut out the middleman and apply this property directly to the sentence itself? In other words, the viability of this kind of solution presupposes that we have already solved the semantic problem that is the topic of this book.

This is often lost sight of, and I think the reason is a preoccupation with attitudes like belief. After all, it is relatively easy to know (or at least to think we know) what it is to utter a sentence; so there does not seem to be a problem about the *objects* of indirect discourse. Because of this, we come to think that there is no problem about the *contents* of indirect discourse. And that is a mistake, because the problem of the contents of indirect discourse is as hard as the problem of the contents of belief sentences.

The trouble is that there are various hard *extra* problems about belief. And it is these problems that make the question of the objects (as opposed to the contents) of beliefs difficult. The computational theory of belief is often addressing these problems: Can beings without a language have beliefs? (No analogous problem about indirect discourse. Beings without a language cannot say anything.) Can one have contradictory beliefs? (No analogous problem about indirect discourse. One can certainly make contradictory statements.) These problems are certainly difficult, but they are not the general problem of the semantics of propositional attitudes.

This is what seems to have misled Moore and Hendrix (1982) into claiming that the computational model of belief solves the problem of the semantics of belief sentences. Moore and Hendrix certainly realize that these are separate questions, and in the early part of their paper they defend the view that believing is to be understood in terms of the manipulation of expressions in an internal language. I do not have the competence to comment on this claim and will only repeat that I do not need to deny it. Moore and Hendrix then say (p. 117),

> In light of the foregoing, there is a truly remarkable fact: although the psychology of belief is relatively clear conceptually, the semantics of belief sentences is widely held to suffer from serious conceptual problem. This might be less remarkable if the authors who find difficulties with the semantics of belief sentences rejected our conceptual picture, but that is not necessarily the case.

Then follows a reference to Partee (1979) and Cresswell (1982). It is clear from this reference that Moore and Hendrix take themselves to be solving the problem that forms the topic of the present book. It is also clear that they think that solving the problem of the objects of belief "ought to go a long way" to solving the problem of the contents of belief.

So what is Moore and Hendrix's solution? In fact, they give it in stages, as they realize the problems that arise. Its general form, though, is this:

'A believes that S' is true iff the individual denoted by "A" has in his belief set a formula that has the same meaning as S.

Moore and Hendrix make a few suggestions about how to analyze the relation "has the same meaning as," but, to say the least, their suggestions are extremely programmatic. They appear to concede (p. 119) that the details are not worked out, and they suggest that Lewis's work on structured meanings (1972, 182–186) may help. What they do not seem to realize is that *this* is the question that semanticists have been concerned with, not the analysis of what goes on when someone believes something. This despite the fact that they explicitly refer to a passage in Cresswell (1982) in which I was making, if briefly, just the points I have been stressing at greater length in this chapter. I have discussed the Moore and Hendrix paper at this length in part because they argue explicitly that internal representations help to solve the problem of the semantics of propositional attitude sentences, but in part also because, perhaps unwittingly, their article gives the strong impression that workers in the computational sciences feel able to provide answers to questions that logicians had been unsuccessfully fumbling about with for many years. It is important to realize, therefore, that the questions these workers have answered are not the questions that logicians have been asking.

The general form of answer that Moore and Hendrix have proposed for the question of the semantics of belief sentences can be put using the distinction made earlier between the objects and the contents of propositional attitudes. The idea is that the content of a sentence (when it occurs as the complement sentence in a propositional attitude sentence) is an equivalence class of all the objects that count as representations of that sentence. Some of these objects, the objects of mental states like belief, would presumably be in an internal language, while others would be in a public language. Others, such as the object involved in the sentence

(5)   The map indicates that it is 12 kilometers to Lower Moutere,

would be in a representation system that might not qualify as a language at all.

That two sentences should have the same content is just (ignoring indexicals) that they should have the same meaning. I have already mentioned one way of explicating this in chapter 5. Given a language $\mathscr{L}$ and an associated value assignment V, α and β, in languages $\langle \mathscr{L}_1, V_1 \rangle$ and $\langle \mathscr{L}_2, V_2 \rangle$ (maybe the same or maybe different) have the same meaning iff $V_1(\alpha) = V_2(\beta)$. But, as I pointed out there, this explication depends on each sentence already having a meaning, in which case the attitude may be taken as an attitude simply to that meaning. Obviously, this would enable Moore and Hendrix's program to work only if we had already solved the semantic problem.

If the relation $\approx$ of synonymy is not determined in this way, then one would need a semantic theory in which $\approx$ was built up directly for all expressions of all languages on the basis of synonymies for the simple expressions. I at least have no idea how this could be done, and it is not what Moore and Hendrix do. What Moore and Hendrix do is to show how to obtain the truth conditions of

(6) x ϕs that α

from the synonymy class of its complement sentence. But on the account they require, the meaning of a sentence is not its truth conditions but its synonymy class; and nothing they say shows how the synonymy class of (6) is determined. The recipe for determining (6)'s truth conditions would only work if the meaning of (6) were determined by its truth conditions. But the problem of the semantics of propositional attitudes only arises in the first place because it seems that meaning is *not* determined by truth conditions.

In any case it seems unlikely that merely knowing synonymies will give us any information about the relation between language and the world. And this, to which we now turn, is what the study of meaning is all about.

Chapter 7
Possible Worlds

So far I have said very little about what meanings are. In chapters 1 through 5 I stated that they form a functionally compositional system and illustrated this using a rather simple arithmetical language. In chapter 6 I argued that meanings are not internal (or external) representations. In this chapter I want to say what kinds of things meanings can be taken to be.

Meanings will turn out to be complex senses made up, as described in chapter 3, from simple parts. The simple parts will all be functions that are combined in such a way that by applying them one to another a reference as well as a sense may be obtained.

Functions are a special kind of set-theoretical entity. In fact, functions were introduced in chapter 1 through the idea of an infinite list. My first task will be to redescribe that idea in slightly more technical vocabulary that will provide the extra precision now needed. Consider first a one-place arithmetical function: let f be the successor function (in other words, the function that adds 1 to any number); thus, $f(0) = 1, f(1) = 2, ..., f(n) = n + 1, ...$ In set theory this function is just considered to be the (infinite) class of ordered pairs of the form $\langle n,n + 1\rangle$, that is, the class $\{\langle 0,1\rangle,\langle 1,2\rangle,...\}$. (A class is just any collection of any kind of thing whatever; in part I we called this class an *infinite list*.) If $f(0) = 1$, we say that the function f *has the value* 1 *for the argument* 0. The argument of a function can be thought of as the input number and the value the output number. The numbers that form the arguments of the function are called its *domain* and the numbers that form its values its *range*. In this case the domain of f is all the natural numbers, and its range is all the numbers except 0. In the case of the function g such that $g(n) = n \times 2$, the domain is still all numbers but the range is just the even numbers. A function is often said to be *defined* for those things that are in its domain and *undefined* for those that are not.

What makes a collection of ordered pairs a function is that for every first member of a pair in the function there is just one second member. That is, if both $\langle n,m \rangle$ and $\langle n,m' \rangle$ occur in the function, then $m = m'$. This is so that we can speak of *the* value of the function for that argument. An example of a function outside arithmetic is 'mother of'. For every human being x, there is exactly one human being y who is the (biological) mother of x. So if y is the mother of x and so is z, then y and z are the same. Of course, many different people can have the same mother, so there is no restriction that prevents $\langle m,n \rangle$ and $\langle m',n \rangle$ from both being in a function even though $m \neq m'$. (A function that does have this restriction is called a *one-to-one* function.) A function like the successor function operates on just one argument to give a value. It is called a *one-place* function. A function like $+$ operates on two arguments. $+$ is a set, not of pairs but of triples. $\langle n,m,k \rangle$ is in $+$ iff k is the sum of n and m. The domain of $+$ is the set of all pairs of numbers. The requirement of functionality here is that for any particular pair of numbers there is exactly one number that is their sum.

So much for technicalities for the time being. I hope it can be seen how the arithmetical language of part I can have its semantics described in these set-theoretical terms.

Some arithmetical functions are said to be *computable*. This means that there exists a device (which could in principle be realized by an actual machine) that operates on numerals that represent the input numbers and, in a finite number of mechanically determined steps, ends up producing a numeral that represents the output number. Now it is often suggested that for an organism or machine to know a function is just for it to have in it, in some sense, a device for computing that function. No doubt this is a very simple-minded view of things, and it may even be wrong, but I would like to go along with it for a while to see how far it will take us.

First we should note that there can be different devices that compute the same function. So the function itself cannot be identified with the device that computes it. (In the terminology of chapter 6 this makes the function like a content and the device like an object. That will turn out to be important.)

Now consider a community of language users who want to talk about arithmetical functions. We assume that they cannot look into each others' heads and so cannot refer directly to the mechanisms by which they are able to compute functions. There are, it seems to me, just two ways in which they can learn a new function. One way is by being given an explicit definition of it. In this case it seems plausible to suppose that what they have learned can be represented by a complex structure that reflects the definition of the function. The other way they can learn is by being given examples.

We can now recall a point once made by Wittgenstein (1953) about the learning of a mathematical sequence. Wittgenstein noticed that when a mathematical sequence is presented by giving a selection of its terms, there is always the possibility of getting the formula that defines it wrong. Nevertheless, we often get it right and somehow know that we and the person who has presented the sequence to us have the same function in mind. Presumably such understanding is only possible because we each have an internal mechanism for computing the function. But since we cannot look into each other's heads, it seems plausible to say that it is the function itself that is this common meaning.

I want now to take this a little further. If a number-theoretical function can be learned by example in this way, then that function, I would argue, can itself become an object of knowledge. And that raises the possibility of a language in which there are higher-order functions that take as their arguments the lower-order functions that are learned directly from the numbers. This leads to a system of hierarchical categories of meaning. And in fact the system of meanings I shall argue for will be of just this kind.

The process of learning a function by being presented with a number of its examples I shall call *learning by ostension*. This is perhaps a somewhat abstract notion of ostension, since it places no restrictions on the method of presentation or the kind of things that can be presented. Examples can be presented by using direct perception, pictures, memory, imagination, or linguistic description. I want to impose no limits on this. The important feature of learning a function by ostension is simply that what is learned is just the function and not any particular way of representing it.

The mathematical language discussed in part I had not only arithmetical function symbols but also predicates like '='. Function symbols denote functions from numbers to numbers. What about predicates? I suppose they denote functions from numbers to propositions, it being left unspecified just what propositions are. In the mathematical case there seems no reason why propositions cannot simply be identified with truth values. Consider after all what the job of the predicate '=' is. $x = y$ is to be true when x and y are the same, and false otherwise. In functional terms, then, the meaning of '=' will be a set of triples in which $\langle n,n,T \rangle$ occurs for every n and $\langle n,m,F \rangle$ occurs for every pair of distinct numbers n and m. T (or 'yes') is truth and F (or 'no') is falsity. An almost equivalent way of putting this is to say that the meaning of '=' is just the set of pairs $\langle n,n \rangle$ for every number n. In general, for every set A there is a characteristic function C_A such that $C_A(x) = T$ if $x \in A$ and $C_A(x) = F$ if $x \notin$

A. These approaches are not quite equivalent, for it would be possible, say, to have a function from numbers to truth values whose domain is not all of the numbers. This function would be undefined for some numbers. In the case of a set, by contrast, every number is either in it or not in it. This difference will be important later.

We can thus speak of a predicate as being computable in just the same way as any number-theoretic function.

The strongest sense of knowing a (one-place) number-theoretic predicate would be to be programmed to compute it—that is, to contain an algorithm that, when presented with a representation of a number, computes 'yes' or 'no' depending on whether the number does or does not satisfy the predicate. This depends on having a way of representing numbers, and it is presumably an idealization, in that we often count people as knowing what addition is even if they do not always, or even often, get their sums right. Nevertheless, I think it makes plausible the view that the meaning of a simple one-place arithmetical predicate is just a function from numbers to truth values.

This of course has the consequence that any two *simple* predicates P and Q that are true of the same set of numbers are identical in meaning. Is this plausible? In the case of mathematics I think that perhaps it is. For even though this simple predicate must no doubt be represented to one somehow, perhaps by an algorithm that computes it, yet the claim that the predicate is simple is just the claim that how it is represented is not part of its meaning.

However, it is time now to move to empirical cases. One constraint on structured meanings would seem to be that they are finite and that therefore one ought to be able to arrive at a simple empirical predicate P whose meaning, on this view, would be just the set of things that satisfies P. Now we are supposing that P is an empirical predicate. That is, we are supposing that it is a contingent matter that any given thing that is P is so. Let us now add to the language a predicate Q that is to be the predicate that holds, of necessity, of just those things that P holds of contingently. That is, where $a_1, a_2, \ldots$ is the (infinite) list of things that are P, then Q is just the predicate 'is a_1 or is a_2 or ...'. If it is plausible to suppose that there could be a simple predicate of that kind, then it is clear that the meaning of P and Q cannot be just the set of things that satisfy the predicates. P and Q are satisfied by the same things and so would have to have the same meaning, which they obviously do not.

Could there be such a P and Q? It is surely implausible to be forced to suppose, from the nature of one's semantic theory, that there could not. And in fact certain perceptual predicates seem to me to be examples. Let us suppose that there is an organism capable of detecting perceptually whether something is red and whether something is round. Now suppose that (unknown to us and unknown to the organism) it turns out that *in fact* the things that are red and the things that are round are precisely the same. This fact clearly does not mean that the organism cannot perceive the difference between red and round, and so the ability cannot be encoded in an algorithm that says 'yes' or 'no' when presented merely with an object. Rather, it is represented by a pair of algorithms or devices, one of which, when presented with the object in a certain physical situation, delivers a yes or no answer depending on whether the object is red or not, and the other of which does the same for round. The devices are different because, although in fact they are going to give the same result for red as for round, yet in certain possible though not actual situations they might not. Further, although no doubt it is not the total physical situation that is relevant to how the organism reacts, no harm can come from allowing consideration of more features than necessary. A total physical situation comes pretty close to what has come to be called in semantics a *possible world,* and I want to produce a simple model of a system that might be said to "know" an empirical predicate, using the idea of how the mechanism would react in this or that possible world. I shall use the example of a thermometer reacting to the temperature around it. How should we describe in completely general terms what it is to do this? The answer seems to go something like this: The system will perform one act (by this I just mean will go into one internal state) in certain possible worlds and will go into another state in others.

I have deliberately introduced the term 'possible world' because, as noted in the introduction, I *am* interested in developing a semantics based on possible worlds. In fact, part of my aim is to make the notion of possible worlds legitimate by using it in the formal semantics of propositional attitudes. I believe that the notion of a possible world required for *that* purpose will show itself to be the right one. At this stage I want to dwell on the notion of possible world required in my description of a system like a thermometer because it seems to me to be a notion that ought to be acceptable to anyone, whether they claim to believe in possible worlds or not.

What I shall in fact try to show is that everyone ought to believe in *some* kind of entities that do the job possible worlds do and therefore that, at least in this use of possible worlds, the metaphysical questions about them, although they can be pursued for their own sake, can be left aside if they are not the main concern.

Everyone I hope will agree that a system like a thermometer reacts differently in different circumstances. Further, it is I think often possible to say what these circumstances are. They may be local circumstances, and indeed mostly probably are, though they may be global circumstances. In fact, we may as well say that it depends on the total circumstance, for nothing is lost by allowing a reference to more than we need, since we are not just now in the game of saying just *what* circumstances the thermometer depends on. One thing is clear, though: they are all *physical* circumstances, and so will be describable in whatever physical theory turns out to be the best one. I have defended elsewhere an account of possible worlds based on physical theories and in other places an atomistic version of theories like this. Bill Lycan (1979) has called views of this kind *combinatorialist views of modality,* and the standard objection is that this procedure may not give enough worlds, in that it seems at least logically possible that the world *not* be made up in this way. Whatever the merits of this objection may be in general, it does not apply here, because we are only interested in a system that reacts selectively to physical differences in its environment. If you will, this is taking a stand on the side of physicalism right at the beginning. Or, to put it better, it is seeing what a semantics for propositional attitudes would come to in the case of a system that *is* purely physical.

But it is not enough simply to require that the system react selectively to its environment. What is needed is the idea of its being right or wrong. Consider the thermometer. The thermometer tells us that it is 15°C. The thermometer is *right* if it *is* 15°C. Note that I am not attributing to the thermometer even the most minimal concepts in itself of what rightness and wrongness are. The point is that *we take* the thermometer to be right in certain circumstances but not in others. What does it mean for the thermometer to "say" that it is 15°C? It may mean that the mercury is by that number (or it may mean that the mercury is by the number 59°F). What it really means seems to be this: We suppose that we are given a complete physical world w. In this world w are all the facts, including the facts about the internal state of the thermometer. Whatever decision we have made about how to read the thermometer, there will have to be a set of worlds that would make the thermometer right; and the others would make it wrong (with the possibility of borderline cases because the machine is not sensitive enough).

The first point that emerges is that the worlds that determine the rightness or wrongness of the reading should be no more discriminating than the worlds that the machine is reacting to. Otherwise, there would be *no way in principle* whereby the machine could be expected to be reliable. Or rather, it is not even clear that we would know what it *means* for it to be reliable. For in general the machine is reliable in a world w iff w is in the set of worlds that represent how the machine says in w that things could be; for instance, the set of worlds in which the temperature is 15°C.

There is no loss in taking the worlds that represent how things are said to be to be *exactly* as discriminating as the worlds to which the system is reacting, because if they were less discriminating, then they could always be replaced by collections of worlds corresponding to each of the many "discriminating" worlds that could realize one of the undiscriminating ones.

I have discussed this question as if it had something to do with the nature of perception and therefore might appear to be defending a form of verificationism. This is true only in the following sense: that the meaning of a noncomplex contingent statement is limited only by what an organism with no spatiotemporal limitations could in principle detect.

The meanings of empirical predicates then may be thought of as functions from things and worlds to truth values. An individual a will be said to satisfy the predicate P in world w iff the value of $\langle a,w \rangle$, according to the function that is the meaning of P, is T, and it is said to lack the property if that value is F. Of course, the predicate may be undefined for many objects. Ryle once remarked (1938, 194) that it makes no sense to ask whether Saturday is in bed. It does seem plausible to suppose, though, that if a is in the domain of P, then the question whether it is P or not has an answer in each world. At least that is a simplifying assumption that it will prove convenient to go along with. The assumption is simplifying in that it lets us replace T and F with sets of possible worlds. A property (i.e., the meaning of a (noncomplex) one-place predicate) then becomes a function from things to sets of worlds. Where ω is such a function, then ω will represent the meaning of P in the following way. A thing a will have the property P in a world w iff w is in the set of worlds $\omega(a)$ that is the value of the function ω operating on a. This set of worlds can be considered as the proposition that a is P. So we now have an answer to the question of what a proposition is. It is a set of possible worlds. This answer will need refinement to take care of tense and other types of context dependence. These refinements will be incorporated into the formal semantics to be developed in part III, but the next task is to examine what sorts of entities emerge as meanings on the basis of the considerations raised in this chapter.

Chapter 8
A System of Intensions

In chapter 7 two points were made. The first point was that the meanings of the simple predicates out of which the complex predicates are made are functions from things to sets of worlds. (We can regard mathematical predicates as having as their value either the set of all worlds or the empty set. We should also allow a class of functions from things to things.) The second point was that any function that can be known might itself be eligible as an argument for further functions. I want to begin this chapter by describing what a system of noncomplex meanings based on these principles would look like.

I shall use D_0 to refer to the set of all sets of possible worlds and D_1 to refer to the universe of "things." What is a thing? Obviously, anything at all is a thing. I do not mean only physical objects but anything our language can talk about: numbers, sets, properties, events, attitudes of mind, and the like. Of course, there are all kinds of interesting questions about what these things may be, but these are not my questions. I shall use $D_{(\tau/\sigma_1,\ldots,\sigma_n)}$ to indicate a class of n-place functions whose domains are taken from $D_{\sigma_1},\ldots,D_{\sigma_n}$, respectively, and whose range is in D_τ. Thus, $D_{(0/1)}$ will be a class of (one-place) functions from things (members of D_1) to sets of worlds (members of D_0) and so on. The σ in D_σ may be called its *semantic category*. Thus, 0 is the semantic category of propositions and 1 the category of things. (0/1) is the category of functions from things of category 1 into things of category 0. Such functions are the meanings of one-place predicates. Semantic categories are cumulative in the sense that where we already have things in categories $\tau,\sigma_1,\ldots,\sigma_n$, then we have functions from things in categories $\sigma_1,\ldots,\sigma_n$ into category τ. In part III a language whose syntax reflects this arrangement will be produced.

Where σ is a semantic category, then, the members of D_σ are called *intensions* of category σ. The reason for using this word can be illustrated with the example of the category $D_{(0/1)}$ of functions that represent one-place predicates. Suppose that a function ω represents the predicate 'is P'. Then for any a in the domain of ω (i.e., any a for which P is meaningful), any world w either will be a member of $\omega(a)$ or will not. Put in another way, for any given world w there will be the set of those a's such that $w \in \omega(a)$. This is the set of all those a's that satisfy the predicate P in world w. Following the terminology of Rudolf Carnap, we can say that this set is the *extension* of the predicate P at world w. By contrast, the *intension* of P is just that which, at each world, determines its extension. It is clear that this is just what ω does: the extension of P at w is just $\{a : w \in \omega(a)\}$. A predicate P then has an intension, and in the case of a simple predicate its meaning is nothing more than its intension. That is what the arguments of chapter 7 were intended to show.

The intension/extension distinction must be contrasted with the sense/reference distinction introduced in chapter 3. As I am using these terms, the intension/extension distinction is being made within the realm of reference. In fact, I want to argue that the reference of any linguistic expression is just an intension (indeed, I shall have very little to say about extensions), and by this I shall mean just something that is a member of some D_σ. Senses will then be complex structures made up out of intensions in the same way as the structures in chapter 3 are made up out of numbers and number-theoretic functions.

Other authors have adopted a different terminology. For instance, Richard Montague used the sense/reference distinction in more or less the way I am using the intension/extension distinction. In terms of Frege's original intent there are, I believe, reasons for going either way; so there is no question of which terminology is the more correct. For the purpose of expounding the account of propositional attitudes defended in this book the two distinctions are obviously necessary, and Frege's terminology seems a convenient one to set against the intension/extension distinction.

The intension of a predicate is a function from things to sets of possible worlds. In the case of a simple predicate its meaning is just its intension, and therefore its intension is what is known by one who knows the meaning of the predicate. This view of things has sometimes been held to have been upset because of recent work by Kripke and Putnam. Their work, it is alleged, shows that meanings are not "in the head" and that speakers do not always know their own language. I am not sure myself just what it means to say that meanings are or are not in the head, and so I am not sure whether the view I am defending is supposed to be incompatible with Kripke's or Putnam's work. What I will do is to go through Putnam's example about the meaning of the word 'water' to show how it fits in perfectly happily with the semantics I am advocating. (I have already discussed the question of proper names in chapter 5.)

My goal is not to produce or defend an account of the correct semantics of 'water' that takes account of Putnam's argument. In fact, I know of two approaches, and there may be others. I only want to say enough to show that the framework I am using has enough resources to tackle the problem.

Putnam's example (Putnam (1975)) is that water on Earth is H_2O but that on a planet Twin-Earth that looks just like Earth there is a substance XYZ that is found in all the places water is found on Earth and that is, at the macroscopic level, indistinguishable from water. Putnam's point is that it is not water because it is not H_2O and that this is so *whether or not* a community of users of the word 'water' know that water is H_2O.

This is so because (roughly) 'being water' means 'having the same internal structure as that', where 'that' is an example of water (i.e., H_2O). XYZ does not satisfy this and so is not water. Further, it is a necessary truth that water is H_2O, even though the speaker of a language may not know this.

How can these facts be accommodated? There are at least two possibilities. First, that the meaning of 'water' just is the function that, in every world, picks out water in that world. In this case the user of the word, in a certain sense, does not know the meaning of the word. But does this matter? Suppose you are talking about someone I don't know. Surely I can agree to use the name for whoever it is that you are talking about. The point is that provided you are talking about a definite person, there can be no doubt about which person I claim to be talking about too, even though I don't know who it is. At any rate, I see no reason why this should show that the thing I agree to be understood as talking about is any different from the thing you are using the name for.

The other possibility is to say that 'water' means something that plays a certain role, but that the thing that plays that role in our world not only is H_2O in this world but would be H_2O in any world in which it existed. Thus, Twin-Earth is not a world in which what is water in our world is XYZ. It is a world in which some quite different thing is water.

Both these approaches, with varying degrees of sophistication (using double indexing and so on), seem to me to provide ways of dealing with the problem. At any rate, I see it as unconnected with the questions I am interested in.

The advantage of regarding the meaning of simple properties as intensions is that a straightforward semantics is then often available.

Detailed work done by possible-worlds semanticists in the tradition of Montague Grammar and allied approaches should show this. One particularly pretty way of illustrating it is to note how the semantics of truth-functional words like 'not' and 'and' come out. The intension of 'not' is just the function, in $D_{(0/0)}$, that turns any set of worlds into its set-theoretical complement. The meaning of 'and', in $D_{(0/0,0)}$, forms the intersection of two sets of worlds. The semantics for most of a language (in fact for all of it except the parts involved in propositional attitudes) seems to be obtainable in a function-and-argument way from the intensions of the simple parts. Thus, in a sentence like 'α and β', where a is the set of worlds that is the intension of α and b is the set of worlds that is the intension of β, the intension of 'and' is just the function ω such that $\omega(a,b)$ is the intersection of a and b. Thus, the worlds in which 'α and β' is true are just those in which both α is true and β is true. (A sentence of course being true in a world iff that world is in the set of worlds that is its intension. This is why the extension of a sentence is sometimes said to be a truth value—presumably why Montague identified reference with extension, since Frege held that the reference of a sentence was a truth value.) The reason why this composition of intensions is possible is that once one has learned an intension, it is itself available for presentation as the argument of a higher-level intension, and knowing an intension involves having the ability on occasion to work out the value of the intension for a variety of arguments.

In the rest of this chapter I want to say something about theories in which worlds are not taken as primitive but are built up out of other things. For example, worlds may be maximal consistent sets of propositions or of situations, where the latter either are taken as primitive or are themselves built up out of something still more primitive. (I shall take it that the principles of construction are those of set theory. I suppose this could be questioned, though I would be willing to conjecture that any principles that could be precisely formulated could be mirrored in set theory.) If this is a purely ontological enterprise, then I have no quarrel with it. I have myself very little to say about the ontological status of possible worlds. In fact, the burden of chapter 7 was that almost everyone has to believe in something that will do the work that possible worlds have to do.

The kinds of approach I do need to say something about are those claiming that the reference of a sentence just is a proposition or is a situation. These approaches do not use possible worlds at all except derivatively. Let me sketch how an approach would work that takes propositions as basic. I shall call this the theory of *hyperintensional* propositions. This is the simplest approach of this kind, and many of the comments on it will be applicable *mutatis mutandis* to other such approaches. On this approach a one-place property would be a function from things to propositions, and so on.

The first problem with approaches of this kind is that unless something more is said, we are left in the dark about what it is for a proposition to be true or what it is for two propositions to be incompatible or to stand in various logical relations with one another. Of course, as Richmond Thomason (1980b) has noted, one can always add this information to the proposition. Perhaps the simplest way is to postulate, in addition to the set of propositions, a set of worlds and a function that associates with each proposition a set of worlds. Where p is a proposition, we could let $I(p)$ (the intension of p) be the set of worlds in which p is true. Then p is true in w iff $w \in I(p)$, p and q are incompatible if $I(p) \cap I(q) = \emptyset$ (i.e., if $I(p)$ and $I(q)$ have an empty intersection), and so on. There are other ways of reaching the same result; for instance, if one has a notion of consistency so that any set of propositions is consistent or not, one can define a world as a set of propositions that is maximal consistent in the sense that any proposition not already in the set would make the set inconsistent if added. A proposition is true in a world iff it is a member of a world and the intension of a proposition is just the set of worlds in which it is true.

An approach like this is held to solve the problem of propositional attitudes in the following way. The problem arises because in possible-worlds semantics one might easily have two sentences α and β that are true in exactly the same set of worlds and yet are such that

(1) $x \phi$'s that α

is true, but

(2) $x \phi$'s that β

is false. A schematic example would be a case where

(3)   Desmond says that α

is true, but

(4)   Desmond says that not-not-α

is false. (This rather stilted example is chosen for simplicity of discussion. Some more realistic examples are given in chapter 9.) Assuming that the meaning of 'not' is just the complementation function in the set of all possible worlds, then the set of worlds in which α is true is exactly the same as the set of worlds in which not-not-α is true. So if propositions just are sets of worlds, these two sentences express the same proposition. (Of course, the solution I am defending in this book allows the possibility of a structural ambiguity, so that 'says' does not have to operate on this whole proposition but can operate on the parts that make it up. This kind of solution does not require extra entities like propositions separate from sets of worlds.) If the meaning of 'says' operates on the intension of not-not-α, then it must give the same result as when it operates on the meaning of α. But this would require that (3) and (4) never differ in truth value, and clearly they sometimes do.

Hyperintensional propositions solve the problem by saying that although α and not-not-α have the same intension, yet they express different propositions, there being no requirement that distinct propositions cannot have the same intension.

But although this appears to solve the problem, a few remarks will show that things are really no better. The first is that whereas the intensional meaning is quite clear for 'not'—it is simply complementation in the set of possible worlds—its hyperintensional meaning becomes obscure. For let $\sim$ be the function that forms the negation of a proposition. If $\sim$ is any kind of negation, then $I(\sim p) = W - I(p)$, but beyond that what? The reason I find this unsatisfactory is that it seems to me that the meaning of $\sim$ is completely exhausted by its truth-conditional description. I find it very odd to imagine that $\sim$ is a propositional operator whose meaning I only partially know.

What is worse, there are, it seems, some things $\sim$ cannot be, for whatever $\sim$ does, the difference in truth value between (3) and (4) seems to require that it cannot be a function two applications of which return to the original proposition. Why couldn't $\sim$ be such an operator? I have not seen any argument to show this, and I find it hard to imagine what kind of an argument there could be. In a way this last remark is merely an echo of the point made in chapter 1, that the problem about propositional semantics is not a problem about any particular view of what propositions are but is a general problem about compositional semantics. Since this is so, there seems no reason for leaving the intensional theory of propositions.

The same point emerges in a different way if we define possible worlds as maximal consistent sets of propositions. We can then add to such sets various different inconsistent sets of propositions. It is not hard to express every propositional operator as an operator taking sets of worlds (whether consistent or inconsistent) into sets of worlds. Different propositions with the same intensions then become sets of worlds that coincide on the consistent ones but differ on the inconsistent ones. Let a negation operator be any operator that behaves as complementation in the set of *possible* worlds. Obviously, among these there will be some that make $\sim\sim p$ different from p. But now consider what might be called a *super-strict-negation*—an operator that is complementation on the set of *all* worlds, whether possible or not. In the case of *this* operator ∼∼*p is* the same proposition as *p*. And why can't ∼ mean this? Surely the existence of this operator means that all the others are not true negations. If that is so, then it means that (3) and (4) differ in truth value only because ∼ is not a genuine negation. But one does not need impossible worlds for that. There is no reason why a function from sets of worlds to sets of worlds could be almost like negation but not quite and so give α a different intension from ∼∼α. Of course, that does not solve the problem at all. The problem is how (3) and (4) can differ in truth value even when ∼ *is* a genuine full-blooded negation.

All the solutions just discussed have the feature that they require a reworking of what has been done within possible-worlds semantics. By contrast, the structured-meaning approach being defended in this book has the consequence that all such work will automatically carry over and can be incorporated as it stands into a semantics for propositional attitude sentences. It also shows *why* there is a problem of propositional attitudes and why that solution is the right one. In the next chapter I shall consider how the structured-meaning solution works out when the structures are based on a system of intensions.

Chapter 9
Structured Meanings Again

In chapter 3 a distinction was introduced between sense and reference. The sense of an expression consists, roughly, of the meanings of the parts of that expression combined in a structure that reflects the structure of the sentence. The reference is the result of letting the parts operate on one another in a function-and-argument way. All this was illustrated using the arithmetical language. The purpose of the present chapter is to illustrate the use of structured meanings when the simple parts out of which the structures are made are members of a system of intensions of the kind described at the beginning of chapter 8. This view of meanings is not new. It is found in David Lewis's "General semantics" (Lewis (1972)) and has its origin in Carnap's account of intensional isomorphism (Carnap (1947, 56–59)). I shall argue that, despite certain technical difficulties, it is nevertheless the right approach to the semantics of sentences about propositional attitudes.

I shall begin by considering cases in which a propositional attitude verb seems sensitive to the structure (as opposed merely to the intension) of its complement sentence. The first example is this. Kerwyn is being set a logic problem. She is given some information and asked to deduce something from it:

(1) Kerwyn is given that there is a burglar in the house who is either stealing the spoons and forks or stealing the spoons but not stealing the forks.

The question is

(2) Is the burglar stealing the spoons?

Kerwyn, having obtained an A in PHIL 103, comes up with the right answer:

(3) Kerwyn deduces that there is a burglar in the house who is stealing the spoons.

I claim that if 'deduces' in (3) is replaced by 'is given', then the resulting sentence is not true. This means that the meaning of 'is given' is sensitive to the structure of what follows it. I further claim that (1) would serve as a perfectly adequate report of a logic problem given to a non-English-speaking person. That is, I can imagine the sentence

(4)   During a logic course at the Sorbonne, where no English is ever spoken, Kerwyn is given that. . . .

So 'is given' in this sentence (recall it is part of my thesis that that-clauses are ambiguous) does not seem to be a quotational operator.

In this example the context is one in which Kerwyn is expected to make certain logical deductions. Presumably she is expected to apply the principle of the propositional calculus that is embodied in the law

(5) $((p \wedge q) \vee (p \wedge \sim q)) \equiv p$.

It is not hard to express the complement sentences of (1) and (3) in such a way that they contain corresponding parts that have the form of the left-hand side and right-hand side, respectively, of (5). Using $\sim$ for 'not', $\wedge$ for 'and', $\vee$ for 'or', and $\exists$ for 'there is a', they take the following form:

(6) $\exists x(burglar\ in\ the\ house\ x \wedge ((steal\ spoons\ x \wedge steal\ forks\ x) \vee (steal\ spoons\ x \wedge \sim steal\ forks\ x)))$

(7) $\exists x(burglar\ in\ the\ house\ x \wedge steal\ spoons\ x)$

with *steal spoons* x as p and *steal forks* x as q, we can see that (7) results from (6) by replacing the left-hand side of (5) by its right-hand side.

In part III I shall be looking at a formal language in which the underlying logical structure of a sentence might plausibly be expressed. Here I shall say only that if the underlying structure is revealed by formulae like (6) and (7), then it is not too difficult to produce structured meanings for them based on a system of intensions. In fact, it is only necessary to consider the subparts

(8)   *(steal spoons x ∧ steal forks x) ∨ (steal spoons x ∧ ~steal forks x)*

and

(9)   *steal spoons x.*

Assuming that a particular value is given for x (I shall reserve the technicalities of the treatment of bound variables for part III), *steal spoons* x will be true in some particular set of worlds (call it p) and *steal forks* x will be true in some other set, q. Then, tolerating a use-mention confusion by which $\wedge$, $\vee$, and $\sim$ now represent the intensions of 'and', 'or', and 'not', we have (8) and (9) as the two sides of (5).

In some cases it might be tempting to treat a sentence of the form

(10) x is given that α and β

as equivalent to

(11) x is given that α and that β

and to treat the latter in turn as a reduced version of

(12) x is given that α and x is given that β.

If this is done, there would be no need to use a that-clause that is sensitive to the conjunctive structure of $\ulcorner\alpha$ and $\beta\urcorner$. However, (1) cannot be so treated as a reduced form because the phrase 'a burglar' acts as a sort of quantifier over the whole complex sentence. The 'and's and 'or's are inside its scope, and the phrase 'a burglar' is itself inside the scope of 'that'. There is no burglar about whom Kerwyn is given some information. This means that there is no way of replacing (1) by means of a number of distinct 'Kerwyn is given that . . .' sentences. The only conclusion is that what Kerwyn is given has to be picked out by a complex structure manufactured out of intensions.

The context of this particular example makes plausible, I think, that it is not necessary to dig more deeply into the structure of *steal spoons* x and *steal forks* x, and that the intensions of these expressions can be our stopping place. A little care is necessary, though. Suppose one replaces 'stealing the spoons' by the intensionally equivalent 'stealing the spoons and either eating the cheese or not eating the cheese'. Such a replacement would seem to affect the truth value of (1). But the use of such a sentence would almost certainly indicate that a different logical form is being assumed. Although the theory *allows* for a logical form in which the more complex sentence can replace the simpler one, it is often the very use of the more complex sentence that indicates that a more complex structure is involved.

Perhaps this point is more general. For there is a sense in which a sentence like

(13)   Miriam steals the spoons and either eats the cheese or does not eat the cheese

splits up into a number of very easily identifiable subsentences or subclauses. One could then formulate some kind of restriction stating that the meaning of a propositional attitude sentence almost always takes account of at least this macrostructure of the complement sentence, so that although 'steals the spoons' or 'eats the cheese' might be taken as denoting a single intension, the whole sentence never would.

My conclusion is that in nontechnical discourse most propositional attitude sentences are to be construed in such a way as to make the attitude verb sensitive to what I have called the *macrostructure* of the complement sentences. I am deliberately leaving this a little vague. In fact, it has to be, because one of my principal claims is that there is a large amount of ambiguity in propositional attitude sentences and so the theory cannot tie down at all precisely what the limits are. Applied to (1), the *Macrostructure Constraint*, as I shall call it, ensures that whereas 'steals the spoons' is taken as a basic unit, 'steals the spoons and forks' is not. How much structure is taken into account must depend on the particular context in which the sentence is used. Some support for the Macrostructure Constraint from outside the area of propositional attitudes comes from recent work by Arnim von Stechow (1981b) on the analysis of topic and focus, and work on the semantics of by-phrases in passive sentences (to be discussed in chapter 15) also suggests operators that work on large chunks of sentences rather than on whole sentences or on words.

The Macrostructure Constraint seems to me to be almost universal, though I think one can imagine some, admittedly a little peculiar, situations in which it can be set aside. One situation is this: There is a railway signal that can be in one of two positions. One position (up) indicates that a train is coming, and the other position (down) indicates that the line is clear. (Of course, the signal may malfunction, and we can then say either that what it indicates is not the case or that it does not after all indicate that a train is coming, and does not indicate that the line is clear either. My own view is that 'indicate' is normally used nonfactively and that the factivity, in its factive uses, is obtained by means of a factive complement. Nothing turns on whether this is so, or on the mechanics of its incorporation into a semantic theory.)

Consider now the following case. You are being set one of those logical puzzles in which you are given some information about what the signal indicates, but in such a way that you are not told it directly but are obliged to work it out. You are told to answer whether the signal is up or down in each of the following cases:

(14)   The signal indicates that either a train is coming and the sky is blue or a train is coming and the sky is not blue.

(15)   The signal indicates that every train coming down the line contains a married bachelor.

I would claim that the correct answer to (14) is 'up' and to (15) is 'down'.

The reason for the peculiar setting is simply that it would be very odd just to report the state of the signal by a sentence like (14) or (15). The isolated use of a sentence like (14) or (15) suggests that the signal is capable of giving more information than in fact it is. So I set up for you a situation in which it was natural to suppose that the (intensional) content of the embedded sentence was concealed.

If I am right about this example, it shows that the meaning of 'indicates' in these sentences depends only on the intension of the sentence following 'that' even in a case where the complement sentence has a macrostructure that would normally be taken into account. Since the verb 'indicate', as was argued in chapter 4, does seem on occasion to be sensitive to the structure of its complement sentences, the present example may provide a case where the reference of the that-clause is nothing but the intension of the complement sentence.

In technical discourse I believe that a great deal more structure is often involved. And often we must attribute a structure to the meaning of single words and not just to complex expressions. I would suggest that in technical subjects—and mathematics is one par excellence, for one might indeed say that that is all it is—and in technical subjects alone, do we have lexical items introduced by explicit definition. Each of these items actually abbreviates a complex structure and can be so treated in dealing with the semantics of propositional attitude sentences.

Lexical decomposition has had a rather checkered history in linguistics. One of the most frequently discussed examples is (or was) the decomposition of 'kill' as CAUSE BECOME NOT ALIVE. I may say right away that I do not believe this sort of decomposition works. It is no part of my program to suggest that the meaning of every word can be described in terms of a small number of semantic primitives. My claim is in fact rather the opposite, *viz* that lexical decomposition is restricted to certain rather special situations, to technical words in fact. It is the fact that these are *not* the usual situations that causes the semantics of mathematical and logical sentences to appear different.

In giving an example of a propositional attitude sentence involving lexical decomposition, I shall continue to use the attitude verb phrase 'is given that'. The example involves the two ways of defining 'finite'. Call a set *inductive* iff it can be put into one-to-one correspondence with a proper initial segment of the natural numbers; and call a set *finite* iff it cannot be put into a one-to-one correspondence with any of its proper subsets. Let us suppose that Imogen has just gone through Euclid's proof that if p is the nth prime, then $p! + 1 > p$ and $p! + 1$ is prime, and that therefore there is an $n + 1$'th. In other words, Imogen has mastered a proof that the primes are not inductive.

Harold takes this as given. That is,

(16)   Harold is given that the primes are not inductive.

Harold was once a student of set theory and tries to recollect the proof that all inductive sets are finite. At last he shouts 'Eureka' and claims success:

(17)   Harold concludes that the primes are not finite.

I claim that if 'finite' replaces 'inductive' in (16), then (16) is false. Harold was not given that; he concluded it. Yet 'inductive' and 'finite' are intensionally equivalent. If we look at what makes (16) and (17) true, by imagining for instance how they could be paraphrased for someone who is a bit unclear just what is going on, we would find that the paraphrases would give two different structures.

But notice that this situation can only occur when the terms 'finite' and 'inductive' have been introduced by explicit definition. One can imagine someone being taught the term in some kind of almost ostensive way. The subject is presented with a set and the teacher says, "No—bigger than that." Indeed, this is surely how it has to be. For I suspect that what mathematics does is to replace the informal way in which terms are learned by an explicit definition. Where the terms are learned in this informal way, then, I would claim that a situation of the kind outlined in (16) and (17) could not arise. In such a case I claim that the meaning of the word is no more than its intension.

This explains why the semantics of mathematical attitudes may appear to be so different. But perhaps it is not quite so different as all that. Certainly, if one supposes that the attitude verb operates on just the intension of the whole sentence, then there would not seem to be any interesting mathematical attitudes. However, it may be that the Macrostructure Constraint provides enough sensitivity. Take the following:

(18)   Gwendolyn has proved that the predicate calculus is undecidable.

The minimal structure (short of none at all) that we could attribute to the embedded sentence in (18) would seem to split it up into a subject 'the predicate calculus' and a predicate 'is undecidable'. Presumably (18) would survive changing into a sentence that referred to the predicate calculus by some other (intensionally equivalent) name. The meaning of the predicate in this case would reduce, in effect, to the class of all undecidable systems. It seems to me not implausible that (18) would still be true when replaced by a term that denoted the same class. One does have to be careful, though. If a predicate is used like 'either is the LPC or is undecidable', then this predicate is extensionally (and therefore intensionally) equivalent to 'is undecidable', yet

(19)   Gwendolyn has proved that the LPC either is the LPC or is undecidable

might well be true without (18) being true. Such a case would seem to violate the Macrostructure Constraint, however, in that the structure that would now have to be attributed to the complement sentence would not be the same as that attributed to the complement of (18).

Whatever else the considerations of this chapter have shown, I hope that they have made clear how much scope there is for maneuver in the use of structures made up from intensions, as the meanings of that-clauses.

Chapter 10
Iterated Attitudes

In this chapter I shall discuss certain technical problems that arise in applying the idea of structured meanings to the semantics of propositional attitude sentences. The problems come up most clearly (though not exclusively) in considering sentences involving what I shall call *iterated attitudes*, such as

(1) Mortimer believes that Natasha believes that the earth is flat.

This sentence contains two (not necessarily distinct) propositional attitude verbs and two that-clauses; moreover, one that-clause is embedded in the complement sentence of the other. I deliberately excluded sentences of this kind from the examples in part I, where the complement sentences were formulae in the language of arithmetic. I want to show that in certain cases the structured-meaning analysis of sentences like (1) can cause problems.

In order to state these problems I must set out the structured-meaning account in somewhat more detail. I shall first take a sentence that does not involve any propositional attitudes at all and show how to assign to it a sense made up of the members of a system of intensions of the kind described at the beginning of chapter 8. The sentence is

(2) Oliphant does not sing.

I am going to consider a somewhat idealized version of this sentence. Syntactically the idealization will assume that it has the structure

(3) *not* (*sing Oliphant*),

in which *sing* is a one-place predicate, *Oliphant* a name, and *not* a "sentential functor," an expression that operates on a sentence to produce another that is its negation. In chapter 11 the syntax of a formal language (called a "categorial" language), based on these principles, will be presented. This chapter may help in setting out the idea behind such languages.

A name like *Oliphant* in (3) is intended to be a word whose sole meaning is captured by its reference, and its reference is a thing. (In chapter 5 we considered sentences in which names could also occur in a more complex role. I shall assume that is not happening in (3).) I will take *sing* to be a one-place predicate whose syntactic role is to convert a name into a sentence. I will assume that the meaning of *sing* is just its intension. By the principles of chapter 8 this will be a function from things to sets of worlds. Here emerges the respect in which (3) is a semantic idealization; for I have ignored the contextual dependence of tense and other features. The meaning of *sing* will be the function ω such that for any thing a in its domain (anything of which it makes sense to suppose either that it sings or that it does not) $\omega(a)$ is the set of worlds in which a sings. The intension of *not* will be the function ζ from sets of worlds to sets of worlds such that if a is any set of worlds, then $\zeta(a)$ is just $W - a$; that is, $\zeta(a)$ is the set of all worlds *except* those that are in a.

A convenient symbolism here is to refer to the function that is the intension of *sings* as ω_{sings} and to the function that is the intension of *not* as ω_{not}. Now assume that o is Oliphant (so that o is the meaning of the name *Oliphant*). It is now possible to state both the sense and the reference of (3). The sense of (3) is just the structure

(4) $\langle \omega_{not}, \langle \omega_{sings}, o \rangle \rangle$.

In (4) the intensions of the words in (3) are put together in a way that mirrors (as indicated by the bracketing) the syntactic structure of (3). The reference of (3), in other words the intension of that sentence, is just

(5) $\omega_{not} (\omega_{sings}(o))$,

where by this is meant the result of first obtaining the set a of worlds in which Oliphant sings, by taking the value of the function ω_{sings} for the argument o (o being Oliphant) and then obtaining the set of worlds, $W - a$, in which Oliphant does not sing (which is just the complement of the set of worlds in which Oliphant sings) by taking the value of the function ω_{not} for the argument a (i.e., for the argument of the set of worlds in which Oliphant sings). The intensions of ω_{sings} and ω_{not}, as described, yield the set of worlds in which Oliphant does not sing.

Structure (4) is what I have called the *sense* of (3), and (5) its *reference* or *intension* (an intension being simply a reference that is a member of a system of intensions). But actually the framework is capable of a much finer range of distinctions than a mere sense/reference dichotomy. For there are intermediate cases in which part but not all the structure is taken into consideration. That possibility was used in the Macrostructure Constraint discussed in chapter 9. In (3) there is not much room to maneuver, but one could give it the structure

(6) $\langle \omega_{not}, \omega_{sings}(o) \rangle$.

This structure is the ordered pair consisting of ω_{not} together with the set of worlds in which Oliphant sings. If we call this set of worlds a, then (6) is just $\langle \omega_{not}, a \rangle$. This is because although when we write $\omega_{sings}(o)$ it looks as if we can refer to ω_{sings} and o separately, yet this expression denotes just the set of worlds that results when ω_{sings} operates on o. In (6) we know that the sentence is a negative one, but we cannot recover any of the structure of the sentence that has been negated. It is because of this flexibility that the semantics for propositional attitudes argued for in this book is not the same as, although similar in some respects to, a Fregean sense-and-reference framework. The flexibility is just that it is up to the syntax of the propositional attitude sentence to determine how much structure is to be taken into account. (There is another structure that the language here is not yet capable of expressing. That is the ordered pair consisting of the intension of the predicate 'does not sing' together with Oliphant. In a moment I shall need to make use of this structure. The language to be introduced in part III has a mechanism for expressing this.)

I want now to illustrate what happens when (2) is embedded in a that-clause. Such a sentence would be

(7) Petula says that Oliphant does not sing.

In part I I argued that that-clauses are syntactically ambiguous and that the ambiguity is in the word 'that'. That is why (7) is in surface form. In the case of (3) there are three different candidates for its meaning, indicated by (4), (5), and (6). This means that there are three different underlying structures for (7), making use of three different 'that's.

I shall call the three different symbols that underlie the 'that' in (7) in its three interpretations $that_0$, $that_{((0/0),0)}$, and $that_{((0/0),(0/1),1)}$, respectively. The indices are not so arbitrary as they may seem. The number 0 indicates the semantic category of propositions in the sense of sets of possible worlds. Now the meaning of (3) taken as (5) is just a set of possible worlds. So if we consider the meaning of (7) in which 'says' operates only on the intension of its complement sentence, we can represent its that-clause as

(8) $that_0(not(sing\ Oliphant))$.

The intension of $that_0$ is just the function ω such that where a is any set of worlds, $\omega(a) = a$. This is just as described in chapter 4. Syntactically, as noted in chapter 3, the function of the that-clause is to convert a sentence into a name.

In chapter 4 I contrasted $that_0$ with $that_s$, which operated on the individual parts of the complement sentence. As just noted, there are various intermediate cases. One is $that_{((0/0),0)}$. This is the symbol associated with (6). Recall from chapter 3 that one task of 'that' can be to make the *reference* of the that-clause the same as the *sense* of the sentence which follows it. In the case of $that_{((0/0),0)}$ its *intension* is a two-place function operator that takes as its first argument a function in category (0/0) (that is, a function from sets of worlds to sets of worlds) and takes its second argument from category 0 (that is, its second argument is a set of worlds). If ω is a function in category (0/0) and a a set of worlds, then the meaning of $that_{((0/0),0)}$ is the function ζ such that $\zeta(\omega,a)$ is $\langle \omega,a \rangle$.

Syntactically the that-clause of this reading of (7) is

(9) $that_{((0/0),0)}$ *not (sing, Oliphant).*

With the intension of $that_{((0/0),0)}$ as just described, it should be clear that the *intension* of (9) is just (6).

The intension of $that_{((0/0),(0/1),1)}$ is a three-place function that operates on functions in categories (0/0), (0/1), and 1, respectively. Where this intension is ζ operating on ω, ω', and a, we have $\zeta(\omega,\omega',a) = \langle \omega,\omega',a \rangle$. This means that the *intension* of

(10) $that_{((0/0),(0/1),1)}$ *not sing Oliphant*

is just (4).

In chapter 12 I shall give an account of the semantics of the two-place predicate *say.* Here I have only tried to show how to use the notion of an intension to make precise the rather vague remarks made in chapters 3 and 4.

Now at last comes the problem of iterated attitudes. In fact, the problem was already raised in chapter 3 in the discussion of (5 + 7) + 2. The point made there was that although there is no problem if + is a function that operates on numbers (that is, if + operates on the *references* of numerical expressions), yet there are grave problems if + operates on structures (that is, if + operates on the *senses* of numerical expressions.) Recall why there is no problem about multiple embeddings where + is a function that operates on the reference of '5 + 7'. In such a case + is just a function from pairs of numbers to numbers. The situation is exactly the same when the references involved are intensions. There is no problem in the semantics of

(11)   *not (not(sing Oliphant))*.

In (11) ω_{not} operates on the set of worlds in which Oliphant sings, to produce its complement. This complement is the set of worlds in which Oliphant does not sing, and there is nothing to prevent ω_{not} from operating on this set of worlds to get back to the set of worlds in which Oliphant sings.

Provided we consider only complement sentences involving *that*$_0$, there need be no more trouble with iterated attitudes than with double negations. Suppose that the following formula is the underlying structure of (1):

(12)   *believe Mortimer that$_0$ (believe Natasha that$_0$ (the earth is flat))*.

In (12) I have ignored the question of what logical structure 'the earth is flat' has.

The reason (12) gives no problem is simply that ω_{that_0} is nothing more than a function from sets of worlds to sets of worlds. It is the identity function, and so the intension of

(13)   *that$_0$ (believe Natasha that$_0$ (the earth is flat))*

is just the set of worlds in which Natasha believes that the earth is flat. In this chapter I offer no semantics for *believe* except to observe that the view of propositional attitudes I am advocating is that their contents, though admittedly sometimes being structured meanings, yet on occasion are nothing more than simple intensions. Or perhaps it would be better to say that the limiting case of a structured meaning made up from intensions is just a single intension. At any rate, I assume that $\omega_{believe}$ is defined for at least some sets of worlds. The intension of (12) is just the result of the intension of *believe* operating on the intension of *Mortimer* (which is just Mortimer) and on the intension of the that-clause. In fact, the intension of *believe always* operates on the intension of the that-clause, though the intension of the that-clause is not always the intension of the complement sentence.

The problem cases are those in which the outermost 'that' in an iterated attitude sentence operates on the *sense* of the complement sentence. For then we get into the same trouble that we would have gotten into in chapter 3 had we allowed + to operate on structures instead of just on numbers. The trouble was that + would then have to be a function that contains itself as one of its arguments, which is obviously objectionable.

The same situation can arise here. Consider the following underlying structure for (1):

(14) *believe Mortimer that*$_{((0/1,1),1,1)}$ *believe Natasha that*$_0$ (*the earth is flat*).

First, some comments. Both *Natasha* and *that*$_0$ (*the earth is flat*) are in category 1; that is, they are both names (remember that any 'that' turns a sentence into a name). *That*$_{((0/1,1),1,1)}$ is a 'that' which operates on the three separate parts of its complement sentence, *believes*, *Natasha*, and *that*$_0$ (*the earth is flat*). (The points being made here are not affected by the choice of *that*$_0$ to underlie the innermost 'that' in (1).) The intension of the outermost 'that' is just the function ζ such that $\zeta(\omega,a,b) = \langle \omega,a,b \rangle$. This means that where ω is the intension of *believes* and a and b are the intensions of *Natasha* and *that*$_0$ (*the earth is flat*), respectively, then the intension of

(15) *that*$_{((0/1,1),1,1)}$ *believe Natasha that*$_0$ (*the earth is flat*)

is just $\langle \omega,a,b \rangle$.

Now comes the problem. The intension of (14) is obtained by letting the intension of *believe* be a function from persons and structured meanings to sets of possible worlds, and by requiring this function to operate on $\langle \omega,a,b \rangle$. But ω was supposed to be the intension of *believes*. To evaluate (14), then, we have to suppose that *believes* has an intension that involves a structure containing itself as one of its own arguments. Clearly there would be a vicious regress in supposing anything of the sort to be possible.

There are certain technical devices for enabling self-reference like this to be admitted, but I do not think that such tricks solve the intuitive difficulty that it seems, if a sentence like (14) is to be admitted, that we must already know what *believe* means in order to say what it means. It seems to me better just to say that (14) is semantically anomalous and expresses no proposition—that whatever the intension of *believe* is, it does not have itself as one of its arguments.

What do we do then about (1)? First, note that the problem is not with (1) but only with one version of (1). There is no problem if the iterated sentence is construed purely intensionally, as in (12). So we could say (as in effect I once did say in an article on this subject (Cresswell (1975))) that any that-clause that contains another propositional attitude verb must be construed purely intensionally. However, this is surely too restrictive. I now believe that that-clauses must be allowed a great deal of flexibility. The problem is that since (14) is not semantically interpretable, what is to be done with (1) in cases in which it seems to be the right reading?

Such cases would have to be ones in which the outer 'that'-clause refers to more than just the intension of its complement sentence. But this does not mean it has to be sensitive to the *whole* structure of the complement sentence. In chapter 9 I introduced what I called the Macrostructure Constraint, which says that typically an attitude verb is sensitive to the macrostructure of the complement sentence, but only to the macrostructure. If we consider the complement sentence of (1),

(15)   Natasha believes that the earth is flat,

we see that there are a variety of ways of splitting it up without 'believes' being a constituent on its own. One way is to split it into *Natasha* and

(16)   *believes that$_0$ (the earth is flat)*,

where (16) is regarded as a one-place predicate. In chapter 11 I will provide a mechanism for doing this. This mechanism will ensure that the intension of (16) is just the function ω from things to sets of worlds such that where a is in ω's domain, $\omega(a)$ is the set of worlds in which a believes that the earth is flat. The 'that' used would then be *that$_{((0/1),1)}$*, and the reading of (1) involved would be

(17)   *believes Mortimer that$_{((0/1),1)}$ ((believes that$_0$ (the earth is flat)),Natasha)*.

The content of the belief in (17) would just be $\langle \omega, \text{Natasha} \rangle$, where ω is the intension of (16). In this case the intension of *believe* does not appear as its own argument.

It seems to me that most cases of iterated attitudes can be accommodated in this way. The remaining ones appear to have a 'believe' that really does make reference to itself. The discussion of (14) showed, however, that there could not genuinely be such cases. If it really appears that there must be and if the intension of 'believes' really does appear to be one of its own arguments, then presumably one would have recourse to some sort of type theory (of the kind involved in, for instance, the formalization of Frege proposed by Alonzo Church (1951)), and claim that there is really a hierarchy of meanings of 'believes'. The first is a function that operates on structures with no meaning of 'believes' in them; the second a function that operates on structures with only the first-level 'believes' in them; and so on.

I consider it possible that this solution may sometimes have to be invoked, but I do not think that it should always be so, and, as I have tried to show, a judicious use of the independently motivated ambiguity of that-clauses will almost always avoid the need for any self-reference.

A hierarchy of 'believe' predicates is just as awkward for quantified sentences as it was for the 'is true' predicate discussed in chapter 4. The problem is that a sentence like

(18)   Several of the things Rupert believes are quite astounding

runs into trouble if some of these things are, say, among Rupert's first-level beliefs and some are higher-level beliefs. Some of the trouble can be avoided if the hierarchy is cumulative, in that all the higher-level beliefs include the lower-level ones, but problems arise even here since the utterer of (18) may not know how far to go up the hierarchy.

I have to admit that I have no real solution to problems of this kind. However, I do not find this particularly worrying because it seems to me (as I noted in chapter 4) that these difficulties are inherent in the nature of semantics itself. For we can certainly form sentences like

(19)   Syllabub believes that all of her beliefs are false.

Such sentences raise difficulties for any semantic theory. In fact, it seems that we have to live with the fact that we just cannot quantify over everything we would like to. The only thing I will say is that the rather more flexible Fregean-style theory, in not requiring the level of the attitude verb to be upped at every iteration, ensures that most iterated attitude sentences are straightforwardly interpretable without the need for any higher-level attitudes. The latter only come in when forced to by the facts. They are not required to be there by the theory.

PART III
Formal Semantics

Chapter 11
λ-Categorial Languages

I have tried to keep the discussion in this book at a reasonably informal level. This is partly because I hope that has made the book easier to read, but partly too because the main aim of the book has not been formal. Instead, it has been to show what an adequate semantic theory of propositional attitude sentences would have to look like. But the matter cannot be left there. We have to know whether such a theory is possible. That means we have to know that a formal syntactic and semantic description of a language can be constructed that incorporates the views proposed up to this point. I will not be able to do this, of course. No one has produced a complete syntactic and semantic description of any single natural language. Within truth-conditional (model-theoretic) semantics, formal fragments of language have been produced, mostly in the tradition of Montague Grammar. But I do not want to commit myself to any particular fragment, and in any case the illumination, as far as the semantics of propositional attitude sentences goes, would not be worth the complexity. (Montague Grammar can be very terrifying.) Instead I shall set out the theory of propositional attitudes argued for in this book using a framework I have worked in extensively myself, namely, a λ-categorial language. Such languages seem to me to combine the virtues of a powerful formal language with relative ease of comprehension. λ-categorial languages seem to have as much power as transformational grammars; thus, it is highly likely that the formalization to be offered can be translated reasonably easily into any truth-conditional and model-theoretic semantical framework.

The best way of approaching a λ-categorial language is to look first at the formation rules of the propositional calculus. All well-formed expressions of this language are what we might call *sentences* (or, if you like, well-formed-formulae, or wff). *Sentence* is a *syntactic category*. In chapter 8 I introduced the symbol 0 for the semantic category of propositions. Since propositions are the intensions of sentences, I shall use the same symbol 0 to indicate the syntactic category *sentence*. (Some authors use the letter 's', and some 'S'. In chapter 4 I used s' for 'sense', so I prefer not to confuse things by using it again.)

In the propositional calculus the propositional variables are simple symbols in category 0. Now consider truth functors like *and* and *not* (which can be represented by a variety of symbols). We recall from chapter 10 that *not* is a functor that makes a sentence (an expression in category 0) out of another sentence. Its syntactic category is (0/0). The functor *and* makes a sentence out of two sentences, so its syntactic category is (0/00).

But the propositional calculus is a relatively meager language. For general purposes we need another basic syntactic category. The other basic category is that of *name*. A name in a λ-categorial language is an expression whose semantic function will be to do no more than denote something. Imagine that *Frodo* is a name. Since names denote things, the category of names will therefore be referred to as 1. One-place predicates are of category (0/1), because a one-place predicate makes a sentence out of a name. Examples might be the symbols for verbs like 'whistles' (in chapter 10 the example was *sings*), though no doubt words like 'whistles' should be represented by rather more complicated expressions when phenomena like tense and aspect are taken into account.

The set of syntactic categories can be built up by the following rules:

S1   0 and 1 are syntactic categories.

S2   If τ and $\sigma_1,...,\sigma_n$ are syntactic categories, then so is $(\tau/\sigma_1,...,\sigma_n)$.

We can see how S1 and S2 work by stating the formation rules. Expressions are either simple or complex. Each simple expression is in (no more than) one syntactic category, and (at least normally) there are only a finite number of simple symbols in each category (with some categories being empty).

Where δ is an expression in category $(\tau/\sigma_1,...,\sigma_n)$ and $\alpha_1,...,\alpha_n$ are symbols in categories $\sigma_1,...,\sigma_n$, respectively, then the sequence

$$\langle \delta, \alpha_1,...,\alpha_n \rangle$$

is an expression in category τ.

For example, given *Frodo* in category 1, *whistles* in category (0/1), *and* in category (0/00), and *not* in category (0/0), the following expression is a well-formed sentence:

(1) $\langle and, \langle whistles, Frodo \rangle, \langle not, \langle whistles, Frodo \rangle \rangle \rangle$.

This corresponds to the following phrase marker:

(2)

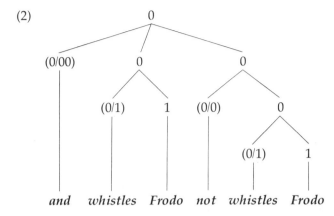

and   whistles   Frodo   not   whistles   Frodo

Often certain rearrangements do not affect the categorial structure. Thus, we might have

(3) $\langle\langle Frodo,whistles\rangle,and,\langle\langle Frodo,whistles\rangle,not\rangle\rangle$.

In (3) the syntactic categories of *and* together with the other expressions make it clear that *and* is operating on two sentences even though it is put between them and not in front. It is equally clear that *not* is operating on $\langle Frodo,whistles\rangle$ even though it is put behind this sentence and not in front of it. Liberties of this kind will be taken from time to time.

A language of this kind is called a *categorial language*. I want now to describe an extension that enables the manufacture of complex predicates. (This is the mechanism referred to in example (16) of chapter 10.) The mechanism is called λ-*abstraction,* and its addition to a categorial language—by adding an *abstraction operator* λ together with an infinite set of variables for each syntactic category— produces a λ-*categorial language.* The formation rule is that if x is a variable in category σ and α is an expression in category τ, then

$\langle\lambda,x,\alpha\rangle$

(called an *abstract*) is an expression in category (τ/σ). As an example, consider x to be a variable in category 1. Then the following abstract is in category (0/1):

(4) $\langle\lambda,x,\langle not,\langle whistles,x\rangle\rangle\rangle$.

This may be read as 'is an x such that x does not whistle'. It can be seen that it is a complex predicate. In fact, making complex predicates out of sentences is one of the principal uses of the abstraction operator.

This book is not the place to demonstrate how much of natural language can be expressed in a λ-categorial language. Nor is it the place to go into the question of the precise role a λ-categorial language might play in a formal description of a natural language. In an earlier book (Cresswell (1973a)) I argued that it should be thought of as giving the underlying "deep" structure of natural languages. Other authors have suggested that it is the language of semantic representation into which the structures underlying the natural language should be interpreted. (That is certainly the way Montague (1974) regarded his "intensional logic.") I now prefer to think that the function of a λ-categorial language is to test a semantic theory, in the sense that if the theory is to be plausible, it must be formalizable in such a language.

In a λ-categorial language, common nouns are in category (0/1), as are intransitive verbs. Transitive verbs are probably in category (0/11) (though Montague put them in category (0/1(0/01))). Adverbs and adjectives are in category ((0/1)/(0/1)) (though some adverbs are in category (0/0) along with such other sentential operators as *not* and the various tense operators). Prepositions are in category (((0/1)/(0/1))1).

An important class of expressions is those in category (0/(0/1)). In Cresswell (1973a) I called expressions in this category *nominals*. (A more common term in linguistics in *noun phrase* or *NP*.) Simple nominals are words like *someone* or *no one*. Words like this are higher-order functors on one-place predicates. If α is a one-place predicate, then $\langle someone,\alpha \rangle$ is a sentence that says that this predicate is true of someone, $\langle no\ one,\alpha \rangle$ says that α is true of no one, and so on. An ordinary name like *Geraldine* can also be thought of as a nominal. $\langle Geraldine,\alpha \rangle$ would mean that α is true of Geraldine. But, although a name can always be treated as a nominal, a nominal like *someone* cannot be treated as a name. If syntactic uniformity is wanted, then, we must treat names as nominals, not vice versa. Many problems can be solved by realizing that definite descriptions are nominals, not names.

These category assignments are the simplest categories that such expressions can be in. Sometimes more complex categories can be argued for. A great deal of work has been done in trying to give semantics for a variety of these expressions. I mention this in order to show that the discussion of that-clauses in the next few chapters will be integrated into a very wide-ranging framework for the semantics of the whole of a language.

The next task is to specify the meanings of expressions in a λ-categorial language. The idea is that the meaning of a functor—that is, the meaning of an expression in a category of the form $(\tau/\sigma_1,...,\sigma_n)$—

is a certain kind of function. Assume that we already know what kinds of things can be meant by expressions in categories $\sigma_1,...,\sigma_n$, respectively, and what kinds of things can be meant by expressions in category τ. Then, following the principles established in chapter 8, the meanings of expressions in category $(\tau/\sigma_1,...,\sigma_n)$ would be functions whose arguments come from $\sigma_1,...,\sigma_n$ meanings and whose values come from τ meanings. (Of course, the "meanings" we are now speaking about are in fact intensions. It will emerge in a moment how the structured meanings are to be incorporated.) As in chapter 8 I shall use the symbol D_σ to indicate the domain of meanings for category σ.

Suppose now that the meanings of $\alpha_1,...,\alpha_n$ are $a_1,...,a_n$ and the meaning of δ is the function ω. Then the meaning of $\langle \delta,\alpha_1,...,\alpha_n \rangle$ is simply $\omega(a_1,...,a_n)$, that is, it is the item associated with $a_1,...,a_n$ in ω (where ω is a list that associates something in D_τ with $a_1,...,a_n$). The meaning of abstraction is a little more tricky. The idea is that a predicate abstract like $\langle \lambda,x,\langle not,\langle whistles,x \rangle \rangle \rangle$ is understood as a function ω such that for any individual a, $\omega(a)$ is to be whatever value $\langle not,\langle whistles,x \rangle \rangle$ has when x has the value a. (That is, ω is the function from a to the proposition that a does not whistle.) The system of intensions used in interpreting a λ-categorial language is represented by a function D that assigns to every syntactic category σ a domain of things that can be the meanings of expressions in category σ. As noted, where σ is a functor category—say, $(\tau/\sigma_1,...,\sigma_n)$—$D_\sigma$ will contain functions from $D_{\sigma_1} \times ... \times D_{\sigma_n}$ into D_τ. These will have to include partial functions that may be undefined for certain members of $D_{\sigma_1} \times ... \times D_{\sigma_n}$, in order to avoid certain paradoxes.

This means that the kind of things in each D_σ will be specified provided D_0 and D_1 are specified. In one way D_1 is easy. It is everything that there is. In another way this is hard. What is there? In this book I am interested only in modeling the way natural language talks about the world. In natural language we talk about many things that give lots of philosophers the willies. We talk not only of concrete individuals but also of events, processes, states, numbers, conditions, tendencies, and points of view. I regard all these as being capable of being named—because we *do* name them—and as being in D_1. Of course, it is then up to those who care about such matters to tell me what kind of ontological status these entities have. No doubt they are engaged in a philosophically important enterprise. But it is not my enterprise. As with the functor categories, certain restrictions on D_1 are necessary to prevent set-theoretical paradox. Perhaps it is not even possible to hold it fixed once and for all.

D_0 is the domain of propositions; that is, it is the domain of the things that are the meanings of sentences. And what are they? At the end of chapter 7 propositions were introduced as just sets of possible worlds, though I remarked there that tense and other kinds of context dependence make extra complexities. It turns out that although tense is crucial, one can at least postpone other kinds of context dependence. Most of the phenomena of tense can be accounted for by having a sentence that can be true (or false) in a certain possible world and at a certain time. The time should be not just an instant but rather an interval. Thus, a proposition is a set of pairs $\langle w, t \rangle$ in which w is a possible world and t a time interval. It is likely that the situation is more complicated than that, but this will do for the purpose of this chapter and the next two.

Now suppose we are given a λ-categorial language $\mathscr{L}$ and a system D of domains of possible meanings for each category. We want to show how meanings for each expression of $\mathscr{L}$ may be determined. Recall that we are assuming that a language is a system of expressions with which may be associated a system of meanings. More specifically, a language $\mathscr{L}$ can be specified without reference to the meanings of its expressions, and a system D of meanings can be specified independently of $\mathscr{L}$. This is what has been done so far. To interpret $\mathscr{L}$ in D is to assign values to the simple symbols of $\mathscr{L}$ from which may be calculated the values of all expressions. What any expression of $\mathscr{L}$ means is therefore relevant to some particular assignment of meanings to its symbols. Obviously, different meaning assignments can give the same expression different meanings, and what one expression means in one assignment may be the same as what another expression means in another assignment. Let F_σ denote the (normally finite and possibly empty) set of symbols of category σ. A *meaning assignment* for $\mathscr{L}$ is a function V such that where $\alpha \in F_\sigma$, then $V(\alpha) \in D_\sigma$. There are obviously many different possible V's, even when $\mathscr{L}$ and D are fixed. This reflects the fact that the same words in a language can be given different meanings or that different words can be given the same meanings.

In addition to F (the system of symbols or words) we have a set X_σ, for each category σ, of *variables*. This is because the abstraction operator plays the role of a variable binder in much the same way as do the quantifiers in ordinary first-order logic. In fact, it could be said that the abstraction operator is nothing but a variable binder (David Lewis (1972, 171) indeed called them *binders*), and quantifiers are represented by functors operating on an abstract.

As in ordinary logic, bound variables play only a structural role in obtaining the meaning of an expression. It will be required that each variable must eventually be bound by an abstraction operator. This just means that a variable x must always occur in some expression α that occurs in an abstract of the form $\langle \lambda, x, \alpha \rangle$. For this reason the value to be assigned to a free variable is given not by V but by a separate value assignment to the variables. We add a system N of value assignments to the variables. Where $\nu \in N$ and $x \in X_\sigma$, then $\nu(x) \in D_\sigma$. Where $a \in D_\sigma$, then $\nu(a/x)$ is the function μ exactly like ν except that $\mu(x) = a$.

Given all this, we show how to define an assignment V_ν to every expression. (The reference to ν is needed for expressions with free variables. When all the variables are bound, the dependence on ν ceases.)

If $\alpha \in F_\sigma$, then $V_\nu(\alpha) = V(\alpha)$.
If $x \in X_\sigma$, then $V_\nu(x) = \nu(x)$.
If α is $\langle \delta, \alpha_1, \ldots, \alpha_n \rangle$, then $V_\nu(\alpha)$ is $V_\nu(\delta)(V_\nu(\alpha_1), \ldots, V_\nu(\alpha_n))$.
If α, in category (τ/σ), is $\langle \lambda, x, \beta \rangle$, then $V_\nu(\alpha)$, if it exists, is the function ω in $D_{(\tau/\sigma)}$ such that for any $a \in D_\sigma$, $\omega(a) = V_{\nu(a/x)}(\beta)$.

This, then, is the basic framework. Readers who wish to see it at work in areas not connected with propositional attitudes should look at the works referred to in the bibliographical commentary. The point of mentioning this other work is not just to show how powerful a framework it is, and how semantically profitable: it is to make plausible the requirement that the correct solution to the problem of the semantics of propositional attitudes ought to be able to be accommodated within it. In particular, the nature of $\mathscr{L}$, D, and V ought not to be essentially changed.

One thing to notice about the assignment function V is that its values are all intensions and that the whole semantics is referential. Nothing has been said about senses. And that is as it should be. Although I have been speaking throughout this book of senses and structured meanings, yet the formal semantics has all been purely compositional on the references or intensions of the expressions. The trick of course is the flexibility in the syntactic category of the symbols that underlie the surface word 'that'. As indicated in chapter 10, this word is represented by a variety of symbols in different categories. Here I shall show how it can be incorporated into a λ-categorial language.

I argued in chapter 3 that that-clauses are names. It is possible that they might have to be treated as nominals, but it is simpler to proceed for the moment as if they are just names. This means that every 'that' is a name-forming operator. The simplest one is in category (1/0). This is the one called $that_0$ in chapter 10. The index indicates that it operates on a sentence as a whole.

The semantics of $that_0$ is very simple. It is the identity function; that is, $V(that_0)$ is the function ω in $D_{(1/0)}$ such that for $a \in D_0$, $\omega(a) = a$. Here use is being made of the fact that anything at all can be named and is therefore in D_1—even propositions. Intuitively a that-clause names the proposition expressed by the sentence following 'that'. In other words,

(5) $\langle that_0, \langle Frodo, whistles \rangle \rangle$

is a (complex) name, whose meaning is just the intension of

(6) $\langle Frodo, whistles \rangle$.

But suppose the 'that' is sensitive to the intensions of the parts separately. In this case *that* would have to be in category (1/(0/1)1); that is, it would make a name out of a predicate and a name. To represent this, I have chosen to index *that* by using the category of the expressions it can operate on. This is because, as suggested earlier, no symbol should be in more than one syntactic category. This is a good rule because it guards against the possibility of syntactic ambiguity. It is true that syntactic ambiguity will occur at surface level, but it should be ruled out at the level of logical form. Sometimes, as here, we are tempted to put the same symbol into more than one category. Rather than do that, I have preferred to index *that* with the category of its argument. So $that_0$ indicates a symbol in category (1/0). The expression $that_{((0/1)1)}$ is in category (1/(0/1)1) and can be used to form

(7) $\langle that_{((0/1)1)} \, Frodo, whistles \rangle$

as a that-clause. The meaning of *that* would be the function ω from $D_{(0/1)} \times D_1$ such that for $a \in D_{(0/1)}$ and $b \in D_1$, $\omega(a,b) = \langle a,b \rangle$; that is, it is the sequence of its two arguments. Thus, the meaning—which is to say the *intension*—of (7) is just the sequence that is the intension of *whistles* and the intension of *Frodo*.

The general rule is that, where $\sigma_1,...,\sigma_n$ are any syntactic categories, then $that_{((0/\sigma_1,...,\sigma_n)\sigma_1,...,\sigma_n)}$ is in category $(1/(0/\sigma_1,...,\sigma_n)\sigma_1,...,\sigma_n)$, and, where $a_1,...,a_n$ are in categories $D_{\sigma_1},...,D_{\sigma_n}$, respectively, and ω is in $D_{(0/\sigma_1,...,\sigma_n)}$, then $V(that_{((0/\sigma_1,...,\sigma_n)\sigma_1,...,\sigma_n)})(\omega,a_1,...,a_n) = \langle \omega,a_1, ...,a_n \rangle$. The idea is that any *that* operates separately on expressions that by themselves can combine to form a sentence, making out of them a name of the sequence consisting of the meanings of the separate parts.

This seems to me the best method of incorporating sensitivity to the structure of complement sentences in an ordinary λ-categorial language. (It does of course only deal with cases arising from a that-clause. Other sources of hyperintensionality will be discussed in chapter 15.) However, it still needs a little more refinement to account for those that-clauses that seem to be partly quotational. Such cases will be important in chapter 12, when we consider the semantics of 'say'.

Quotation can be incorporated into a λ-categorial language in a variety of ways. In a sentence like

(8)   Elinor said 'I was here'

a relation is stated to hold between Elinor and the sentence 'I was here'. One way to represent this is to have a quotation symbol. The idea is that a quotation symbol (which can have a variety of surface realizations—including none at all, as in spoken language) is simply a device that turns an expression α into an expression that is the name of α. Put more formally, qu is a quotation symbol for a language $\mathscr{L}$ with respect to a value assignment V iff for any expression α, $V(\langle qu,\alpha \rangle) = \alpha$.

This would allow (8) to be represented as something like

(9) $\langle Past, \langle say, Elinor, \langle qu, \langle I\ was\ here \rangle \rangle \rangle \rangle$.

In (9) the internal structure of the complement sentence is left open.

In direct quotation the meaning of the quoted sentence seems not to be involved. What is more difficult is to deal with the partly quotational uses of that-clauses, for in these cases the attitude seems sensitive to both the form and the meaning of the complement sentence.

The easiest technical solution seems to be to allow two kinds of quotation operators, a strict quotation operator that behaves as described, and a sort of mixed operator that delivers both the intension and the linguistic item. qu^* is a mixed quotation operator (under V) iff

$$V(\langle qu^*,\alpha \rangle) = \langle V(\alpha),\alpha \rangle.$$

We can regard $\langle qu^*,\alpha \rangle$ as in the same category as α provided we realize that in this case the meaning of an expression in category σ is not in D_σ as set out before. (The alternative is to insist that all quotations be in category 1.)

The use of quotation symbols of both these kinds allows a formal account to be given, in a λ-categorial language, of all that has been said about propositional attitudes in parts I and II. The next two chapters illustrate how this is done by considering the semantics of the verb 'say' and the formalization of indirect discourse.

Chapter 12
Indirect Discourse (I)

In this opening chapter on the semantics of the verb *say* in a λ-categorial language, I shall consider only occasions on which it is used with a that-clause whose meaning is no more than the intension of the complement sentence. The simplest example of a sentence of this kind is

(1) $\langle Elinor, says, \langle that_0, \langle Dugald, whistles \rangle \rangle \rangle$.

(In (1) and in the formulae that follow I shall make no distinction between *say* and *says*. I take this difference to be a surface phenomenon and therefore cite the underlying symbol in whatever form makes for easiest reading. I also make use of the liberalization of the formation rules that allows a functor to go between its arguments.)

Example (1) is to be understood as a sentence in a λ-categorial language $\mathscr{L}$ that in some sense "underlies" English. Associated with $\mathscr{L}$ is a meaning assignment V that gives to the symbols of $\mathscr{L}$ meanings of the appropriate kind that are supposed to reflect the meanings that the corresponding words have in English. The language actually spoken is the "surface" form of this λ-categorial language, and a fully worked out linguistic theory on this basis would have to spell out what would count as a surface realization of a λ-categorial expression. As noted in chapter 11, a properly worked out linguistic theory might well take a more complicated base, so the picture presented here is a somewhat idealized one.

In (1) $V(that_0)$ is just the identity function so that

$$V(\langle that_0, \langle Dugald, whistles \rangle \rangle) = V(\langle Dugald, whistles \rangle).$$

In other words, $V(\langle that_0, \langle Dugald, whistles \rangle \rangle)$ is the set of pairs $\langle w, t \rangle$ such that in world w Dugald whistles at time t. The problem of this chapter is the meaning of *says*.

$V(says)$ will be a function ω from $D_1 \times D_1$ into D_0; that is, it will be a two-place operation, both of whose arguments come from D_1 and whose value is in D_0. Its domain will obviously not be the whole of $D_1 \times D_1$. The first argument will be a person (or any kind of entity that can be held capable of saying things). The second argument will be anything capable of being the meaning of a that-clause. In this chapter I am considering only cases where the second argument is an intension—that is, a member of D_0, or in other words a subset of the set W of all pairs of the form $\langle w,t \rangle$, where w is a possible world and t a time interval.

The framework assumes that all possible meanings of all possible languages are described in λ-categorial languages with semantic interpretations using a system of intensions as described in chapter 11. A semantic description in a different framework might well look different. My question is: given this framework as a mechanism for linguistic description, how can one give an account of the meaning of *says?*

Suppose that V(*says*) is the function ω, that a is a person, and that b is a set of worlds. The requirement is that $\omega(a,b) \in D_0$. This means that to specify just which function ω is, it must be stated, for any $\langle w,t \rangle \in W$, whether or not $\langle w,t \rangle \in \omega(a,b)$. My suggestion is this:

$\langle w,t \rangle \in \omega(a,b)$ iff a produces in w at t a surface realization of a sentence α in a λ-categorial language $\mathscr{L}^*$ such that, where $\mathscr{L}^*$ together with a meaning assignment V* is the language a is speaking at $\langle w,t \rangle$, V*$(\alpha) = b$. (Note that V* and $\mathscr{L}^*$ do not have to be the same as V and $\mathscr{L}$. Indirect discourse can report utterances made in a different language.)

In this book I do not wish to be more specific about how to decide which $\langle \mathscr{L}^*, V^* \rangle$ is the speaker's language. Some writers claim it is the speaker's intentions that are relevant on a given occasion. Others deny this. (Can a parrot say that necessity is the mother of invention?) These are interesting questions, but it is sufficient for my purposes that they *have* answers—since we can decide when people say things and what it is they say—even if I am not able to say what those answers are. Since they have answers, then ω will fall out in accordance with what those answers are.

I must make a general point, however, about the role of V* (and $\mathscr{L}^*$) in this definition. In chapter 5 I objected to giving the meaning of 'say' as 'utters a sentence that is synonymous with' on the ground that synonymy is language relative, and words that are synonymous in one language might fail to be so in another. Yet it appears that the meaning of 'say' as specified just now involves the very same language relativity. Why is reference to V* here not equally objectionable?

The answer, in technical language, is that V* is playing the role of a bound variable. The idea can perhaps be made clear by a simple example. It will, I hope, be conceded that the word 'admires' expresses a two-place relation. One cannot give a sensible answer to the question whether 'x admires' is true or false. One could describe its truth as relative. The expression 'x admires' could be said to be 'true relative to y', meaning by that no more than that x admires y. Technically this is just to say that 'admires' is a two-place predicate and needs two arguments to make a complete sentence. Now consider the sentence 'x admires someone' and the predicate 'admires someone'. In this case, for any given x, it is either true or false that x admires someone. The phrase 'admires someone' is not relative in the same way. It is a one-place predicate. Or take the phrase 'admires the person next door'. Forgetting for the moment that the person next door to x may not be unique, the same is true. Any x either does or does not admire the person next door. There is no extra relativity in these cases as there is in 'x admires'. One cannot say that 'x admires the person next door' is true relative to y, or true relative to z.

Of course in *explaining* the one-place predicate 'admires the person next door', one may undoubtedly use the two-place predicate 'admires' in the explanation. One could use a formula of predicate logic and say

(2)   ($\exists^1 y$) *y lives next door* $\wedge$ ($\exists y$)(x *admires y* $\wedge$ *y lives next door*).

In this case the y to which 'x *admires*' is related is bound by the existential quantifier in the middle of the sentence. In an informal exposition one could speak of y being the person who lives next door and of x admiring y, but the y would be in bound position and the whole expression (2) would have a meaning dependent only on the value provided for the free x.

The same is true in the explanation of V(*says*). In this explanation V* occurs only as a bound variable. The function ω that is the meaning of *says* under assignment V is just a two-place function. Its value does not depend in any way on V*. Of course, in describing *what* function it is, the explaining sentence does make use of V*, but only in the way in which y occurs in (2).

What I have said so far is enough to show that the meaning of V(*says*) is not formally dependent on language. But of course its meaning does have something to do with language. This is not unexpected, since the meaning of the word 'says' does put a person into some relation with a language, but it does raise questions about how one might learn such a meaning. To be sure, *says* can be treated as a single lexical item and therefore its meaning does not have to be worked out on the basis of the meanings of its parts. (That fact allowed a distinction to be made between the function that is the meaning of *says* and the metalinguistic explanation of what this function is.) Nevertheless, it does seem to require that a person using the word 'say' should have a grasp not only of what 'say' means but also of what all sorts of other expressions mean.

What it comes to is that what a person is able to say in a language depends on what other expressions mean. In certain cases one can actually show that a sentence that appears to report someone as saying something cannot actually do so. The most acute form of such cases arises in what is in fact a version of the liar paradox. The usual type of liar paradox is illustrated by sentences like

(3)   This sentence is false.

In (3) the predicate 'is false' is a predicate of sentences, and although it was suggested in chapter 4 that words like this should not be treated as equivocal, yet it is often considered that predicates like 'is true' and 'is false' do have different meanings when applied to propositions than the meanings they have when applied to sentences. In the latter case, at least in cases where meanings are no more than intensions, they are held not to be paradox-generating.

But the liar paradox can be stated in indirect discourse. The title of a recent collection of essays on the subject (Martin (1970)) was

(4)   What I am now saying is false,

and many years ago Jonathan Cohen (1957) produced the example of a policeman who testifies that nothing the prisoner says is true, while the prisoner says that something the policeman says is true. In both cases it could plausibly be held that 'what is said' is a proposition rather than a sentence. (That at any rate is how I understand Arthur Prior (1961) to have taken Cohen's example in his discussion of it. Prior formalizes similar paradoxes, in a logic with variables for proposition-forming operators that are syntactically like truth functors but semantically need not even respect logical equivalence.)

I want to show exactly how it is that a sentence like (4) becomes paradoxical when the meaning of *says* is the function described earlier in the chapter in the case where its second argument b is a set of world-time pairs. Because b is just an intension, we should not expect that, as happens with the ordinary liar sentences, the problem is with *is true* or *is false* (recall the discussion at the end of chapter 4). The sentence I shall consider is

(5)   What Felicity says is false,

said on a particular occasion on which (5) is the only thing Felicity says. This occasion will be represented by a world-time pair.

Syntactically, *what* is an expression that makes a nominal out of a predicate, which is to say that it is in category $((0/(01)/(0/1))$. As in chapter 4, I shall treat *is false* as a single one-place predicate. Thus, in a λ-categorial language (5) becomes

(6) $\langle\langle what, \langle \lambda, x, \langle Felicity, says, x\rangle\rangle\rangle, is\ false\rangle$.

I shall assume that what Felicity says is being reported only to within logical equivalence. This means that the meaning for *is false* is simply the function that turns every subset of the set W of all world-time pairs into its complement in W. The only task, then, is to specify $V(what)$.

$V(what)$ is the function ζ in $D_{((0/(0/1))/(0/1))}$ such that where ω_1 and ω_2 are in $D_{(0/1)}$, then $\langle w, t\rangle \in (\zeta(\omega_1))(\omega_2)$ iff there is some $a \in D_1$ such that

(i) a is the unique member of D_1 such that $\langle w, t\rangle \in \omega_1(a)$

and

(ii) $\langle w, t\rangle \in \omega_2(a)$.

Assume that $\langle w, t\rangle$ is a context at which the only sentence Felicity utters is a surface realization of (6). Suppose further that the meaning assignment for the language Felicity is speaking at $\langle w, t\rangle$ is V. Then a contradiction may be deduced in the following way:

Evaluate first the meaning of

(7) $\langle \lambda, x, \langle Felicity, says, x\rangle\rangle$.

This will be the function ω_1 such that for $a \in D_1 : \omega_1(a) = V(says)(Felicity, a)$. That is, $\langle w, t\rangle \in \omega_1(a)$ iff Felicity produces at $\langle w, t\rangle$ a surface realization of a sentence α in a λ-categorial language such that where V^* represents the meaning assignment to α in the language Felicity is speaking at $\langle w, t\rangle$, $V^*(\alpha) = a$.

Suppose that ω_2 is $V(is\ false)$. Then for any b in D_1 in the domain of ω_2 (by which can be understood any $b \in D_0$, i.e., any set of world-time pairs), $\omega_2(b) = W - b$. So $\langle w, t\rangle \in V((6))$ iff Felicity produces at $\langle w, t\rangle$ a surface realization of a sentence α of a λ-categorial language and, where V^* represents the meaning assignment in the language Felicity is speaking at $\langle w, t\rangle$, $\langle w, t\rangle \notin V^*(\alpha)$.

But we are assuming that the only sentence Felicity produces at $\langle w, t\rangle$ is (6), so that α is (6), and that $V^* = V$. So $\langle w, t\rangle \in V((6))$ iff $\langle w, t\rangle \in V^*(\alpha)$. So $\langle w, t\rangle \in V((6))$ iff $\langle w, t\rangle \notin V((6))$, which is our contradiction.

It may seem strange for logic to prohibit Felicity from saying something. Felicity is not of course prohibited from producing a realization of (6). She is prohibited merely from saying anything by it if the language she is speaking has the same meaning assignment as the language reporting it. (The reason why (4) is more dramatic than (5) is that this is built into the meaning of 'I' and 'now'.) If Felicity is saying anything, she would have to say more than one thing. Prior (1961) formalizes in a very simple logical system a proof that if a Cretan says that nothing said by a Cretan is true, then at least two things must be said by a Cretan. What all this shows—indeed, what any consideration of liar sentences shows—is that the formulation of the meaning rule of a word like *says* requires care. Certain assignments for *says* are definitely ruled out as not possible. The problem about liar sentences is to say which ones are ruled in. The moral to be drawn from this consideration of the semantic paradoxes is that certain semantic features that one might naively expect *say* to have cannot be possessed by any function. That is in fact typical of the general lesson to be learned from these paradoxes. The hard work then is to see how close one can come to the impossible desideratum. This book is not concerned with the semantic paradoxes, and I have no more to say about what to do with cases like (6). I shall assume that V(*says*) is a function that gets as close as is consistently possible to what is desired.

Example (1) ($\langle$ ***Elinor,says,*** $\langle$ ***that***$_0$,$\langle$ ***Dugald,whistles*** $\rangle$ $\rangle$ $\rangle$) requires in its semantics that Elinor utter a sentence whose meaning is precisely the proposition that Dugald whistles—that is, it is true precisely at those $\langle w,t \rangle$ pairs in which t is an interval of Dugald's whistling in world w. This makes the reference to Dugald part of Elinor's *linguistic* ability, and it may seem too stringent a requirement for successful *de re* reference, for we might be unwilling to attribute such a meaning to Elinor's sentence unless she knew just which worlds these were, and to do this might require that she have knowledge of the whistler's essence. In fact, *de re* attitudes, as described in chapter 2, work a little differently, and I shall formalize some examples of *de re* discourse in chapter 13. It will emerge there that the *de re* correlate of sentence (1) requires a more elaborate ***that.***

De re attitudes are frequently linked with quantification into intensional contexts, and though it is true, in the formal account to be offered in chapter 13, that a typical *de re* sentence containing a quantificational phrase will have the quantifier outside the scope of the attitude operator, it is not this fact alone that gives rise to the *de re* interpretation. In fact, quantification into attitude contexts is automatically taken care of by the semantical rule for abstraction stated in chapter 11, and it poses no special problem. To indicate this, I shall show how to quantify into the that-clause in sentence (1). Consider a quantified version:

(8)   Elinor says that someone whistles.

This sentence can be represented in two ways, the first of which is

(9) $\langle Elinor,says,\langle that_0,\langle someone,whistles \rangle \rangle \rangle$.

This differs from (1) only in that *someone* is a symbol in category $(0/(0/1))$, whereas *Dugald* is in category 1.

Where V is a value assignment and $\langle w,t \rangle$ a world-time pair, then $\langle w,t \rangle \in V((9))$ iff Elinor produces in w at t an utterance of a sentence that has as its semantic value in the language she is speaking $V(\langle someone,whistles \rangle)$.

But (8) can also be analyzed in such a way that *someone* has wide scope:

(10) $\langle someone,\langle \lambda,x,\langle Elinor,says,\langle that_0,\langle x,whistles \rangle \rangle \rangle \rangle \rangle$.

(10) will be true at $\langle w,t \rangle$ iff there is some person a in D_1 such that where $\nu(x) = a$, $\langle w,t \rangle \in V_\nu(\langle Elinor,says,\langle that_0,\langle x,whistles \rangle \rangle \rangle)$. By V(*Elinor*) and V(*says*) this will be so iff, where V^* is the language that Elinor is speaking in w at t, Elinor produces a sentence α such that $V^*(\alpha) = V_\nu(\langle x,whistles \rangle)$.

Now if $\nu(x) = a$, then $V_\nu(\langle x,whistles \rangle)$ will be the set of worlds in which a whistles. So Elinor will say that someone whistles iff there is a person a such that Elinor's sentence means that a whistles.

This shows that there is no problem for quantification into a *that*-clause. And the procedure here can be carried through with reference to a clause introduced by any *that*, however complicated its index. This is because each *that*, however complicated (provided only that quotation is not involved), is a purely intensional operator, admittedly not always operating on the intension of the complement sentence taken as a whole, but always operating on the intensions of its arguments.

One feature that distinguishes indirect discourse from direct discourse is that certain changes of tense in the attitude verb require a change of tense in the complement verb. For that reason there is perhaps some interest in indicating what happens when such sentences are considered in a λ-categorial framework. Consider how to formalize

(11)   Cynthia said that Bruce sang.

(11) is I think ambiguous in that it may be what would most naturally be reported by

(12) Cynthia said that Bruce was singing

when it means that Bruce was reported to be singing at the same time as Cynthia's utterance. Alternatively, it may mean that Bruce was understood to have sung (been singing) at a time previous to that utterance. I will take the former interpretation, though I hope it will be easy to see how to formalize the latter. (I am also ignoring completely the question of aspect. Luckily I can plead that a great deal of very detailed work has been done elsewhere on the formalization of truth-conditional semantics for tensed sentences; see the bibliographical commentary.)

I will take it that the past tense is normally represented in a λ-categorial language by a propositional operator. Thus, (11) can be formalized as

(13) $\langle\langle Cynthia,say, \langle that_0, \langle Bruce,sing \rangle \rangle \rangle, ed \rangle$.

The *ed* is reflected on the surface by the past forms of both *say* and *sing*. For present purposes its semantics can be expressed as:

V(*ed*) is the function ω in $D_{(0/0)}$ such that for any $a \in D_0$, $\langle w,t \rangle$ $\in \omega(\alpha)$ iff there is some interval t' such that every moment in t' precedes every moment in t and $\langle w,t' \rangle \in a$.

(13) will be true at $\langle w,t \rangle$ iff, at some $\langle w,t \rangle$ in which t' is completely prior to t, Cynthia produces an utterance that, in her language at $\langle w,t' \rangle$, is true in just those possible worlds in which Bruce is singing at t'.

Chapter 13
Indirect Discourse (II)

In this chapter I want to consider cases in which the meaning of *say* operates on something more elaborate than just the intension of the complement sentence that follows. The discussion in part I leads us to expect that there should be cases in which the structure of the complement sentence is involved.

Some of these will be cases of *de re* reference. Suppose Cynthia utters the sentence

(1)   The man in the blue coat is singing.

If the man in the blue coat is Bruce and if Cynthia can be construed as making a *de re* statement about him, then (1) could be plausibly represented by means of a *that* which, if the approach argued for in chapter 2 is accepted, could operate on a name and a predicate separately. This would be *that*$_{(0/1)1}$, and a report of what Cynthia says might be

(2) $\langle Cynthia, says, \langle that_{(0/1)1}, Bruce, sings \rangle \rangle$.

In (2) the reference of the that-clause is $\langle \omega, b \rangle$, where b is Bruce and ω is the function in $D_{(0/1)}$ such that for any a in its domain $\langle w,t \rangle \in \omega(a)$ iff a sings in w at t. So the task is now to extend the account of $V(says)$ for the case where its second argument is such a structure. This extended account would be something like this (for any a and b in D_1, and ω in $D_{(0/1)}$):

$$\langle w,t \rangle \in V(says)(a, \langle \omega, b \rangle)$$

iff there is a sentence in a λ-categorial language of the form $\langle \alpha, \beta \rangle$ in which α is a nominal that picks out b for a at $\langle w,t \rangle$ and $V^*(\beta) = \omega$ where V^* is the meaning assignment for the language a is speaking at $\langle w,t \rangle$.

To say that α picks out b for a at $\langle w,t \rangle$ is to say something like this: α is a nominal, and the kind of nominal that picks out something is a phrase like 'the tallest spy in the world'. If b is the tallest spy in the world, and if a intends to refer to b by this description (if Donellan

(1966) is right, sometimes only the second condition may be required), then α can be said to pick out b. A great deal of work has been done recently about what it is to intend to refer to something. For my purposes I merely assume that the phenomenon occurs and that some account can be given of it.

The pattern of analysis suggested here for *say* when it operates on *that*$_{(0/1)1}$ is obviously capable of generalization to cases where *that* has a more complex index. The general idea is that each separate argument of such a *that* must be represented by an item in the speaker's language.

In mathematical cases reference to numbers is typically by numerals. This would give the following analysis of

(3)   Cynthia says that 59 is prime.

Taking *is prime* as a simple predicate, we have

(4) $\langle$ *Cynthia,says,* $\langle$ *that*$_{((0/1)1)}$*,59,is prime* $\rangle$ $\rangle$.

This will be true in $\langle w,t \rangle$ iff Cynthia utters a realization of sentence $\langle \alpha,\beta \rangle$ in which (at $\langle w,t \rangle$) α is a numeral, V* is Cynthia's language at $\langle w,t \rangle$, V*(α) = 59, β is a one-place predicate, and V*(β) is the function ω such that $\langle w,t \rangle \in \omega(a)$ iff a is prime. β might of course not be a single word, but V(say) in these cases might nevertheless require that it not be too complex. For instance, suppose Cynthia recalls being told (erroneously) that every number is either prime or an even factor of 10. Now in fact the predicate 'is either prime or an even factor of 10' has exactly the same intension as the predicate 'is prime'. So what happens if Cynthia produces the following sentence?

(5)   59 is either prime or an even factor of 10.

By the account given of (4) one would be forced to say that Cynthia had said that 59 is prime. But has she?

My intuitions are divided, but what is important is to see what these intuitions are about. What is going on is a sort of complement to the Macrostructure Constraint discussed in part II. That constraint was to ensure that the complexity of the *reporting* sentence was reflected by assigning a sufficiently complex structure to be the meaning of its that-clause. The restriction involved in (5) would prohibit the object sentence (the sentence that, if uttered by Cynthia, makes the report true) from being too complex. A restriction of *this* kind would be part of the meaning of *say*. That is why I am not worried about my divided intuitions. Perhaps indeed the word *say* is used slightly differently on different occasions.

Of course, the situation is even more complicated because what Cynthia produces is actually what I have called a *surface realization* of a λ-categorial sentence. Presumably such a notion must take account of the various levels in a grammatical theory. Some of this is just the phenomenon mentioned earlier that the function that is the value of *says* is given within the context of a particular theory. But not solely. For instance, if the explanation of V(*says*) is correct, it would seem that if it is plausible to suppose that two distinct surface sentences have the same λ-categorial level, then they function equivalently as the arguments of V(*say*). The following examples are adapted from Barbara Partee (1982) (by changing 'believes' into 'says'):

(6) Mary says that for John to leave now would be a mistake.

(7) Mary says that it would be a mistake for John to leave now.

If these are just different surface realizations of the same λ-categorial sentence and if the meaning of *says* is not quotational, then (6) and (7) would have to have the same meaning. Of course, this is a question about the meaning of *says.* It is not at all clear that the synonymy results in (6) and (7), if any, would be the same as in Partee's examples involving *believes.* So one answer is to let the facts fall as they may.

It is not the whole answer, however, because if (6) and (7) are not synonymous, then the that-clause will have to be at least partly quotational. We must consider quotation in any case, if only because the word 'say' occurs in both direct and indirect speech. Thus, we have both

(8) Elinor said that I whistled

and

(9) Elinor said 'I whistled'.

(8) and (9) have quite different meanings. If I utter (8) at time t, it means that at some time in the past of t, Elinor said that I (Cresswell) whistled at t'. If I utter (9) at t, it means that at some time t' in the past of t, Elinor uttered a certain sentence ('I whistled'), and what this sentence says is that Elinor whistled at some time t'' in the past of t'.

In written language we can indicate the difference by using 'that' in (8) and quotation marks in (9). But the word 'that' is often omitted, particularly in informal spoken language; and quotation marks do not occur in spoken language. So we get

(10)   Elinor said I whistled.

This might suggest that the difference between (8) and (9) is not part of their meaning but only reflects an orthographic convention. (Just as the difference between 'manoeuvre' and 'maneuver' is hardly of semantical interest.) However, even if (10) is used, it is quite clearly susceptible of interpretation either as (8) or as (9), and these two interpretations are quite different. (Actually, I suspect that in spoken language there are rather subtle intonational differences between the two interpretations, but whether this is so or not, it is clear that two different underlying logical structures are involved, and it is with these structures that I am concerned.)

In this chapter I want to ignore the contextually dependent meaning of the pronoun 'I', so I shall imagine versions of (8) and (9) that contain a proper name. I shall also use present tense.

Consider first, then, a present tense version of (9):

(11)   Elinor says 'Dugald whistles'.

Assume that qu is a quotation symbol with respect to the assignment V that is the intended interpretation of $\mathcal{L}$. The underlying structure of (11) is then represented as

(12) $\langle Elinor, says, \langle qu, \langle Dugald, whistles \rangle \rangle \rangle$.

In (12) both *Elinor* and $\langle qu, \langle Dugald, whistles \rangle \rangle$ are in category 1. And since qu is assumed to be a quotation operator in V, then $V(\langle qu, \langle Dugald, whistles \rangle \rangle) = \langle Dugald, whistles \rangle$. Notice the difference between qu and $that_0$, $V(\langle that_0, \langle Dugald, whistles \rangle \rangle) = V(\langle Dugald, whistles \rangle)$.

This means that, if $V(say)$ is the function ω in $D_{(0/11)}$, the case now to be considered is the one in which its second argument is a sentence in a λ-categorial language. In view of what has been said already this case is relatively simple:

$\langle w, t \rangle \in \omega(a, b)$ iff a produces a surface realization of b.

It is important to see that this does not make *says* ambiguous. $V(says)$ is defined for a wide range of things as its second argument. When b is a set of worlds, interpretation proceeds as stated in chapter 12; when b is a structure made up from intensions, interpretation proceeds as stated earlier in this chapter; and when b is a λ-categorial sentence, interpretation proceeds as stated just now. Further, the general pattern is the same, namely, that a should produce a sentence as close to b as b's structure allows. The limiting case of this is where b actually is a sentence.

In chapter 12 it was shown how to formalize past tense sentences in indirect discourse. It is perhaps worth pointing out here that the sentence

(13)   Cynthia said Bruce sang

is treated differently depending on whether it is treated as (11) was there or as

(14)   Cynthia said 'Bruce sang'.

In the former case (13) could be analyzed as the formula (13) in the last chapter, but it would be impossible to get this meaning with direct speech. For example, (14) would have to be formalized as

(15) $\langle\langle Cynthia, say, \langle qu, \langle\langle Bruce, sing, \rangle ed\rangle\rangle\rangle, ed\rangle$.

In (15) the claim is not only that Cynthia's utterance is supposed to have taken place in the past, but also that it has to be a realization of the sentence $\langle\langle Bruce, sing\rangle, ed\rangle$.

Using a structure-sensitive *that* produces mixed cases in which some expressions are quoted but others are not. Consider:

> There's a little proverb that
>   you really ought to know:
> Horses sweat and men perspire
>   but ladies only glow.

Suppose we have the sentence

(16)   Bill says that Arabella perspires.

This sentence can be used to report Bill as making a statement that, even if a trifle impolite, might well be true about Arabella's bodily state. But one could also imagine (16) being uttered in a shocked voice by someone who wanted to report that Bill used an indelicate word in describing a lady. In this case 'perspires' would be quoted. But (16) may make no claim that Bill picks out Arabella by that name. For that uncouth fellow may say

(17)   Doesn't that dame in the corner perspire?

In this sense (16) could be represented as

(18) $\langle Bill, says, \langle that_{(0/1)1}, Arabella, \langle qu, perspires\rangle\rangle\rangle$.

A slight technical problem here is that $\langle qu, perspires\rangle$, being a quotation, is presumably in category 1, and its meaning *perspires* is in D_1, rather than in $D_{(0/1)}$. There are various solutions. One is to change the category of *that* so that it operates on two names. Another is to let the category of the quotation be the same as the category of the symbol quoted. At any rate, whatever device is adopted, the meaning of the that-clause in (18) ought to be the pair consisting of Arabella and the word *perspires*. What must be done, then, is to specify what V(*says*) is when its argument is a pair consisting of a word or thing and a one-place predicate. Presumably it will be something like this:

$$\langle w,t \rangle \in \omega(a,\langle b,\alpha \rangle)$$

iff at $\langle w,t \rangle$ a produces a sentence $\langle \beta,\alpha \rangle$ in which β is a nominal that picks out b for a at $\langle w,t \rangle$.

This semantics would make (18) true even if Bill is using the word 'perspires' to mean something quite different from its ordinary meaning. Often, as in the case of the little rhyme quoted above, a sentence may take note both of the meaning of its words and of the words themselves. If that is happening in (16), then we would need a way of referring *both* to the expression Bill uses and to its meaning. This would need to make use of the qu^* operator introduced in chapter 11. Recall that

$$V(\langle qu^*,\alpha \rangle) = \langle V(\alpha),\alpha \rangle.$$

With qu^* replacing qu in (18), the meaning of its that-clause would be the pair whose first term is Arabella and whose second is itself a pair in which the first member is the meaning of *perspires* and the second is *perspires* itself. V(*say*) would have to be extended for all such arguments, presumably as follows:

$$\langle w,t \rangle \in \omega(a,\langle b,\langle c,\alpha \rangle \rangle)$$
iff at $\langle w,t \rangle$ a produces a sentence $\langle \beta,\alpha \rangle$ in which β is a nominal that picks out b for a at $\langle w,t \rangle$ and, where V* is the meaning assignment for the language a is speaking at $\langle w,t \rangle$, V*(α) = b.

Some very pretty examples of these mixed cases, involving words like 'holler' and 'giggle', have been given by Barbara Partee (1973); and of course we can embed the celebrated

(19)   Giorgione was so called because of his size

of Quine (1953) into a sentence of indirect discourse:

(20)   The guide told us that Giorgione was so called because of his size.

In (20) we can suppose that the guide spoke only Italian, so that most of (19) when embedded in (20) is not quoted. But presumably some of it is, on the ground that replacing 'Giorgione' by any other name distorts what the guide says.

One way to deal with (19) is to suppose that the 'so' in 'so called' is what has been called a *pronoun of laziness* (Geach (1962, 125)); by this is meant that (19) is short for

(21)   Giorgione was called 'Giorgione' because of his size.

This turns (20) into

(22)   The guide told us that Giorgione was called 'Giorgione' because of his size.

In (22) the first occurrence of 'Giorgione' is not quoted, though the second is, but the methods described earlier in this chapter would seem adequate to the case. So if (22) is a good rendering of (20), there is no problem.

But there is another way to deal with the problem, namely, to say that the predicate 'is so called' is a property of pairs $\langle a, \alpha \rangle$ that holds iff α is the name of a. Such a solution would use qu^* in giving a direct account of (19). Whether a solution along these lines would be plausible I am unsure. I hope, though, to have said enough in these two chapters to indicate both the problems and the possibilities of giving an account of indirect discourse in a λ-categorial framework.

Chapter 14
Discourse *De Se*

In a recent article (Lewis (1979a)) David Lewis has argued that many attitudes that appear to be attitudes toward propositions are really not. His most persuasive example is the following:

> Consider the case of the two gods. They inhabit a certain possible world, and they know exactly which world it is. Therefore they know every proposition that is true at their world. Insofar as knowledge is a propositional attitude, they are omniscient. Still I can imagine them to suffer ignorance: neither one knows which of the two he is. They are not exactly alike. One lives on top of the tallest mountain and throws down manna; the other lives on top of the coldest mountain and throws down thunderbolts. Neither one knows whether he lives on the tallest mountain or on the coldest mountain; nor whether he throws manna or thunderbolts. (1979a, 520f.)

Lewis discusses the problem in terms of knowledge. I shall continue in the style of the last two chapters in considering it in the context of indirect discourse, and I shall try to use the analysis of *say* offered there. Lewis does not give his gods names but we might appropriately call the manna-throwing god *Jehovah* and the thunderbolt-throwing god *Zeus*. I shall focus on the sentences

(1) Zeus says that he throws thunderbolts

and

(2) Zeus says that he is Zeus.

In Lewis's terminology sentences like these would be examples of *de se* attitudes because they are attitudes that something takes toward itself. The question is how we are to analyze these sentences. I shall consider various possible structures for (1) in a λ-categorial language. The first makes use of *that$_0$*:

(3) $\langle$*Zeus,*$\langle \lambda, x, \langle$*says,x,*$\langle$*that$_0$,*$\langle x,$*throws thunderbolts*$\rangle \rangle \rangle \rangle \rangle$.

(I shall take *throws thunderbolts* as a one-place predicate without regarding its internal structure. If Carlson (1978) is right, *throws* could be just a two-place predicate and *thunderbolts* the name of a kind.)

I have used λ-abstraction in (3) as a way of marking the use of the pronoun 'he' in (1) as a bound variable, for that is what I think it is doing here. However, on the assumption that *Zeus* is a name rather than a nominal, principles of λ-conversion make (3) equivalent to

(4) $\langle Zeus, says, \langle that_0, \langle Zeus, throws\ thunderbolts \rangle \rangle \rangle$.

If (4) is evaluated according to the recipe given in chapter 12, we have that it is true at any $\langle w,t \rangle$ (with respect to the intended meaning assignment V) iff Zeus at $\langle w,t \rangle$ produces a surface realization of a sentence α in a λ-categorial language such that $V^*(\alpha) = V(\langle Zeus, throws\ thunderbolts \rangle)$.

But clearly this will not give the right results. If Zeus speaks the same language we do, he could well make (4) true by uttering a realization of

(5) $\langle Zeus, throws\ thunderbolts \rangle$.

But suppose that Zeus mistakenly thinks that he is Jehovah. In such a case we are surely not entitled to take his utterance of (5) as evidence for his saying that *he* throws thunderbolts. If this example is not persuasive, consider the case of (2), where the analogue of (5) would make (2) true if Zeus said 'Zeus is Zeus'. Saying 'Zeus is Zeus' in the posited case would not make (2) true because the deluded Zeus might go on to say 'Zeus is Zeus but I am Jehovah'. So his saying 'Zeus is Zeus' cannot count as his saying that he is Zeus.

What seems to have gone wrong is that in (1) it is required that Zeus be referring to himself. This suggests that a *de re* attitude might be involved. The sentence to be considered is therefore

(6) $\langle Zeus, says, \langle that_{((0/1),1)}, Zeus, throws\ thunderbolts \rangle \rangle$.

Applying the account of V(*says*) given in chapter 13, we see that (6) is true at $\langle w,t \rangle$ iff there is a nominal α, which picks out Zeus for Zeus at $\langle w,t \rangle$, and a predicate β such that $V^*(\beta) = V(throws\ thunderbolts)$, where V^* is the language Zeus is speaking at $\langle w,t \rangle$.

Sentence (6) is better than (5), for suppose that Zeus thinks he is Jehovah. In such a case one might say that the name *Zeus* would not pick out Zeus for Zeus, and so an utterance of (5) would not count as a saying that Zeus throws thunderbolts.

This might be sufficient to close the matter. If so, it would mean that the *de se* cases of indirect discourse could be accommodated by the framework so far developed. But perhaps there is more to be said.

David Kaplan imagines watching someone in the mirror and saying 'His pants are on fire'. A few seconds later he thinks 'My God, it's me'. Kaplan considers this to be a case where he knows *de re* of Kaplan that Kaplan's pants are on fire, but, not realizing that he is Kaplan, does not know that his own pants are on fire.

What would be the analogue of this for indirect discourse? It would be that there is an interpretation of

(7)   Kaplan says that his pants are on fire

in which it is not sufficient that Kaplan use a description that picks out Kaplan for Kaplan, for in Kaplan's example that would only give us the case where Kaplan says of Kaplan (not knowing that he himself is Kaplan) that his (Kaplan's) pants are on fire.

The difficulty about (7) is where to locate the source of the *de re/de se* ambiguity. It seems undesirable to make *say* ambiguous; indeed, that would go against the whole tenor of this book. A clue is that the surface form of the genuine *de se* cases often involves some qualification of the pronoun in the embedded sentence. One could make this interpretation of (7) more likely by using

(8)   Kaplan says that his own pants are on fire.

And (1) could be replaced by

(9)   Zeus says that he himself throws thunderbolts.

(In my explanation of (7) I referred to Kaplan's not knowing that he himself was Kaplan.)

So tagging the pronoun in the reporting sentence seems to indicate a preferred way of referring to oneself. Typically in (1), Zeus, if an English speaker, would use a sentence like

(10)   I throw thunderbolts,

and Kaplan would say

(11)   My pants are on fire.

In (10) and (11) the speakers use variants of the first person pronoun. Of course, we cannot insist that those lexical items be used, because it is only in English that they are so used. What is needed is a semantic criterion for this privileged way of referring to oneself.

To show how such a criterion could be supplied, I shall consider an analogous problem about temporal reference. Consider the sentence

(12)   Zeus says that it is four o'clock.

There are, I believe, two interpretations of (12). One corresponds to the *de se* case—it is what might be called the *de nunc* case, in which Zeus is asked what the time is. (One has to imagine a sort of combination of the time service and dial-a-prayer.) The other corresponds to the case where someone says

(13)   At what time does the train arrive?

and receives (12) as an answer.

The ambiguity in (12) seems to depend on a corresponding ambiguity in the complement sentence

(14)   It is four o'clock.

The *de nunc* use is indicted if the word "now" is inserted, to get

(15)   It is now four o'clock.

(This is why I claim that it parallels (10) and (11).) In this way of taking (14), 'it' seems to play a rather special role. Following Castañeda (1968), one could use the symbol *it**. Actually, I shall not go into the details of how the semantics of (14) is to be worked out, so the * on 'it' will mark a property of the sentence as a whole:

(16)   *it* is four o'clock.*

For any $\langle w,t \rangle \in W$, $\langle w,t \rangle \in V((16))$ iff t is four o'clock. (Of course, 'four o'clock' is itself a context-dependent expression. I shall assume at the moment that there is simply a class of times that we can call four o'clocks.) With (16) we can analyze (12), using *that*$_0$, as (17). (Of course, a more complicated *that* may still be needed for other reasons, but not for *de nunc* reasons.)

(17) $\langle$ *Zeus,says,* $\langle$ *that*$_0$,*it* is four o'clock* $\rangle \rangle$

$\langle w,t \rangle \in V((17))$ iff there is a sentence α such that $V^*(\alpha) = V($*it* is four o'clock*$)$ where V^* is Zeus's language at $\langle w,t \rangle$ and Zeus utters α at t in w.

In this case the sentence *it* is four o'clock would* do, if V represents Zeus's language at $\langle w,t \rangle$, for it would count as a saying that it is four o'clock.

Also it seems that this case is not plausibly on a par with the temporal *de re* case. At least there seem some grounds for thinking that Zeus is not saying, of a certain moment, that it is four o'clock.

If this kind of solution is to be applied to the *de se* examples, then we need to complicate our notion of propositions. The set W will now be not just the set of world-time pairs but the set of triples $\langle w,t,p \rangle$ in which w is a possible world, t a time interval, and p a person. The idea is that we are thinking of world w at time t from the point of view of the person p. The idea behind Lewis's examples might be seen by thinking of desire. Suppose that I desire to be Archimedes at the moment when he said 'Eureka'. I do not just want to be in a world w in which Archimedes said 'Eureka'. I want to be in it at the time t when he said it, and I want to be him, p. So my desire can be expressed as all those $\langle w,t,p \rangle$ triples in which p is Archimedes and t is a time at which in world w he said 'Eureka'.

Given this, we can go back to a formalization of (1) using only *that*$_0$. This formalization will make use of a symbol *he**. This symbol will combine with a name (e.g., *Zeus*) to form a nominal (e.g., *he**,*Zeus* $\rangle$). This means that it is in category $((0/(0/1))/1)$. It has the following semantics (recalling now that D_0 contains sets of $\langle w,t,p \rangle$ triples):

V(*he**) is a function ζ such that for $a \in D_1$ in its domain and $\omega \in D_{(0/1)}$ in the domain of $\zeta(a)$, and any $\langle w,t,p \rangle \in W$, $\langle w,t,p \rangle \in \zeta(a)(\omega)$ iff $\langle w,t,a \rangle \in \omega(a)$.

The idea is to make $\langle \langle he^*,Zeus \rangle,\alpha \rangle$ true at $\langle w,t,p \rangle$ iff Zeus satisfies the predicate α at $\langle w,t,\text{Zeus} \rangle$, that is, if Zeus is α at t in world w when Zeus is regarded as the speaker.

Being a nominal, *he** can of course occur in a variety of positions. I claim that it has different surface realizations depending on whether it has wide scope (with regard to attitude verbs) or narrow scope. When it has wide scope with regard to all attitude verbs in the sentence, it is realized as 'I'. When it has narrow scope, it is realized as 'he' or 'she' (or possibly 'they' or 'it'). This allows a solution to the problem of (1) to be given along the following lines. On this account the underlying formula for (1) becomes

(18) $\langle Zeus,says,\langle that_0,\langle \langle he^*,Zeus \rangle,throws\ thunderbolts \rangle \rangle \rangle$.

(18) will be true at $\langle w,t,p \rangle$ iff Zeus produces a surface realization of a sentence α in a λ-categorial language such that, where V* is the language Zeus is speaking at $\langle w,t,p \rangle$, then V*(α) = V($\langle \langle he^*,Zeus \rangle$, *throws thunderbolts* $\rangle$). Since *he** has wide scope in the complement of (18), then, if Zeus speaks English, a realization would be (10). Thus, we have given a semantic characterization of the pronoun 'I'. (18) is not open to the objections brought against (4) because (5) is not semantically equivalent to

(19) $\langle \langle he^*,Zeus \rangle,throws\ thunderbolts \rangle$.

It is also not open to the objections brought against (6), since (18) requires a very special way of referring to Zeus. The constraint on surface realizations also gives the right result for the surface sentence

(20)   Zeus says that I throw thunderbolts.

Since 'I' indicates a wide scope he^*, then, if I am speaking, the underlying structure of (20) is

(21) $\langle\langle he^*,Cresswell\rangle,\langle\lambda,x,\langle Zeus,says,\langle that_0,\langle x,throws\ thunderbolts\rangle\rangle\rangle\rangle\rangle$

(21) is true at $\langle w,t,p\rangle$ iff when the free variable x is assigned Cresswell,

(22) $\langle Zeus,says,\langle that_0,\langle x,throws\ thunderbolts\rangle\rangle\rangle$

is true at $\langle w,t,\text{Cresswell}\rangle$; this in turn is true iff Zeus produces at $\langle w,t,\text{Cresswell}\rangle$ a sentence α such that where V* is Zeus's language at $\langle w,t,\text{Cresswell}\rangle$, then V*($\alpha$) is true at any $\langle w',t',p'\rangle$ iff Cresswell throws thunderbolts at $\langle w',t',p'\rangle$. This means that Zeus could make (20) true by uttering

(23)   Cresswell throws thunderbolts.

This analysis should help to explain the difference between (8) and (9) in chapter 13 with respect to direct as opposed to indirect speech.

Something similar to the 'I' case happens with temporal words like 'now'. 'Now' seems to represent a temporal adverbial referring to t in the way 'I' refers to p when in wide-scope position. In narrow-scope position it becomes 'then'. The reference to p in the semantics may also help to establish the spatial 'here' (here is the place where p is at t in w) and to solve the problem about four o'clock mentioned earlier (it could mean that t is four o'clock at the place where p is in w).

The remark just made about the semantics of 'here' may be used to allay any fear that the introduction of the "person coordinate" may lead to a potentially infinite list of contextual coordinates to be taken into account in evaluating the meaning of an expression. I and others have argued against this approach to context dependence, and in Cresswell (1973a, 110–119) I set out an alternative approach in terms of properties of utterances. Since then a number of different approaches to context dependence have been canvassed, and it is not my intention in this book to take sides. The phenomenon of tense in natural language is so ubiquitous as to make the addition of a time coordinate well-nigh inevitable, and the only question is whether the same inevitability attends the speaker coordinate. I have tried to show in the preceding pages why it may be necessary. I shall now argue that there is no need to fear a proliferation of indices. I shall do this by showing why there need be no "person addressed" coordinate to deal with *you,* no spatial coordinate to deal with *here,* and no "indicated object" coordinate to deal with *this* or *that.* The argument in each case will be the same: that all these other coordinates can be defined with reference to the world, time, and speaker.

The speaker index appeared necessary because the difference between being Zeus and being Jehovah, and therefore the content of what was said when someone said this, could not be sufficiently identified as a set of world-time pairs, since one could know what the world was like at any particular time and still not know what god one was. Does this argument apply to the semantics of *you?*

Suppose a case that parallels Kaplan's. Kaplan watches someone in a mirror at the same time he is talking to someone. He says to the person he is addressing 'His pants are on fire'. A few seconds later he shouts 'My God, it's you'. The way to proceed here, I think, is to say that what has happened is that Kaplan has suddenly recognized that it is the person he is addressing whose pants are on fire. In other words, the semantics of *you* is sufficiently described in terms of its relation to the speaker. In fact, it is not hard to see how this would work. We need to treat *you* as a nominal in category $(0/(0/1))$.

$V(you)$ is the function ζ in $D_{(0/(0/1))}$ such that for any $\omega \in D_{(0/(0/1))}$, and $\langle w,t,p \rangle$, $\langle w,t,p \rangle \in \zeta(\omega)$ iff there is some a in the domain of ω such that a is being addressed by p in w at t, and $\langle w,t,p \rangle \in \omega(a)$.

The case of *this* and *that,* when they are used deictically, can be dealt with in the same way as indicating the "most salient" object in the discourse (for a detailed discussion of salience in this context, see Lewis (1979b)). *Here* of course indicates where the speaker is, though as in the case of 'I', it sometimes takes different forms when embedded. For example,

(24)   Roger said that he was there

might report the sentence

(25)   I am here.

A "context" is after all a "context of use," and this typically means a context in which a person or other language user produces an utterance token of a linguistic expression. Given the person, the time, and the possible world, we ought to have as much information about the properties of the utterance as we need to evaluate the expression.

For this reason there seems no call for supposing that the addition of a speaker index foreshadows a further increase.

It may be that even the speaker coordinate is not required, for it may be that, as I indicated above, the purely *de re* account will do for Kaplan's example. And in fact I shall mostly continue to speak as if the $\langle w,t \rangle$ analysis were sufficient, while reserving the right to introduce the speaker index if it should prove necessary.

The last three chapters have been concerned with the verb *say*. Indirect discourse provides useful examples of propositional attitude sentences. But it has another function as well. For suppose that those who claim that the objects (as opposed to the contents) of *all* propositional attitudes are expressions in a system of representations are right. Then the semantics given for *say* in the last three chapters will automatically carry over to each attitude. In fact, where the representational system in question is an internal one, there will not be a quotational element in the attitude (for the simple reason that what is quoted is in the public external language, not the private internal representational system); thus, the analysis will in that respect be simpler than that given for indirect discourse.

I shall indicate the adaptations needed for the case of *that*$_0$. The generalization to more complex 'that's should then be obvious.

Suppose that Φ is an attitude. Then, if Fodor (1975) and others are right, for every person a at time t in world w there will be a collection of "sentences" in the representation system appropriate to Φ for a at $\langle w,t \rangle$. If Φ is belief, then this set will be the representations of everything that a believes at $\langle w,t \rangle$; if Φ is knowledge, then it will be the set of representations of all the things a knows at $\langle w,t \rangle$; and so on. Nothing need be presupposed about the nature of the representation system except that it *is* a representation system. And that means that an expression ϕ in the representation system appropriate to Φ for a at $\langle w,t \rangle$ must have an intension, which is what ϕ represents for a at $\langle w,t \rangle$. This is V*(ϕ) in the case of indirect discourse.

Suppose now that α is the verb in the public and common language that has Φ as its meaning. Then V(α), for the case in which α is followed by a *that*$_0$-clause, can be defined as the function ω such that

Where a is a person, $b \in D_0$, and $\langle w,t \rangle \in W$, then $\langle w,t \rangle \in \omega(a,b)$ iff there is an expression ϕ in the representation system appropriate to Φ for a at $\langle w,t \rangle$ that has b as its intension.

Several points should be noted about such a system. I have made no claims whatsoever about what the nature of formulae in such a system might be. All that is required is that they be states of the subject of the attitude. Further, whether a person (or other entity capable of having propositional attitudes) is or is not in such a state may well depend on features external to the person. (For instance, whether a ϕ will be in a's knowledge set will depend, among other things, on whether its intension is true at $\langle w,t \rangle$.) Nor does this account deal only with episodic attitudes. To say, for example, that a formula is in a's knowledge set at $\langle w,t \rangle$ may mean no more than that a is in such an internal state that the formula can be called up if required.

The detailed questions of the nature of the representation systems involved in each attitude are the proper subject of study for the various disciplines involved in cognitive science. In chapter 6 I criticized Moore and Hendrix's attempt to solve the semantic problem of propositional attitudes. But nothing I said there is intended to dispute the value of their analysis of the nature of belief or of any other attitudes. My purpose has been to show how the division of labor between semanticists and cognitive scientists should be appointed.

In Cresswell (1982) I argued that if it were not for the problem of propositional attitudes, semantics could be seen as an autonomous discipline not reducible to psychology or any other cognitive science. The present book is intended to show that the semantics of propositional attitudes does not require that assumption to be given up.

Chapter 15
Semantics in the Picture

I have argued in this book that that-clauses are semantically ambiguous and that this fact is a key to understanding the semantics of propositional attitudes. Thus, hyperintensionality is assumed to occur only in the complement sentences of that-clauses. In this final chapter I want to consider various other ways in which hyperintensionality can arise. My aim in each case will be to show that wherever hyperintensionality is found, there will also be the kind of ambiguity that occurs in that-clauses.

One very important source of hyperintensionality arises in what Jeff Ross (in an unpublished thesis) calls *semantic prepositions*. An example is

(1)   According to the map it is 7 + 5 kilometers to Lower Moutere.

In chapter 4 I argued that an analogous sentence involving 'that' was structurally ambiguous. The ambiguity involved whether 7 + 5 was interpreted as a structure or just as a number. Exactly the same ambiguity seems to be involved in (1).

Semantic prepositions occur in phrases like 'in the story', 'on television', or 'over the air'. In these cases the phrase that follows the preposition denotes what Ross calls a *medium*—the story, television, or "the air" (= radio). Ross is undertaking a detailed and general study of media prepositions and so I will confine my remarks to a single example that I have discussed elsewhere. But one general point that should be made is that these prepositions seem to be used in an almost metaphorical extension of their literal spatial uses. I do not want to suggest that they are used metaphorically—I think they are not. But this extended use means that it might be plausible to locate the structural ambiguity in sentences like (1) in the preposition itself. At any rate, I shall try to show that a discussion of the phrase 'in the picture' requires reference to a structured meaning. In particular, I shall try to show that this has to be the correct analysis of what is represented by certain "impossible" pictures.

Using a system of intensions based on possible worlds, the logical structure of pictorial representation is fairly straightforward. In Cresswell (1983, 66) I discussed a photograph of early Wellington. That photograph, of course, was causally produced by how things were in Wellington at the time. And if one asks the question 'What is that a picture of?', one can be given an answer in terms of the causal ancestry of the picture. But perhaps the picture has been faked. Or perhaps we are watching a television program in which things are not as they ever were in reality. There is still a legitimate answer to the question of what a picture is a picture of. This answer can be thought of as the answer to the question of what the world would have to be like in order for things to be as the picture shows them to be. A picture of a purple cow would demand at least a world in which there was a purple cow.

Worlds in which things are as the picture shows may be described as worlds that *realize* the picture. If I look at the photograph of Lambton Quay in 1910 and I see a man about to board a tram bound for Tinakori Road, then a world in which there is such a man about to board such a tram is one that realizes the picture. Not all such worlds, of course, because they have to be worlds in which things are as the rest of the picture portrays. For instance, there must be a man and a woman walking along the pavement under the verandah of shop number 290, and so on.

Now, as far as the picture is concerned, the only person visible on the tram is the motorman. We cannot see whether the tram is empty or crowded, and there are any number of ways of filling the tram, compatible with what we see in the picture, whatever the situation was like in the actual world.

We can now give an analysis of what it means to say that in the picture there is a tram outside the Gresham Hotel. It is to say that there is a tram there in all the worlds that realize the picture. By contrast, one cannot say that the tram in the picture is either full or empty, because in some of the worlds that realize the picture it is full, but in others it is empty. So we say that a world realizes a picture in those and only those possible worlds in which what the picture represents is so. This set of worlds can be taken to be the representational meaning of the picture.

There is, however, an important class of pictures whose treatment requires something more elaborate. These are the "impossible pictures" of the kind made famous by M. C. Escher and others. In one Escher drawing (plate 69 of (1967)), water from the bottom of a waterfall flows down until it reaches the top of the very same waterfall. Another drawing shows (plate 68) a succession of monks continually ascending or descending a staircase, yet paradoxically always reaching again a point where they were before. There are no worlds in which things are as either of these pictures show, yet clearly something different is going on in each.

A simpler example is what is known as *the devil's tuning fork:*

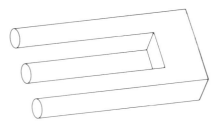

Since there is no set of worlds in which such an object exists, how are we to describe what we see? What seems to happen is that parts of the picture are perfectly consistent but contradict other parts of the picture. We can see this quite easily by putting the edge of a piece of paper across each part of the tuning fork:

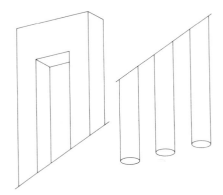

The result is a perfectly consistent pair of pictures. This suggests that we can explain what the picture represents by thinking of two sets of worlds, the sets that respectively realize each part of the picture. The same is true, though in a more complex way, in the Escher drawings of the waterfall and the monks.

How, then, should a semantics be given to the following sentence?

(2)   In the picture there is at least one monk going both up and down at the same time.

The situation (2) describes is Escher's picture. I use the quantifier to prevent (2) from being reexpressed as

(3) In the picture there is at least one monk going up and in the picture there is at least one monk going down.

If what I said above about what Escher's picture represents is correct, there seems no way of avoiding a structure in which there are sets of worlds with each monk going up, and sets of worlds with each monk going down. And this is certainly one of the structures that could be assigned to the sentence in (2) that follows 'In the picture'.

Semantic prepositions form a limited class that can be reasonably easily identified and isolated. So there seems no block to allowing them to indicate how much structure is to be assigned to the sentence that follows the prepositional phrase. Each semantic preposition would be indexed, in a λ-categorial language, in much the way *that* is.

Semantic prepositions might not be the only prepositions that are structure-sensitive. Fred Dretske (1972) has considered phrases like 'by mistake' in cases of contrasting stress. He argues that although there may be no truth-conditional difference between

(4) Clyde gave me THE TICKETS

and

(5) Clyde gave ME the tickets

(though there is, he argues, a semantic difference of some kind, to be analyzed in terms of an implied contrast), yet if (4) and (5) are followed by the phrase 'by mistake', then a truth-conditional difference emerges. If Clyde is instructed to give the tickets to Harry but gives them to me by mistake, then, says Dretske,

(6) Clyde gave me THE TICKETS by mistake

is false but

(7) Clyde gave ME the tickets by mistake

is true. Arnim von Stechow (1981b) has argued that cases like this should be accounted for by splitting the sentence up into topic and focus. The phrase 'by mistake' would then operate on this structure in such a way that the part selected as the focus would be the part involved in the contrast.

Another kind of by-phrase that has been argued to be structure-sensitive is the one used in passive sentences. The problem is how to recover

(8) Harriet discovered Ian

from

(9)   Ian was discovered by Harriet.

In (9) the intension of the phrase 'was discovered' seems to be that of 'was discovered by someone', and (if I understand him correctly) Keenan (1980) argues that in cases like this the intension is not sensitive enough to allow the intension of 'by Harriet' to operate on it and produce the meaning of (9) that makes it synonymous with (8). He argues that the by-phrase in (9) must be sensitive to the separate parts of the verb phrase it operates on.

Another class of words that induce hyperintensionality includes words like *whether, if,* and *what* as they occur in such sentences as

(10)   Sam knows whether 2 + 2 = 4,

(11)   Tinkerbell is wondering if B+ has the finite model property,

and

(12)   Urs has worked out what 257 − 28 is.

There seems to be no reason why these words cannot be indexed in just the same way as *that.*

The word *if* has problems of another kind, though. Consider

(13)   If what Gödel seems to have proved is true, then we are in for a shock.

Presumably the proposition that Gödel is reported as having proved is either necessary or impossible. If the former, then (13) would seem equivalent to the straight

(14)   We are in for a shock.

If the latter, then it would seem that anything follows, since in that case there are no worlds in which what Gödel proved is true. Yet (13) seems a contingent statement. I have nothing very definite to say about this case except that it seems in some ways like the Phosphorus and Hesperus case. For I do not think we are really imagining a case in which a given noncontingent proposition has this or that value. We are rather imagining a (logically possible) situation in which Gödel does something that is (at a certain level) observationally indistinguishable from proving a certain proposition. The exact formulation is admittedly difficult, but I see no reason why some kind of *de expressione* analysis would not prove possible.

The final class of expressions I want to consider that do not involve a that-clause is a small class of adverbs. I shall examine the adverb 'obviously' in

(15)   7 + 5 is obviously 12.

Like other hyperintensional operators, 'obviously' seems susceptible of semantic ambiguity, as in

(16)   There are obviously 7 + 5 kilometers to Lower Moutere.

Other examples in this class are 'apparently', 'indubitably', and so on. The most attractive way of dealing with these is to postulate a transformational derivation from phrases like 'it is obvious that'. The reason for dealing with them this way is that the meaning of the adverb ('obviously') is closely connected with the meaning of the attitude verb phrase ('it is obvious') that precedes 'that' in the paraphrase. I have argued strenuously throughout this book that the ambiguity found in propositional attitude sentences is not to be located in the attitude verb, and for this reason would very much wish to avoid any suggestion of ambiguity in the adverb itself.

At any rate, none of these cases of hyperintensionality without a that-clause seems to me to indicate any drastic revision of the analysis I have defended in the cases in which a that-clause is involved.

Bibliographical Commentary

I have tried, in the text, to set out and defend a way of accommodating propositional attitude sentences within possible-worlds semantics. In order to preserve the flow of the argument, I have kept bibliographical reference there to a minimum. Many of the issues I discuss have been the subject of considerable controversy in the philosophical literature, however, and it would seem unfair to ignore this entirely. In addition, there is a need to elaborate the sometimes cryptic references I do make in the text. This commentary therefore has a twofold purpose of discussing the work of others and acting as notes for the text, though it is designed to be read straight through.

Introduction

The reference to Wittgenstein is Wittgenstein (1921). 4.024 reads, in the Pears and McGuinness translation, "To understand a proposition means to know what is the case if it is true."

Sentences (2)–(5) are to be found in Bigelow (1978, 103) (his (5)–(8)). Similar examples occur in Partee (1973).

In this book I treat indirect discourse as a propositional attitude. Davidson's account of indirect discourse is set out in Davidson (1969). His basic idea is that, in an utterance of what appears to be the single sentence 'Galileo said that the earth moves', what is going on is in fact two utterances, first an utterance 'Galileo said that' and second an utterance 'the earth moves'. In the first utterance the word 'that' is just a demonstrative. I am taking it that the fact that two utterances are involved means that Davidson thinks that the sentence 'Galileo said that the earth moves' is really two sentences, 'Galileo said that' and 'the earth moves'. If so, then although we no doubt require a semantics of demonstratives, there is no propositional attitude sentence whose meaning has to be specified in Davidson's favored manner (which is an adaptation of Tarski's semantics for first-order logic; see Davidson (1967a)). The view that propositional attitude sentences do not have a meaning that depends on the

meaning of their complement sentences seems to be shared by Johnson-Laird (1982), who produces some examples that he claims establish "that a semantic theory formulated for a language can never be
rich enough to cope with propositional attitudes" (p. 56). I shall not
attempt a discussion of Davidson's theory or of the objections to and
defenses of it that have appeared in the literature (though I do mention it briefly in chapter 6) because my immediate aim in this book
will be to show that a structured-meaning approach allows the problem of propositional attitudes to be solved within possible-worlds
semantics. It is only indirectly that I shall be concerned with evaluating alternative semantical frameworks.

Ignoring vagueness might be thought worse in the case of propositional attitude sentences on the ground that a precise sentence
might report a vague belief. I think this is what Machina (1976)
claims. But I am not persuaded of the correctness of any particular
account of vagueness and so I shall continue with the idealization. I
mention the work done on the linguistic application of λ-categorial
languages and related frameworks in the commentary on chapter 11.

Chapter 1: Compositional Semantics: An Arithmetical Analogy

I regard both the conventionality and the compositionality of language as obvious, and indeed as almost trivial. This would presumably be conceded for conventionality, and, in the sense I intend, it
ought to be conceded for compositionality. For all I intend is to claim
that the meanings of complex expressions are worked out rather than
learned piecemeal. As Partee (1983) recognizes, this claim is hardly
one to be doubted. But, as she also recognizes, any precise articula-
tion of it can make it controversial. Even in the form in which it is
often called *Frege's Principle, viz* that the meaning of a sentence is a
function of the meaning of its parts, it can be contentious; in fact, as
my treatment of quotational contexts shows, its precise meaning, or
even truth, can be questioned. It has been explicitly questioned recently by Hintikka and other proponents of game-theoretical semantics. Hintikka (1982) gives a useful summary of work in this tradition
and disputes the principle of compositionality on p. 230. I do not in
this book wish to take issue with Hintikka on this, though I suspect
that my own inclinations run in the direction of invoking higher-
order entities to deal with phenomena like branching quantifiers, as
Hintikka suggests on p. 231. It is true that the framework I suggest in
part III is compositional in a sense that Hintikka would dispute, and
it is true that I have nothing in particular to say about the problem he

is concerned with. As far as this book is concerned, I would like to think that anything I say about propositional attitudes could be expressed within game-theoretical semantics by those who favor this approach.

In saying that the meanings of words are not compositional, I do not want to take sides on the question of what to do with words like 'beekeeper' (Emmon Bach gave me this example). Compounding of words is an area I do not wish to venture into (see Bauer (1983)). I want only to insist that in language there are certain simple expressions whose meanings are learned and other complex expressions whose meanings have to be worked out.

A final issue on which I do not wish to take sides is the question of "semantic syntax"—the question of whether a language can be syntactically specified independently of its semantics. Here I follow Lewis (1972, 188f.) in assuming that the function of semantically sensitive rules of syntax would be to rule out as ill formed on semantic grounds expressions that the syntactic rules alone would generate.

The view that a proposition of mathematics is really about a linguistic expression, to the effect that it denotes the necessary proposition, seems to be defended in Stalnaker (1976, 88). If propositions of mathematics are really such propositions, then of course they can be true in different worlds. It seems to me, for the reasons given in the text, that this view cannot be right. It seems so also to Field (1978, 15). Of course, the problem of just what it *is* to believe a mathematical proposition, or any proposition, does cry out for an answer. I see my own task as that of first clearing up the semantics of attitude sentences in general so that this other question can then be taken up by others. But more of that later.

I hope it is clear that my use of the term 'propositional attitude' is extremely liberal. Klein (1978, 158) rules out any verbs like 'say' that can take direct quotations as propositional attitude verbs. It is of course true that a verb like 'believe' (as opposed, in my opinion, to 'think') cannot (normally) take a quotational complement. But as I try to show throughout the book, that-clauses with verbs like 'say' should be given the same kind of semantics that they have with verbs like 'believe'.

In offering the semantics I have for numerical expressions, I do not want to suggest that this is how they behave in natural language. Numerals in natural language behave very like quantifiers. Their role has been studied in Boër and Edelstein (1979).

Chapter 2: De Re *Attitudes*

Fodor (1975, 27) states explicitly that computational models are "the only psychological models of cognitive processes that seem even remotely plausible." I return to some of these matters in chapter 6.

An interesting discussion of how we have to rely on empirical information for our confidence in mathematical truths occurs in Kroon (1982). This dependence can become worrying in cases in which the proofs are so complicated that we have to rely on computers.

By a "roughly Russellian" account of definite descriptions I mean, in essence, one that treats a definite description as the same syntactic category as a quantifier, such as 'someone'. Expressions of this category have the property that they can take wide or narrow scope over sentential operators. Thus, 'Someone does not come' does not mean the same as 'It is not the case that someone comes'. Russell saw that in modal and doxastic contexts scope distinctions could matter even with a description like 'the person next door'. For although 'the person next door lives next door' is logically equivalent to 'exactly one person lives next door' and therefore there is a sense in which 'necessarily the person next door lives next door' is true, yet there is obviously a sense in which the person who lives next door might not have lived next door. In the former case the description 'the person who lives next door' is said to have narrow scope with respect to the sentential operator 'necessarily'; in the latter case the sentence 'necessarily the person who lives next door lives next door' would be held to be false because even though a person happens to live next door, this could never be true by necessity of anyone. Here the description has wide scope with respect to the sentential operator. For Russell's account of descriptions in belief contexts, see Russell (1905); for a recent discussion of the issues, see Reeves (1973). Such an account has been defended in Sharvy (1969), and an even more recent defense of Russell is given in K. Bach (1983).

The account of *de re* belief sketched in the latter part of this chapter is discussed in more detail in Cresswell and von Stechow (1982, 506–510) and in von Stechow (1982). In speaking about the "object" of Ralph's beliefs, I mean to claim that the meaning of the that-clause which expresses that belief (in sentence (iii)) is not a proposition. But of course in speaking of the object of Ralph's belief, one might be asking what is the proposition that Ralph "directly" believes that makes (iii) true. On the account suggested by (iii') the proposition he directly believes might be, say, the proposition referred to in (i).

In fact, there is even a third thing if we count the way Ralph represents the belief to himself. This third thing will be discussed further in chapter 6, where it will be called the *object* of Ralph's belief, in contrast with the *content* of that belief. The content of Ralph's belief is just the meaning of the that-clause that reports it. For the time being I shall use the term "content*" for what Ralph "directly" believes. Thus, sentence (iii) now involves three things—the object, the content, and the content*—and the picture I support is roughly of the kind described—that is, when x has a *de re* belief to the effect that y is F, then there is an appropriate relation R in which x stands to y such that there is in x's belief store a representation of the proposition that any y such that xRy is F.

Two comments on this account are in order. First, I have no analysis to offer of what the relation R might be. (Kaplan (1969) suggests an analysis in terms of "vivid" names. Perhaps he is right. Perhaps he is not.) In fact, I never consider the question of the precise nature of belief. Second, as far as the semantics of (iii) goes, all that is needed is an explanation of the content (as opposed to the content* or the object) of the belief. Thus, even if the view I have just sketched of the relation between content and content* should turn out to be wrong, that in itself need not show that the content of the belief in (iii) need be anything other than a thing and a property. One author who seems to want to deny that the relation between content and content* is as I have described it is Bach (1982). On p. 120 and p. 131 he denies that *de re* attitudes are propositional attitudes at all. Part of what he means may be the same as the points I make in distinguishing the *de re* approach from the propositional approach. But in addition, although I do not entirely understand his positi˰ ɛ proposals on pp. 143–148 regarding perceptual *de re* beliefs, I think he would want to deny that there is even a content * that is propositional. Nothing that Bach says, however, seems to me to count against the analysis I have given of content as opposed to content*; thus, even if he is right, the only part of the *de re* semantics that I want definitely to commit myself to would still stand. Van Fraassen (1979, 371) suggests that the appropriate relation is one that involves not the believer so much as the context of the attitudε sentence, in particular the intentions of the speaker, though the details of his theory have been challenged in Reddam (1982).

The distinction between content and content* can help, I think, in looking at certain puzzles about belief. In particular, I have in mind the case in Kripke (1979) of Pierre, who knows London both as the city that he has read about under the name 'Londres' and that he thinks is pretty and also as the city he now lives in that he knows under the name 'London' and that he thinks is ugly. Kripke (rightly, I believe) claims that both of Pierre's beliefs are about London but that his beliefs are nevertheless not inconsistent, and poses the puzzle of how this can be. Lewis (1981) agrees with Kripke's intuitions, but claims that the puzzle has an easy solution. Before looking at what Lewis says, I want to examine what happens to the puzzle when we make the distinction between content and content*, for this distinction will help us to see that there is an equivocation in the notion of inconsistent beliefs. Assuming that 'pretty' and 'ugly' really are (in this instance) contrary predicates, then it is not logically possible for the same thing to be both pretty and ugly; thus, it is not logically possible for the thing of which Pierre believes both that it is pretty and that it is ugly to have both these properties. However, as (iii') and (iv') show, the content* of either of Pierre's beliefs does not contradict the other and so, in that sense, Pierre's beliefs are not inconsistent. What does Pierre believe? Lewis (1981) takes it to be the content*; or at least, assuming that his principle (4) on p. 284 can be taken as saying that Pierre's belief is to be the meaning of the that-clause that reports it, then his denial of (4) can be taken as a denial that Pierre's belief is the content of the that-clause. And his remarks about what Pierre's belief really is suggest that something like content* would do. He considers briefly on p. 288 the view that beliefs might be contents (he puts this by suggesting that we might be characterizing partly the believer's inner state and partly the relations of that state to the outside world) and comments that, in that case, "there is no reason to suppose that a leading philosopher or logician would never let contradictory beliefs pass." (Lewis's reaction to the Kripke puzzle seems also to be shared by Barcan Marcus (1983).)

As Kripke tells the story about Pierre (1979, 254f.), it comes across to me at least as a tale of *de re* belief, and in fact my comments about it make sense on that assumption. On p. 242 (and p. 272f.), however, Kripke claims that he will not be concerned with *de re* belief and insists that the beliefs be taken *de dicto*. So taken, they raise important questions about the correct analysis of proper names in belief contexts. These issues are taken up in chapter 5, and further reference to Pierre will be made in the commentary on that chapter.

The account of *de re* attitudes adopted does not deal with the difficult and embarrassing case of *de re* reference to fictional entities. In his discussion of Pierre, Lewis (1981, 288) imagines him to have been told in France that Père Noël brings presents to all the children, and in England that Father Christmas brings presents only to the good children. (Pierre reckons that good children get double shares.) Lewis assumes that this cannot be a *de re* attitude, given the nonexistence of the *res*. I am less sure. It seems to me that one might well make out a case for saying that sometimes we can make reference to and have attitudes about things that only exist in some other possible world. To be sure, the appropriate relation that the holder of the attitude is required to stand in cannot any longer be a straightforwardly causal one, but that does not mean that there might not be some kind of causal chain linking the holder of the attitude with a certain story. Boër (forthcoming) adopts such a solution to the problem of when and how mythological names can be regarded as the "same," and even Devitt (1981), who eschews completely a possible-worlds account of fictional entities, explains our use of fictitious names on pp. 174–177 in terms of a causal network originating in a story-telling.

More acute difficulties are illustrated by some well-known examples invented by Peter Geach. In Geach (1967, 628) the following sentence occurs:

(i)   Hob thinks a witch has blighted Bob's mare, and Nob wonders whether she (the same witch) killed Cob's sow.

These sentences are difficult, not just because they seem to involve reference to nonexistent entities. (As Pendlebury (1982, 347) observes, the same problem arises when 'lion' replaces 'witch'.) It is rather that they seem to require a quantifier that is both outside and inside the scope of the attitude verbs. I have no particular solution to offer to this problem. One kind of solution that others have offered involves postulating aspects (Geach (1976)), intensional objects (Hill (1976), Kraut (1983)), or the like, all of which, in a sense, act as surrogates for individuals and form the range of a wide-scope quantifier. Pendlebury (1982, 249–254) argues that the puzzles can be solved without the need for such entities, and Saarinen (1978) discusses Geach's problem within the context of game-theoretical semantics. Reference to the nonexistent is also discussed in Lewis (1983).

Burdick (1982) is among those who want to rule out the possibility that one may have contradictory *de re* beliefs. His solution is to say that what goes on in a *de re* belief is that we ascribe properties to something under a mode of presentation and not *simpliciter*. Any apparent contradiction in *de re* beliefs can then be dissolved by replacing the *res* with a pair consisting of the *res* together with a description, since x could easily believe G of $\langle y,F \rangle$ and not believe G of $\langle y,H \rangle$, G, F, and H being construed linguistically. (The idea of "belief-under-a-mode-of-presentation" is also found in Schiffer (1977, 32).) The mode-of-presentation account is of course strictly independent of the question of whether attitudes are relations to linguistic expressions. I take up that question in chapter 5. In fact, Burdick's view of the semantics of purely *de re* sentences is perfectly in accord with the view advocated in the text since, on p. 191, he construes believing *G* of *x* as believing it under some description.

In the fuller account of *de re* belief presented in Cresswell and von Stechow (1982, 506–510), we resolved the contradiction by denying that, in *de re* cases, one could infer from '*x* believes not *G* of *y*' that *x* does not believe *G* of *y*. Burdick (1982, 187), however, imagines a case where *x* has no opinion about whether *y*, under a certain description, is *G*; though he does believe that *y* under some other description is *G*. In such a case we should, he feels, say that *x* does not believe *G* of *y*. Of course, this means that the *de re* belief that *y* is *G* is inconsistent with the suspension of judgment. In fact, this is just the problem discussed on p. 235 of Kaplan (1969). Ralph is still sure that the man in the brown coat is a spy, but he is now inclined to suspend judgment, rather than disbelieve, of the man he saw at the beach (in the grey coat) that he is a spy. Kaplan points out that this cannot be analyzed by saying that he does not believe of the man at the beach that he is a spy, but must be analyzed by saying that there is some way of picking out Ortcutt (I would say by some appropriate relation R; Kaplan would say by some "vivid name" Ralph has for picking out Ortcutt) such that Ralph does not believe that whatever is related to him by R is a spy. In other words, we must deny the principle that Burdick relies on, *viz* that '*x* suspends judgment of *y* that it is *G*' entails '*x* does not believe of *y* that it is *G*'. This principle certainly has a *prima facie* appeal, so much so that Heidelberger (1974, 442), like Burdick, relies on it without argument and requires Devitt (1976) to point out the error.

Klein (1978) calls the problem of apparently inconsistent beliefs the problem of *double vision* (p. 73). His solution (on pp. 171–176) is, very roughly, to construe 'Ralph believes of Ortcutt that he is a spy' as

(ii)   'Ralph believes the proposition that would have been expressed by "he is a spy" in the context Ralph believes that he was in when Ortcutt was demonstrated on the beach.'

In other words, Klein's solution is a version of the solution described by (v) in the text. Certainly Klein has tried to give an account of how this would go, but the reservations I expressed there still remain.

A useful collection of articles, most of which are concerned with *de re* attitudes, may be found in Heny (1981).

Chapter 3: Structured Meanings

That knowledge of meaning is constituted by knowledge of truth conditions is something I have argued for in Cresswell (1978b). It is no doubt simplistic, since in fact the problem of propositional attitudes shows that often we *don't* know truth conditions; for we may not know that '7 + 5 = 11' has the same truth conditions as '56 is a prime'. Perhaps it is better to regard it, as Barbara Partee (1982) suggests, as codifying the consequences of what we know. Partee suggests (p. 97) that we should make a distinction between "what the speaker knows" and "what properties of language are determined by what the speaker knows." At any rate, I take it as an assumption that sentences have truth conditions, and that it is the job of semantics to show how the truth conditions of complex expressions are determined. For that purpose I regard as relevant to semantics all but only those features of an expression that can affect the truth conditions of larger expressions as a part of which that expression may occur. I do not wish to lay down in advance what these features may turn out to be, but I do want to rule out as relevant to *my* project any argument to the effect that such and such a feature is a semantic feature, which does not depend on truth conditions. This is why I have nothing to say here about "conceptual roles" (Harman (1975), (1982)), intention-based semantics (Schiffer (1972), (1982)), or speech act theory (Searle (1969)). I have no wish to argue that any of these views is incompatible with truth-conditional semantics.

Katz's views on semantics are expressed in a wide range of articles. Perhaps they are articulated most clearly in Katz (1972), though he has only recently commented on possible-worlds semantics. As far as truth-conditional semantics is concerned, Katz's criticisms can be reduced to two. The first, expressed on p. 174 of Katz (1982), is that all other approaches to semantics but Katz's own try to reduce meaning to something else, among which he cites truth conditions. Unfortunately, as many of Katz's critics have realized (see for instance Saarinen (1982) and Pelletier (1982)), Katz's criticism depends on already knowing that truth conditions *are* something else. Katz has his own view of what the data of semantics are (see Katz (1972, 4–6) and (1982, 175–177)); they are such facts as the meaningfulness of sentences, the synonymy of pairs of sentences, and the like. In Cresswell (1978b) I suggested that a Katz-type semantics is not so much wrong as incomplete—on the grounds that a truth-conditional semantical theory gives as consequences precisely the kind of information Katz requires. Be that as it may, I am perfectly content for Katz to use the word 'semantics' as he pleases, having made clear how I want to use the word.

Katz's other criticism of truth-conditional semantics is that it predicts that all logically equivalent sentences have the same meaning. He applies this in particular to the possible-worlds version in which the meaning of a sentence is the set of worlds in which it is true. The objection is found, for instance, in Katz (1982, 190). Katz and Katz (1977) realize that attempts are being made to deal with this problem. They say (p. 88f.), "We do not mean to suggest that possible worlds semanticists are unaware of such counter-examples, but only that they are unable to deal with them." They then criticize Lewis (1972) for his attempts. Their own view of what is wrong (pp. 91–96) suggests that they would support some kind of structured-meaning account, though one involving a great deal of lexical decomposition into semantic primitives. The solution to the problem of propositional attitudes defended in this book will I hope meet these criticisms, in at least some measure, though I doubt it would be regarded as completely acceptable.

Taking that-clauses in the way suggested in the text means regarding them as what linguists call *noun phrases* or *NPs*. According to Klein (1978, 43f.), it has been usual in linguistics to regard them as such since the early work of Joan Bresnan (see Bresnan (1970)). Thomason (1976, 83), in an extension of Montague Grammar, treats 'that' as making a term out of a sentence, although in "Universal Grammar" Montague himself generated that-clauses by a syntactic rule (Montague (1974, 238)). There seem to be some adverbial uses of that-clauses—in Cresswell (1973a, 169) I cited the sentence 'I was upset that he came'—but these uses seem distinct. There is another problem, however: although that-clauses seem to fit all kinds of attitude verbs, as do words like 'something', yet some noun phrases are more selective. Thus, although one can say 'Vera knows whether it will rain', one cannot say 'Vera believes whether it will rain'; and although one can say both 'Vera knows what William said' and 'Vera believes what William said', the first means that Vera knows, of a certain proposition, that William said it, whereas the second means that Vera believes, of something William said, that it is true. (See Vendler (1975) and Hintikka (1975a, 21f.).) It is certainly clear that there are some important distinctions here that a full theory of propositional attitudes will eventually have to come to grips with. But it is less clear that they affect the use to which 'that' is being put in the present book.

There is a view, which was held by Arthur Prior (see Prior (1963,

116f.), (1971, 19)), that, instead of taking 'believes' as a predicate that operates on a that-clause, we should regard 'believes that' as a syntactic unit that operates directly on a sentence. Obviously, such a view does not allow the ambiguities in propositional attitude sentences to be put into the that-clause, because on this view there is, strictly speaking, no such thing as a that-clause. Such a view seems to me not to be a plausible one, principally because it fails to take account of cases in which what follows the attitude verb is not a that-clause. Thus, it cannot account for phenomena like the inference in (5). The fragment in chapter 8 of Montague (1974) generates **believes that** and **asserts that** directly. It is not clear how that fragment would deal with (5). Those who advocate the 'believes that' view must go to considerable lengths to deal with inferences of this kind, and I must admit that their maneuvers seem to me semantically artificial and syntactically unmotivated. A theory designed to deal with attributions of truth without making it a predicate of that-clauses may be found in Grover, Camp, and Belnap (1975). Baldwin (1982) takes up the task of integrating Prior's views on indirect discourse within a Davidsonian type of truth theory. (He argues against Davidson's own way of doing this.)

The *locus classicus* of Frege's views on sense and reference is of course Frege (1892). Frege's word 'Bedeutung' in that article is translated as 'reference' in Frege (1952). Alternative translations are 'Nominatum' and 'denotation'. (For a discussion, see Kneale and Kneale (1962, 495).) In recent philosophical literature it is more usual to speak of the 'referent' of a name, but I have preferred to stick with 'reference'. I hope it is obvious that I am not engaged in Fregean exegesis. Van Heijenoort provides in (1977a) a reconstruction of a notion of Fregean sense that involves structure, and discusses in (1977b) some of the things Frege had to say about sense.

Chapter 4: Structural Ambiguity

The ambiguity of belief sentences is recognized in Hill (1976, 215f.). Hill also recognizes that one must locate the ambiguity either in the that-clause, or in 'believes', or in a mixture of both. He opts for an ambiguity in 'believes' but otherwise his theory has many similarities with the one defended in this book. In particular, his long-term aim of showing that these problems have a solution within possible-worlds semantics is one that I wholeheartedly applaud. Hill only recognizes a twofold ambiguity, and he does not consider other attitudes. In my view it is the existence of a parallel multiple and systematic ambiguity in all the attitude-verb phrases that supports locating the ambiguity in the that-clause.

Thomason's argument occurs in (1977) and (1980a). It is based on Montague's proof (1974, 286–302) that modal operators are not predicates of sentences. See also Anderson (1983). The importance of Montague's work on this question has been questioned by Skyrms (1978), who shows that there is certainly *a* sense in which modal operators can be given a metalinguistic semantics. The price Skyrms must pay, however, is a very strictly typed hierarchy of metalanguages. Hintikka's epistemic logic dates from Hintikka (1962) and has been refined in many publications since then (see, for instance, the essays in Hintikka (1969) and (1975a)).

Chapter 5: Attitudes De Expressione

A fuller discussion of attempts to give a quotational analysis of propositional attitude sentences will be found in Cresswell (1980) as well as references to much of the standard literature on the subject. As I point out there, my criticisms of this approach are in essence a sharpening of Church's (1950) translation argument. I believe, however, that it is better to make them without using the notion of translation and, as in (1980), I have tried to do that here. In chapter 6 I discuss the possibility of giving a direct recursive specification of synonymy as a relation between two (interpreted) languages. In the present chapter I confine myself to showing that if we are working with a semantics that proceeds by assigning meanings to expressions, then the "synonymy" approach to propositional attitudes would only work if we already had an adequate semantics for each attitude in terms of a relation between people and meanings.

An intriguing attempt to bring together the quotational approach and the propositional approach is found in van Fraassen (1979). Van Fraassen uses the distinction between pragmatics and semantics drawn by Montague (1974) (see, for example, p. 96 and p. 119f.) in which pragmatics is concerned with the role of contexts such as times and speakers in dealing with such phenomena as tense and personal pronouns. (I prefer to regard this as semantics, but that is a relatively unimportant terminological matter.) Van Fraassen's move is to regard reference to a language (or, as he calls it, "idiolect") as something that can be specified by the context. Unfortunately, he does not have anything to say about precisely how this approach (which is in any case only very briefly sketched on p. 372f.) would work with the arithmetical examples I have discussed in earlier chapters. Grabski (1978) also uses the context to specify the language spoken. He allows words like 'not' (or rather 'nicht') to have nonstandard meanings at some contexts. The purpose of Grabski's paper is to show how hyperintensionality can be canceled by phrases like 'so to speak' ('sozusagen') or 'in effect'. My inclination is to regard these operators as indicating a purely referential 'that', and my feeling is still that it is not really plausible to explain mathematical beliefs in terms of the nonstandard use of words.

Arnim von Stechow's felicitous phrase *de expressione* has not previously occurred in print, but he has used it often in correspondence and conversation. I take it that he invented the phrase, though claims of that kind are often risky.

On a Russellian account there is no particular problem about identity statements when descriptions are involved. To say that the star that appears in the morning is identical with the star that appears in the evening is to say no more than that there is a unique star with both properties. This is clearly a contingent statement, and one not logically equivalent to the statement merely that there is a unique star that appears in the evening. What has been more problematic in the recent literature is the case in which names are involved. In Kripke (1972) and (1979) a clear distinction is drawn between the problem as it applies to names and the problem as it applies to descriptions. If I understand him correctly on p. 279, Kripke does not intend, at least not there, to dispute a Russellian solution in the case of descriptions but only in the case of names. In fact, it is due in large measure to Kripke that the problem which in Frege's work and in the work of many subsequent authors appeared as the problem of the morning star and the evening star turned into the problem of Phosphorus and Hesperus.

A large part of Kripke (1972) is devoted to giving an account of how we can use a name to refer to something. Bach (1981, 313) points out that it is important to distinguish the semantics of names from a theory of uses of names, and indeed it does seem that by far the bulk of the work done recently on names, in particular the controversy over the historical vs. the description theory of reference (and on related issues such as the referential use of definite description, as argued for in Donnellan (1966) and (1972) and elsewhere), is concerned with the latter question. I have nothing to say here on such matters. As far as this chapter is concerned, the only feature I take to be important about causal theories of reference is that the meaning of a name is nothing but its bearer. (This is what Boër (forthcoming) calls the *negative part* of the causal theory of reference.)

The simplest course for one who believes this is to take the hard line mentioned in the discussion of (12) and (16). An example of a hard-liner is Tye (1978), who argues that knowing that Hesperus is Hesperus just is synonymous with knowing that Hesperus is Phosphorus. It seems to me less obvious that one can take a hard line when the attitude verb is 'says', though I suppose one could argue that this is because 'says' might be partly quotational. Of course, on any of the description theories mentioned in the text, the hard-line interpretation is always available by giving the description wide scope. This is what makes the hard-line position less conclusive than its supporting arguments might suggest. For, although one can produce arguments for saying that sometimes a belief about Phosphorus just is a belief about Hesperus, it is much more difficult to argue that there is no way of interpreting a belief sentence involving 'Phosphorus' that makes it different from the same belief sentence except for involving 'Hesperus'.

Loar (1976, 370–373) and Bach (1981) both defend the kind of description theory that would make 'Phosphorus' mean something like 'is called "Phosphorus"'. Loar (p. 371) discusses the objection that the theory might be circular because using a name N to refer to a thing x is part of what is involved in calling something x and so cannot be involved in the meaning of N. (For such an objection, see Kripke (1972, 283, 286).) Loar seems to me to give the right reply to this sort of objection: "It is not as though one were trying to refer to something by saying 'the referent of this very phrase'; rather, on an intrinsic use of N, one means *the F which has been referred to as, or has been dubbed, N;* and there is no more problem with that than there would be had one uttered those very words" (p. 371; Loar's italics). Loar also discusses the modal objection and notes (p. 373) that names are normally read as having wider scope than modal operators (though even this may not always be so if we regard counterfactual contexts as modal: Ziff (1977, 326) shows that there may well be cases in which we want to say things like 'If Harmon had been Gaskin, then . . .'). Kripke (1972) is aware of the "wide-scope" reply to his criticism but responds rather briefly (on p. 279). As I have tried to indicate, I am not myself convinced either way on whether his response succeeds, and I have rested content with showing how the semantics would work in each case.

Bach (1981, 371) calls the theory discussed the *nominal description theory* and defends it against Kripke's objections. A number of authors (e.g., Burge (1979, 412) and Bach (1981, 381)) have pointed out that Kripke (1972) does not address the question of names in belief sentences (he says (1979, 281, n. 44) that he did not "wish to muddy the waters further than necessary at that time"). McGinn (1982, 245) puts it by saying that Kripke's account "gets the modal status right but runs into trouble over the epistemic status." Other comments on Kripke's arguments against a description theory of names may be found in Burge (1979, 412f.).

Kripke (1979) does raise the question of belief and proper names in his example about Pierre who believes that Londres is pretty but that London is ugly. In the commentary on chapter 2 I discussed Kripke's example, if interpreted in a *de re* way, as a belief about London. It should be clear that, if it is interpreted in the *de expressione* way, there is, on the description theory, no problem either. For Pierre does believe that the city he knows as 'Londres' is pretty but that the city he knows as 'London' is not. On this analysis 'London' is not always an accurate translation of 'Londres'. Here 'London' is doing duty for something like 'the city Pierre knows under the name "London" '. This description is relative to Pierre, but it is not any sort of "private sense" that Pierre attaches to the name. Kripke rightly criticizes those whom he calls on p. 277 "extreme Fregeans" who "believe that in general names are peculiar to idiolects" (he claims that Frege and Russell are extreme Fregeans). The problem for them is that, in a sentence that attributes a belief to Pierre, the question of what the names mean is a question for the speaker, not Pierre. The description 'city Pierre knows under the name "London" ' has a public meaning.

Unfortunately, the issue is not *quite* as simple as that. Returning to Phosphorus and Hesperus, if I wish to report an ancient Greek belief, and I use these names, I probably do not use 'Phosphorus' to mean 'heavenly body known under the name "Phosphorus" ', at least not if this is taken to be different in meaning from 'heavenly body known under the name "Φωσφορος" ' in the way in which 'London' and 'Londres' were supposed to be different. (We could easily construct a parallel Phosphorus case with a little bit of science fiction in which Πετρος is transported from ancient Greece and does not realize that Phosphorus is Φωσφορος.) What this does mean is that, although the extreme Fregean does not seem to be right, for the description is a public one, yet there does seem to be a great deal of flexibility about what the description means.

I find this not unwelcome. In the first place, it is one of the principal contentions of this book that sentences of propositional attitudes are ambiguous and are ambiguous in a wide variety of ways. So the ambiguity caused here by the fact that a name can abbreviate a number of different descriptions is just what would be expected. Ambiguity also allows it to be the case that in many cases (perhaps even in most) it *is* legitimate to translate 'Londres' as 'London'. The only cases in which this cannot be done are sentences like the one about

Pierre. And these are just the cases in which we do not want it to be done.

In the second place, what may seem to be a number of different meanings may really be a single meaning that depends on the context (in the way in which the single meaning of 'I' picks out different people in different contexts). Thus, what appears to be an ambiguity would at least in some cases not really be so. Context-dependent descriptions would in any case seem to be necessary to take care of the case of Peter in Kripke (1979, 265) who has learned the name 'Paderewski' under two different circumstances, and of whom it seems to be true, both that he believes that Paderewski had musical talent and that he believes that Paderewski had no musical talent. The most plausible interpretation of this seems to me as a *de re* belief, but if it is *de expressione*, then it would seem that in one sentence 'Paderewski' has to mean something like 'person known to Peter under the name "Paderewski" in circumstances c_1' and in the other 'person known to Peter under the name "Paderewski" in circumstances c_2'. (I think that I would be supported here by Over (1983).)

Description theories have in fact been criticized (see for example Kripke (1972, 291f.) and (1979, 246f.)) on the ground that a description like 'the thing called "Phosphorus" ' may well not be unique. As Bach (1981, 372) notes, there are many people who bear the name 'George Smith'. The reply here is that it is a quite general feature of descriptions that the linguistic meaning of a description does not usually provide the means for singling out a unique thing that satisfies the description in question. My own preference is to adopt some such view as the one presented in Lewis (1979b, 348–350) whereby 'the cat' refers to the most salient cat in the context of utterance. Lewis gives a plausible and entertaining account of how salience can change in a conversation. It is of course a further question exactly how this is to be incorporated into semantics (Bigelow (1975) has some intriguing suggestions on this), but what is clear is that some way must be found, and must be found whatever is the correct solution to the semantics of names and the semantics of sentences of propositional attitudes.

Nute (1978) argues that Kripke's own theory of names provides the right description because it assumes the necessity of an appropriate relation between the speaker, the thing named, and the name in order to use the name in the first place. Nute claims that this relation therefore must be able to give a description adequate to be the meaning of the name. This relation seems to me very like what Devitt (1981, 29) calls a *d-chain*, and it is interesting to note that Devitt, one of the staunchest defenders of the causal theory of proper names, proposes, on pp. 236–243, that in opaque belief contexts a proper name refers to the appropriate d-chain.

In discussions of the description theory of names, one idea has been that 'Phosphorus' means something like 'the thing called "Phosphorus"'. This suggests that a name might be a description in an even stronger sense, for one might argue that it is actually made up from the predicate 'is called "Phosphorus"'. This would make the uniqueness problem even more clearly a case of the problem of how to get from the general predicate 'is a cat' to the unique referent of 'the cat' in a particular context. The idea that names are predicates has been defended by Burge (1973), relying on examples like 'There are relatively few Alfreds in Princeton' and 'All Alfreds are crazy' to show that names are frequently used predicatively. Burge's arguments have been disputed by Boër (1975) (though see Hornsby (1976) for a reply), and it is not my intention to take sides here, except to acknowledge that treating names as predicates would fit very nicely with the description theory of their status. Boër (1978a) suggests that names are ambiguous between a referential use and an attributive use. They are predicates in the attributive use.

The description theory of names might also help to solve a problem raised in Partee (1982, 99f.). The problem is highlighted in the sentence

(i)   Loar believes that semantics is a branch of psychology
      while Thomason believes it is a branch of mathematics.

This sentence could of course be interpreted as expressing a *de re* attitude. Assuming that a discipline is not a branch of both psychology and mathematics, then Thomason and Loar could not both be right. However, I take it that Partee has in mind that the dispute is not about the properties possessed by some agreed thing but is rather about what it is that is being referred to in the first place. There seems to me some plausibility here in using a description theory of names and analyzing the sentence in some such way as

(ii)   Loar believes that the thing called 'semantics' is a branch
       of psychology while Thomason believes it is a branch
       of mathematics.

Such an analysis is only a start, of course, and may not be quite right, at least not without further refinement. As I have said in the text, I do not wish to be specific here about just what descriptions the name corresponds with. The other problem about this sentence is the role of the pronoun 'it'. (Partee's example does not actually use the pronoun, but the problem it raises is worth mentioning.) Pronominalization is another topic I will not be concerned with. In this sentence the pronoun 'it' cannot stand simply for the thing that is semantics, though it might stand for the property of being called 'semantics', or rather for the meaning of the description 'the thing called "semantics"'.

The notion of a "rigidized" description is worth a fuller discussion. Rigidized descriptions are mentioned in Kripke (1977, 259f.). The way a rigidized description works may be seen by comparison with an ordinary description. In the ordinary case 'The F is G' is true in any world w iff the thing that is (uniquely) F in w is also G in w. In the rigid case we want it to be true in w iff the thing that is F in the actual world is G in w, whether or not it is F in w. However, what is actual depends on one's viewpoint. The actual world, from the viewpoint of a world w, is just w. So the semantics of a rigidized description must involve two worlds, for we must say that 'The F is G' is true in w_2 seen from w_1 iff the thing that is F in w_1 is G in w_2. This kind of semantics is sometimes called *double indexing*. I associate that phrase with David Lewis, but although he *almost* uses it in Lewis (1970, 185f.), he doesn't quite. It seems to have been first investigated by Frank Vlach in his UCLA Ph.D. dissertation, but the first published use is in Kamp (1971). It was later used in Åqvist (1973) and Segerberg (1973), who called it *two-dimensional modal logic*. Bäuerle (1983) argues that multiple indexing is required to deal with certain mixtures of quantifiers and intensional operators, and it is explicitly suggested by Stalnaker (1978, 320) as a formalization of Kripke's views on proper names and seems also to be accepted in Kaplan (1979) as a formalization of related views on demonstratives of the kind expressed less formally in Kaplan (1978).

Do we need rigidized descriptions? In the first place we note that in the presence of an intensional operator, such as a modal operator or a propositional attitude verb, the rigidizing can be effected by giving the operator wide scope (though see Bäuerle (1983) for some problems). By this I mean simply that 'Kaplan says that the F is G' can be read as 'Concerning the F, Kaplan says that it is G'. This has to mean that in the worlds in which what Kaplan says is so is so, the thing that is F in the actual world is G in that world. What the rigidizing can do is enable the sentence 'The F is G' to have this meaning even when standing alone. If one regards the principal value of truth conditions (over truth values) as providing the right input conditions for further embeddings, then this fact might be considered of less importance than it would appear at first. For the rigid meaning can always be obtained in such contexts.

The other thing rigidization can do is this. It seems (from the Hesperus and Phosphorus example) that in *modal* (as opposed, say, to belief) contexts a description is always interpreted rigidly. If "ordinary" descriptions are used, then one must have a restriction that insists that they have wide scope over modal operators. If rigid descriptions are used, then the semantics of modal operators can ensure that, wherever the description occurs, it is understood rigidly. (For 'necessary α' is true at $\langle w_1, w_2 \rangle$ iff α is true at $\langle w_1, w \rangle$ for every world w.) In the case of belief we can have a semantics that interprets the description nonrigidly, so that, for instance, 'Pierre believes that London is pretty' can be interpreted as true at w_2 from the point of view of w_1 iff 'London is pretty' is true at w from the point of view of w, where w is any of Pierre's belief worlds. (This makes use of what Stalnaker (1978, 318) calls the *diagonal* proposition.) If the description has wide scope, we can recapture the rigid interpretation. This means that the belief operator treats the description as if it were an ordinary one, whereas the modal operators take it as always rigid. If we are prepared to disallow a rigid interpretation of belief, then we could give up the view that a name is syntactically a description, for in that case scope differences would no longer be called for.

A variant of the multiple-indexing approach is provided by van Fraassen (1979), who uses the notion of "character" found in Kaplan (1979, 84). A character is a function from contexts to what Kaplan calls *contents* and is thus part of "pragmatics" in Montague's sense. Kripke's view of names requires (see van Fraassen (1979, 366)) that in any given context, the content of a proper name is just its bearer; but this does not entail that a name has the same bearer in all contexts. Thus, two names may, in a certain context, have the same content but lack the same character. If we then accept the view (suggested by Kaplan's remarks about Kripke on p. 85) that propositional attitudes attach not to content but to character, we can allow a propositional attitude sentence to change its truth value when a name in it is replaced by another name with the same content.

Another account claiming that the problem is better treated as a pragmatic one is found in Boër (forthcoming) (see also Lycan (1981)). By comparison with the work of these authors, who treat the kind of ambiguity argued for in the text as a pragmatic and not a semantic matter, it may seem a little simple-minded of me just to postulate a scope or a lexical ambiguity. It is, however, consonant with the wider claim of this book that that-clauses are ambiguous in a variety of ways. To be frank, I am not sure how one could decide whether the ambiguity is a semantic or a pragmatic one. Indeed, I am not even sure that this is a genuinely empirical question. (So in that sense it is not obvious to me that I am in clear disagreement with these authors.) I see the question at issue as being whether the ambiguity is systematic enough to be incorporated in the semantics and, in my opinion, it is. Indeed, as I said in the introduction, it seems to me as certain as anything can be in semantics that the meanings of propositional attitude sentences do depend on the meanings of their that-clauses.

In the text I allowed the possibility that, although names might sometimes be used as nominal descriptions, as Bach (1981) suggests, yet they might also be used purely denotatively: in other words, there is a lexical rather than a scope ambiguity. Some evidence for this comes from example sentences provided in Burge (1978). One is (p. 125)

> (iii)   I once believed that some female foxes are not vixens since I thought that a fox wasn't a vixen unless it had had sexual intercourse, but I never thought that some female foxes are not female foxes.

Burge accepts that 'vixen' and 'female fox' are synonymous and argues that therefore replacement of synonyms need not preserve truth in belief contexts. (Kripke (1979, 274, n. 12) gives a similar example involving alienists and psychiatrists.)

Now it seems clear that, in contrast to the case of 'Phosphorus', which might plausibly mean 'is called "Phosphorus"', it does not seem at all plausible to suppose that 'vixen' means 'is called a "vixen"'. Thus, if we do not like to follow Burge in supposing that compositionality fails in belief sentences (and my comments should have made clear that I would indeed not like to do so), then the word 'vixen' must be ambiguous. Or rather, there must be (perhaps nonstandard) contexts in which it does mean 'is called a "vixen"'. If such an ambiguity can occur here, then perhaps we have some reason for allowing it in the case of 'Phosphorus'. This would mean that Kripke's arguments against the description theory could be accepted for most uses of names.

With reference to example (25), it is admittedly much more natural to interpret it in a *de re* way. The *de expressione* sense would be more likely to be expressed by some such sentence as 'Prunella has just learned that the uninhabitable planet is Venus'. This need not be surprising, and it is in fact an instance of a quite general phenomenon concerning ambiguity in natural languages. Certain sentence forms are more sympathetic to a *de re* construal, and others are more sympathetic to a *de expressione* construal. But naturalness is not what is at issue here. The question is simply whether (25) can be used in the circumstances described. And it seems to me clear that it can.

Chapter 6: Why Meanings Are Not Internal Representations

My principal references for the whole tradition that sees the mental life as best modeled by analogy with syntactic or proof-theoretic operations on formulae (which is what I understand by the "computational view") are Fodor (1975), (1981), and (1982). Other references are found in Peters and Saarinen (1982) and the works cited by the contributors to that volume. An early example of the computational view at work in artificial intelligence occurs in Winograd (1972), where semantic processing takes the form of using syntactic rules to get from a natural language sentence to a formula that encodes a television-screen picture of a "world" in which blocks of various shapes and sizes are moved from one place to another.

The place in Fodor's writings where he comes closest to making the distinction I have expressed as that between object and content is in a note on p. 317 of (1981). There he discusses the criticism in Collins (1979) that causes are mental particulars, but anything that has a truth value must be a universal. (Collins puts it (p. 225f.) by contrasting the "temporality" required for mental events with the "propositionality" required of the bearers of truth and falsity.) In a way this point is an old one. It is surely the point of Frege's distinction between an idea and a thought (Frege (1918)). Fodor's reply is to grant Collins's distinction (or at least say that it is "arguably correct") and then to say simply that when we believe something, there is something in us (a representation) that has semantic properties. In fact, Fodor is quite adamant that representations have semantic properties (or contents, as he puts it in Fodor (1982, 100–102)). That is why I am not actually taking issue with Fodor. But the point is that some at least of what Fodor says trades on a confusion between what I have called *objects* and what I have called *contents*. For instance, his proof that attitudes like belief are relational (1981, 178–181) is *in fact* a proof that the meaning of 'believes' must relate a person to a *content*. His argument for this seems to me successful, but it goes no way toward showing that there exists what I have called an *object* of belief.

It is true that Fodor has other arguments to support the existence of internal objects for attitudes like belief, and much of what he says about them may be plausible. All that I want to insist is that, once a distinction between object and content is made, then the question arises of what content is, and no amount of description of what the objects of attitudes are will help with this question. In fact, the burden of my "autonomy" paper (Cresswell (1982)) was, in the object/ content terminology, that the nature of contents is independent of the nature of objects. Fodor might well grant this. Certainly the arguments on pp. 204–224 of Fodor (1981) are in many ways similar to the arguments of the present chapter. And certainly on p. 223 he seems to admit to not knowing just what a *semantic* theory of the content of attitudes would be like. I suspect that the theory defended in this book would not satisfy him, because I suspect that he wants a semantic theory to be also a theory of how an organism could be said to be using a language in which meanings were as a model-theoretic semantics says.

The question of relating a model-theoretic semantics to the use of language is taken up in Lewis (1975). Work such as Bennett (1976) in the Gricean tradition could also be said to be addressing the same question. (See Grice (1957), (1968), (1969) and Schiffer (1972).) The Gricean program of course wants to define meaning directly in terms of psychological states, whereas Lewis wants to attach an account of use to a truth-conditional semantics. Obviously, I support Lewis in principle, if not always in detail (see Cresswell (1978b, 21f.)). Field (1978, 12) sees a theory of belief as having two components: an account of the relation between a person and a representation, and an account of what it is for a representation to mean that p, where p is a proposition. He initially goes along with regarding a proposition as a set of possible worlds, though he notes (p. 14) that structured meanings of the kind advocated in Lewis (1972) might be needed. (On p. 20 he passes off this complication as introducing no new difficulties of principle for the issues that concern him.) At any rate, in Field's terms, what this book is about is solely his second task, that of providing an account of what expressions mean, in such a way as to satisfy the constraints imposed by sentences of propositional attitudes.

The object/content distinction seems to me to throw light on some recent controversies about the role of belief. (The fact that these controversies have all been about belief underscores my point about the confusion that has been engendered by a preoccupation with this one attitude.) For instance, in the case of *de re* beliefs, there is a reason why their contents ought not, or at least not without refinement, enter into a belief/desire explanation of action. For, as noted in chapter 2, one can have contradictory *de re* beliefs without being guilty of an inconsistency. Baker (1982) argues (to my mind cogently) that any belief/desire explanation that allows beliefs to have this feature is incoherent. But if what plays the causal role is the representation rather than its content, then, provided that the explanation is given at that level, belief/desire psychology can perhaps be reinstated.

Part of the objection to using contents in psychological explanation is that what the content of an attitude is may sometimes be determined by factors outside the subject. This conflicts with the research strategy Fodor (1981, chap. 9) (following Putnam (1975, 136)) calls *methodological solipsism*, to the effect that considerations external to the subject should not be involved in a psychological theory of the mental causes of that subject's behavior. Burge (1982) argues that even (the contents of) *de dicto* beliefs are determined by external considerations (Burge's arguments use the "Twin-Earth" example invented by Putnam (1975), which will be discussed in chapter 7), and Prior (1961, 30) is puzzled by a situation in which X, not realizing that he is in room 7, thinks, at six o'clock, that nothing thought by anyone in room 7 at six o'clock is actually the case. Prior is able to prove, in a very simple logic, that in this circumstance X cannot be thinking any such thing, and he wonders how it can be that factors external to X (that he is in room 7 and not, as he believes, in room 8) can determine what he can think. And Collins (1979, 420) argues that belief cannot be an internal state, on the ground that if I want to establish whether I believe that *p*, this is indistinguishable from the procedure I would use to establish that *p*, and different from the procedure I would use to establish whether or not I am in any particular internal state.

The idea that semantics comes on more than one level has had a number of recent defenders. One of the most explicit of these is McGinn (1982). It seems to me that all these views could be seen as involving the distinction between object and content. For they are all concerned to explain both truth conditions and the role that linguistic thinking plays in our mental life. My task is simply to explain how the truth conditions of propositional attitude sentences are determined from the contents of their that-clauses. Nothing in the hybrid or two-level conception of semantics has convinced me that the representations are themselves involved in the contents of propositional attitudes.

I suppose that the kind of "intention-based semantics" defended by Stephen Shiffer could be regarded as claiming that contents could only be defined using objects or could in some way be reduced to objects (see Shiffer (1982, 120)) and, as such, might perhaps be in conflict with my approach. However, intention-based semantics could more neutrally be seen as a theory about how psychology relates to semantics, via the intentions of language users, and as such it is not in conflict with anything I have to say. (This more neutral way seems to be the way McGinn (1982, 243f.) sees Gricean theories.)

On the view I am defending, there is no doubt that content would not determine object. This would mean that a belief/desire explanation could sometimes be underdetermined. Thus, if I say that Ralph shot Ortcutt because he believed that he was a spy, this would be construed, on a language-of-thought model of belief, as saying that Ralph has (in his language of thought) some representation α of Ortcutt and some representation β of the property of being a spy, and that 'α is β' is in Ralph's internal belief store and is causally responsible (at least in part, since Ralph's desires are important too) for his shooting Ortcutt. But the point is that the content (in my sense) of the belief is not sufficient to determine the object.

So far there is no incompatibility with a view like, say, that of McGinn (1982) (see p. 216, for example) in which belief combines two separate elements: the causal element and the truth-conditional element. McGinn does not directly address the question of the truth conditions of propositional attitude sentences, except to suggest (p. 233) that it is only psychological contexts that "are sensitive to the mental representations associated with the expressions in their scope"; so I *suppose* he is claiming that the truth conditions of at least some propositional attitude sentences depend on the representations associated with the complement sentence. As I have said in the text, there are good arguments for denying that particular representations are involved. This is because particular representations, being "in the head," are private and not accessible to the speaker. Putnam (1975, 138f.) claims that psychological states are public in the sense that different people could be in the same state. Unfortunately, no one has produced anything like a recursive specification of how the psychological state-type associated with a complex sentence is determined from the states associated with its simpler parts, though McGinn (1982, 243) suggests that Katz's work might be seen as such an enterprise. Certainly more than just the truth conditions of the complement sentence are involved in determining the truth conditions of the whole propositional attitude sentence, and in fact this whole book is an attempt to say what this more is. But I have seen no evidence to show that psychological state-types would need to be involved. Of course, those who like Katz (whose views were discussed in the commentary on chapter 3) or Harman (see (1982, 247)) deny that truth conditions are essential to meaning will not be interested in the problem of the semantic determination of the truth conditions of propositional attitude sentences. Harman (1975) even suggests that the language of thought just is the public language, though Fodor (1975, 56) criticizes this kind of view.

It is perhaps surprising that there seem to have been no attempts at a direct recursive specification of a synonymy relation, such as the ≈ referred to in the text, since it is an appealing approach for those who do not want to postulate language-independent meanings for linguistic expressions. One might of course deny that the relation ≈ involved is a genuinely semantic one. For instance, Boër (forthcoming) introduces a relation that holds when one locutionary act "captures the gist" of another. Boër says of this relation that, although it "surely has a semantical dimension," yet it "summons nonsemantical resources as well." Boër's account does not actually treat ≈ as relating sentence/language pairs with one another, but rather treats it as relating them with classes of locutionary acts. This brings it closer to Davidson's (1969) analysis of indirect discourse, in which an unanalyzed relation of "samesaying" between utterances is proposed. Davidson (pp. 161–167) actually discusses an account that would involve a synonymy relation between sentences, but discards it because of the relativity to languages that it involves. (He follows Quine (1960) in despairing of giving identity criteria for languages.) His idea seems to be that a token is not language relative. (Davidson is taken to task on this by Arnaud (1976) on the ground, among others, that a sentence like 'What Galileo said, namely, that the earth moves, is true' would require that truth be a property of utterances and that a Davidsonian truth theory for utterances involves the notion of a language just as much as a synonymy relation between sentences does.) Both Boër and Davidson seem to deny that a recursive specification of ≈ is needed, though Boër's views at least seem compatible with the provision of such a specification (mainly because, unlike Davidson, Boër does not object to the language relativity, and even suggests the use of the λ-categorial languages described in chapter 11 of this book). As I said in the Introduction, it is my conviction that the sentences of indirect discourse, like all sentences of propositional attitudes, do have meanings, and that the meanings are dependent on the meanings of their that-clauses. The evidence against this is, it seems to me, better construed as evidence that propositional attitude sentences are multiply and systematically ambiguous, and the semantic theory I am defending in this book is designed to account for this.

Chapter 7: Possible Worlds

There are many good introductions to set theory. One that uses the minimum of formalism compatible with the subject is Halmos (1960). The branch of logic (or mathematics) concerned with effective functions is usually known as *recursive function theory*. My favorite introduction is Hermes (1969), but that is only one among many. The idea that mental operations can be modeled by Turing machines (algorithms) is discussed in Fodor (1981, 13–16). Fodor cites Putnam (1960) as a classic paper.

Wittgenstein's remarks on continuing mathematical sequences are found in the *Philosophical Investigations* (Wittgenstein (1953); see especially §151 but also §§143–154 and §§185–190). Like virtually everything in that work, the precise purpose of Wittgenstein's remarks in these passages is difficult to grasp, and it would be rash of me to claim that he is making exactly the same point as I am.

I suggested in Cresswell (1973b) a way in which possible worlds could be manufactured from the models of a physical theory. And even Quine (1969, chap. 6) suggested a way in which possible worlds could be manufactured out of space-time points. Quine applied this analysis only to the attitudes of animals lacking a language in which to express them. This restriction could presumably be motivated using the terminology of the present chapter by saying that although animals have the capacity to learn by ostension, they do not have the capacity to learn by explicit definition. For such beings, the problem of logically equivalent but distinct attitudes perhaps cannot arise. In Cresswell (1973a) I suggested that possible worlds might be classes of what I called (p. 38) *basic particular situations,* and I mentioned Quine's occupancy of space-time points as one way of taking them. Lycan's discussion of combinatorialist views of possible worlds occurs in Lycan (1979). His discussion of my views of the matter is on p. 307f.

One cannot of course restrict the worlds solely to the ones allowed by one's favorite physical theory; in doing so, one could not allow for the possibility of testing that theory. My claim is that a physical theory of the world must also contain enough resources to define what it would be like for that theory to be false. If you like, there's a sort of bootstrapping going on here, because although the job of a theory of the world is to make sense of our experience, yet it seems that we can only describe that experience with the aid of that theory (perhaps that is the point of chapter 3 of Quine (1969)). The bootstrapping of course does not end with the postulation of the worlds. In my remark about verificationism I spoke of what an organism with no spatiotemporal limitations could in principle detect. That statement itself is certainly vague; worse maybe, it depends on what kinds of detection procedures are "in principle" allowed. Here too, though, all I will say is that the view of the world that we operate with does, in my opinion, give content to such notions.

As I understand Dretske (1983), he argues for the even stronger thesis that what something can be said to know is determined by what that thing can in principle discriminate between. This thesis is obviously compatible with what I argue here. Dretske (pp. 7–9) uses the example of dolphins who can identify cylinders. He then supposes that perhaps the only cylinders the dolphin has been shown are plastic, or perhaps even that all and only things made of plastic are cylinders. This would not show that the dolphin has acquired the concept of plastic because we know that the dolphin has no mechanism that enables it to detect plasticity. On p. 17, interestingly enough, Dretske claims that what he has to say applies only to simple concepts, and not to complex ones. (In fact, on p. 216 of Dretske (1981) he seems to adopt a view of complex concepts that would fit in with the one I am advocating in these chapters.)

In saying that I am taking a stand in favor of physicalism, I mean of course what Fodor (1975, 12) calls *token physicalism*. I see no reason to believe that the principles of semantics can be reduced in any plausible sense to those of physics, or even of psychology (see Cresswell (1982, 71f.)).

In a sense I suppose I am in this chapter, and indeed in this whole book, taking sides in favor of a realist conception of truth, even if it is relativized to possible worlds. Michael Dummett has in many publications (e.g., Dummett (1976)) argued against such a conception of truth and therefore against an analysis of meaning in terms of truth conditions. I shall not argue directly against antirealist views like Dummett's. The aim of my book is simply to show that the semantics of propositional attitudes can be accommodated within a possible-worlds semantics. Of course, as Field (1978, 40) notes, using possible worlds does commit one to a general notion of synonymy. And if we are impressed, as Field is, with the arguments in Quine (1960) against such a notion, then that will be an argument against their use. I am not myself persuaded by Quine's arguments, and it seems to me that there is such a notion. At the same time, of course, there are limits to how far we can *exactly* translate a sentence of one language into a sentence of a language having a very different structure. It is this fact that necessitates the use of that-clauses whose meaning is not always sensitive to the full structure of the complement sentence. In sentences reporting the attitudes of speakers of these very different languages, we may be forced to use relatively insensitive that-clauses.

Possible-worlds semantics allows an immediate account to be given of such notions as entailment, contradictoriness, and the like~ without the necessity for such things as "meaning postulates." Entailment is simply class inclusion in the set of worlds; a contradictory sentence is true in no worlds; and so on. These notions are therefore automatically defined in any semantics that assigns sets of worlds to be the meanings of sentences. This is how possible-worlds semantics delivers the judgments regarded by Katz (1972) as constituting semantic knowledge. For more on this, see Cresswell (1978b) and (1978c).

Chapter 8: A System of Intensions

The notion of semantic category presented in this chapter is very like that set out in Cresswell (1973a, 93–100), with the terminological difference that I now prefer to use $(\tau/\sigma_1,...,\sigma_n)$ in place of $\langle \tau,\sigma_1,...,\sigma_n \rangle$ for the category of functions from $D_{\sigma_1} \times ... \times D_{\sigma_n}$ into D_τ. In saying that everything is a thing, I am being unabashedly Platonistic. It seems to me that, in dealing with the semantics of natural language, this is right. For I think that we *do* speak as if all these things existed, and I follow Emmon Bach (1983) in assuming that the illuminating way to study natural language is to ask what sorts of entities it presupposes. The ontological questions can then be tackled separately. This attitude seems the opposite of one advocated by Bigelow (1981, 403), who suggests that semantics should be as economical as possible. Many philosophers seem to believe that the fewer entities one's ontology admits, the better. This is like saying that Platonism is guilty until proved innocent. I prefer to regard Platonism as innocent until proved guilty, but, with one important qualification, I do want to know how the entities I assume behave, and what structure they have. And therefore I insist that they can be manufactured using the principles of set theory. These principles seem to allow as many entities (or, if you prefer, surrogates for them) as anyone could want.

Does this Platonistic attitude mean that I must believe in fairies, Santa Claus, unicorns, or the perfect Vice-Chancellor? In a sense, yes. The semantical framework I am defending does admit all these things. It is just that they are not actual. They exist in other possible worlds. A belief in fairies is wrong because it mislocates them; just as a belief that Hobbes still exists is wrong because it places him in the wrong century. I will even, if you like, give away the word 'exists' and say that not all of the things I am willing to postulate exist. This does not mean that I want to defend a Meinongian line, of the kind that has recently been defended by such writers as Routley (1980), Parsons (1980), and Zalta (1983). My notion of a fairy, for instance, is of something that exists, but in another possible world. (And also unicorns, even if, as Kripke (1972) suggests, it is part of their *essence* that they do not exist in this world.)

The word 'intension' in English philosophical language (not to be confused with 'intention') is attributed on p. 318 of Kneale and Kneale (1962) to Sir William Hamilton, in the middle of the nineteenth century, as a replacement for the term 'comprehension' used in the Port Royal logic of 1662 to contrast with 'extension'. More recently it was used in Carnap (1947) in more or less the way indicated in the text. Reference is sometimes alternatively called 'denotation', and Montague's use of 'sense' and 'denotation' is explained on p. 228 of Montague (1974). Meaning for Montague is a function from contexts to senses—it is rather like Kaplan's distinction between character and content. Senses in that terminology are what I am calling intensions, and references are extensions.

In my commentary on chapter 5 I have already discussed Kripke's views on names. The Twin-Earth example is introduced on p. 141 of Putnam (1975). Part of the point of Putnam's discussion is connected with the issue of methodological solipsism. For it is argued that if A and B are both in the same psychological state, then they must have the same beliefs (this principle appears to be endorsed on p. 104 of Fodor (1982)), but that if A is an Earth dweller and B a Twin-Earth dweller, then they do not have the same beliefs. Although the issue of methodological solipsism is not my concern, there is nevertheless a question that is of concern here, analogous to the question discussed in chapter 5 about Hesperus and Phosphorus. That water is H_2O appears to be something that Earth people have learned— something that Twin-Earth people could not have learned. This means that the sentence 'Oscar has just learned that water is H_2O' has to be given a semantics that makes its truth conditions different from those of 'Oscar has just learned that water is water'.

I suggest two approaches to the meaning of 'water'. On the first of these, unless one takes a hard line and says that learning that water is H_2O just is learning that water is water, then one will have to posit a lexical ambiguity in the word 'water'. The hard line is not quite so implausible as it might seem if one interprets the sentence in a *de re* manner. For then one would be claiming that there is a description F that picks out water, and Oscar has just learned that whatever is F is H_2O. Here F might be 'the stuff that Oscar is looking at' or some such way of picking out water. One would then argue that, although it would still be strictly *true* that what Oscar had learned was that water is water, it would be misleading to report it that way because it makes it look as though Oscar had discovered only a tautology. The double-indexing approach would say that the *character* of the word 'water' is something that has a different content in the Twin-Earth context from its content in the Earth context. Putnam (1975, 187f.) refers to work "in the tradition of California semantics" as possibly being able to give a solution to the problem, and he mentions David Lewis, though without citing any particular source (presumably he has Lewis (1972) in mind).

Actually, the "character-and-content" solution is really not so far from the possibility suggested in the text of treating 'water' as meaning something that plays a certain role. This is analogous to the description theory of names discussed above, except that it does not seem plausible to say that 'water' means 'that which is called "water"'. Natural-kind terms, unlike proper names, are easily and regularly translatable by completely different and unrelated words in other languages.

Putnam of course no more likes the description theory of natural-kind terms than Kripke likes the description theory of proper names (see Putnam (1975, 148)), and indeed, as just stated, it has its difficulties. One difficulty concerns the sentence 'There is water on Twin-Earth'. Assuming that there is no H_2O on Twin-Earth, then this sentence, *uttered on Earth*, ought to be false. But since there is something on Twin-Earth, *viz* XYZ, that plays the role of water, then the description theory would seem to make the sentence true. The trick here is suggested by Fodor (1982, 111–113). It is that a word like 'water' is in a sense contextually restricted. In using the word 'water' on Earth, we mean something like 'that which plays the water role on Earth'; more generally, 'water' means something like 'that which plays the water role around here'. Fodor's idea is that these restrictions, although relevant to the truth conditions, are not part of the belief, so that Oscar here and his Twin-Earth counterpart can believe the same thing when they utter sentences involving the word 'water'. This allows belief to be classified as a psychological attitude within the constraints of methodological solipsism.

The idea of solving the problem of propositional attitudes by taking propositions as primitive is put forward in Thomason (1980b). Thomason's paper is important in that it indicates what adaptations would be needed for a Montague Grammar based on a semantics of propositions. He seems to feel that reference to truth, if deemed necessary, could be incorporated by simply adding a truth value to each proposition. If this is done for each possible world, then the result is formally equivalent to the function I, which associates a set of worlds with each proposition. With propositions taken as basic, one can define properties as functions from individuals to propositions, though some authors, such as Rescher (1975), prefer to take properties as basic. Rescher's book is worth noting because Rescher is quite explicit about what is going on. Field (1978, 39) banishes propositions but admits properties. Bradley and Swartz (1979) have both propositions and worlds.

A defense of an ontology based on properties, relations, and propositions, even to the exclusion of set theory, is found in Bealer (1982). Among the properties are some, which Bealer calls *conditions,* that are identical if necessarily equivalent. The imposition of this is effected by a family $\mathscr{H}$ of functions H that specify possible extensions of the properties, one of which, $\mathscr{G}$, represents their actual extensions. By this means Bealer is able to define both truth and necessity. (It is worth pointing out that, although Bealer does not mention Kripke's (1959) paper on the completeness of S5, in that paper what later became possible worlds were just assignments of extensions. In fact, even the $\mathscr{H}$, $\mathscr{G}$, H terminology is the same in Bealer and in Kripke.) Bealer claims not to be using possible worlds, but he certainly has world surrogates.

Bealer does not have a discussion of the formal semantics of propositional attitudes, but he does have an intriguing chapter (chap. 3, pp. 69–77) on the paradox of analysis, which indicates that his solution would be one very similar to the structured-meaning solution defended in this book. On p. 74 he recognizes what I have been calling the ambiguity between sense and reference, though he does not use those terms. Bealer's device for marking the ambiguity is to underline an expression when the reference is involved and omit the underlining when the sense is involved. Because he does not use set theory, his senses are not defined quite in the way mine are—his formal account is given on pp. 190–195.

An author who manufactures possible worlds out of states of affairs, together with an undefined notion of logical possibility, is Plantinga (1974). Plantinga, though, is more concerned with modality than with propositional attitudes.

With the notable exception of David Lewis (see (1973, 84)), many philosophers seem to get a little defensive when introducing possible worlds. My own ploy in chapter 7 was to argue that everyone believes in something that does the work of possible worlds, so that we perhaps need not worry overmuch about just what they are. In Cresswell (1973a, 38) I constructed worlds out of "basic particular situations." This construction was atomistic in the sense that it was assumed that whether or not one situation obtains is logically independent of whether or not any other one does. In that work I also tried to solve the problem of propositional attitudes by a complex construction of things I called *heavens* (p. 42). I now believe that the criticisms of inconsistent worlds made in the text also apply to heavens. This is a view I came to by reflecting on the fact that heavens play no role at all in the semantic analysis of English undertaken in parts III and IV of Cresswell (1973a).

In mentioning the idea that worlds can be thought of as maximal consistent sets of propositions, I had in mind theories such as Plantinga's in which propositions are not linguistic entities. To some, however, an attractive way of getting a grip on a possible world has seemed to be via language. For instance, Hintikka (1969, 154) uses the idea of a "complete novel" or maximal consistent set of sentences of some given language (i.e., a set that cannot be enlarged without making it inconsistent). He writes, "A possible world is, in effect, what such a complete novel describes." No modal logician, of course, would want to take issue with Hintikka's use of maximal consistent sets. However, we must step rather more warily if we want actually to define a world by means of such a set. The problem arises because consistency is a notion that is relative to a logic, and if the logic is classical, then all classically equivalent sentences will be true in just the same worlds.

It is sometimes suggested that a solution to the problem of propositional attitudes can be found by using a nonclassical logic, say, one of the "relevance" logics in which "entailment" is so defined as not to coincide with strict implication (see for example Anderson and Belnap (1975)) or a logic based on urn models (see Rantala (1975) and Hintikka (1975b)). But it is not hard to see that *whatever* logic is chosen, it will be possible to make a logical mistake. This was the point made in chapter 1 about all compositional systems. All that nonclassical logics do is study the behavior of symbols that have a nonstandard meaning, and in fact it can be shown (see Routley (1980, 312–325)) that, in a certain sense, all logics have a possible-worlds semantics.

Plantinga, as mentioned above, manufactures worlds out of states of affairs. In Cresswell (1973a) I made them up out of situations, though my situations were very tiny, and mutually independent, states of affairs. Taking situations seriously in semantics is at the heart of what is in fact called *situation semantics* by Jon Barwise and John Perry. Barwise and Perry have been developing their views in a series of articles (Barwise and Perry (1980), (1981a), (1981b), and Barwise (1981)), and they have most recently completed a book (Barwise and Perry (1983)) that I shall take to be the "received" doctrine on situation semantics, though I shall also refer to the earlier articles.

The present book is not the place for a detailed critique of situation semantics, though one would be worthwhile because Barwise and

Perry certainly envisage using it to provide a semantic theory for natural language rivaling theories such as the kind, based on possible worlds, defended in this book (see Barwise and Perry (1983, chap. 2 and p. 4)). However, since Barwise and Perry explicitly deny the principle that logically equivalent sentences are intersubstitutable in attitude contexts ((1983, 175) and (1981b, 676f.)), it is desirable to make at least a brief enquiry into how situation semantics would claim to deal with the problem.

What I shall do is consider two sentences that are logically equivalent in situation semantics, and see whether the semantics that Barwise and Perry offer for attitude verbs enables substitutivity to fail. The sort of case I have in mind as a test case is provided by sentences (3) and (4) in the text (renumbered here (i) and (ii)),

(i)   Desmond says that α

and

(ii)   Desmond says that not-not-α,

where it is to be supposed that one of them (say, (i)) is true but the other (say, (ii)) is false.

In order to discuss this kind of case, I shall have to give a brief description of Barwise and Perry's semantics. On their (1983) account, the meaning of a sentence is a relation between situations. What a situation is need not be relevant here; in essence, it is a collection of individuals having certain properties and standing in certain relations. Where ϕ is a sentence, and u and e are situations, then u $[[\phi]]$ e means that the sentence ϕ, as uttered in situation u, is true in situation e. The situation u is what, in such theories as those of Montague (1974), Lewis (1972), von Stechow (1981a), and others, is called a *context-of-use*. The relation $[[\phi]]$ will not, of course, be defined for all pairs of situations. Typically, u will be a situation that supplies things like a time, a speaker, and so forth, and also the referents for proper names, pronouns, and the like. The two aspects of u are often separated and referred to as d and c. I will continue to use u, since nothing I say turns on its precise nature. The second term, e, will be the kind of situation that Barwise and Perry call a *course of events* (p. 56).

I want now to look at sentence (ii) in situation semantics. In this sentence the word 'not' appears, functioning here as a sentential negation. As it happens, Barwise and Perry (p. 138) find sentence negation a puzzling phenomenon, and they do not give a semantics for such a 'not'. The reason they find it puzzling involves the partial nature of situations. Suppose that e is a situation in which I am sitting at my desk. As Barwise and Perry think of situations, this situation may well be one in which the color of my wallpaper is not specified. (It seems to me that this shows that Barwise and Perry are not, despite their homely talking (e.g., (1981a, 388)), using 'situation' in its ordinary sense—if I am in an actual situation at my desk, then my wallpaper *does* have some determinate color.) So the sentence 'My wallpaper is blue' will not be true. But this ought not mean that it is true that my wallpaper is *not* blue. Rather, nothing is said about the color of my wallpaper. For Barwise and Perry, a situation specifies of some relations that they do hold between various things and of some that they do not, leaving others undetermined. This means that there could be sentences without a determinate truth value in certain situations.

My own preference here would be simply to say that in such a case $\langle u, e \rangle$ is not in the domain of $[[\phi]]$. It is not clear to me that Barwise and Perry do take this line, but if it is taken, then one can give a very simple semantics for 'not'. So I shall simply stipulate that NOT is to be a sentential connective with the following semantics:

(iii) $u[[\text{NOT-}\phi]]e$ iff not $u[[\phi]]e$

I shall further stipulate that $[[\text{NOT-}\phi]]$ has exactly the same domain as $[[\phi]]$. This means that

(iv) $u[[\text{NOT-NOT-}\phi]]e$ iff $u[[\phi]]e$,

in other words, that ϕ and NOT-NOT-ϕ are logically equivalent in situation semantics.

In order to examine (i) and (ii), a meaning for 'say' is needed. Such a semantics is provided in Barwise and Perry (1981b, 684) but criticized in (1983, 278–280). I shall try to show that everything they say about attitude verbs leads to the conclusion that, with the semantics for 'not' just given, (i) and (ii) could not differ in truth value in situation semantics.

The attitude verb that Barwise and Perry discuss in (1983) is SEES THAT, and they claim (p. 176) that a theory adequate for this verb can be easily extended to KNOW, BELIEVE, ASSERT, and DOUBT. The analysis of SEES THAT (p. 211) involves a relation SO, between a situation, a person, and a course of events. For Barwise and Perry a relation may, in any given situation, be true of certain things, false of them, or undetermined. Where u (or d, c) is a situation, a is a person, and e and e' are courses of events, then $u[[\text{SEES THAT } \phi]]a,e$ holds just in case either it is false that, in situation e, u is related to a and e' by SO, or $u[[\phi]]e'$. (This is very like Hintikka (1969, 155), whose semantics for perception makes it true, in a world w, that a perceives that p iff, where w' is any world compatible with what a perceives, then p is true in w'.)

The only feature of this semantics that need concern us at present is that any sentence ψ that has the feature that $u[[\psi]]e$ iff $u[[\phi]]e$ for every u and e will give exactly the same result for [[SEES THAT ϕ]] as for [[SEES THAT ψ]]. In other words, this semantics does not distinguish between sentences that are logically equivalent in situation semantics. In particular, it will not distinguish between ϕ and NOT-NOT-ϕ when NOT has the meaning given to it above. Barwise and Perry produce a more complicated semantics for BELIEVES THAT on p. 256, but it still has the consequence that situationally equivalent sentences are intersubstitutable. So does the semantics they produce for 'says that' on p. 684 of (1981b), and nothing they say in their discussion of its inadequacies on pp. 278–280 of (1983) suggests a repair for this. Of course, it would be possible to amend the semantics to take account of the structure of the embedded sentence. If this were done, then the problem of propositional attitudes could be solved in the same way as in the present book. But there is nothing peculiar to situations, as opposed to worlds, about this, and a solution of that kind could not be claimed as a victory for situation semantics.

In showing that situation semantics does not allow a difference in truth value between (i) and (ii), I chose a semantics for NOT that made [[ϕ]] and [[NOT-NOT-ϕ]] be the same relation. As I mentioned, Barwise and Perry do not give a semantics for sentential negation, and so I have not, strictly, produced a counterexample to anything they say. Two comments on this are in order. First, even if Barwise and Perry do not have a NOT whose meaning is defined as I stipulated, there is nothing in situation semantics to prevent such a symbol, and therefore nothing in situation semantics to prevent the problem of logical equivalence from arising. Second, even if (i) and (ii) as they stand do not provide a counterexample, yet we can find other cases that do. For this purpose we can use examples analogous to those to be discussed in chapter 9. Suppose we are trying to give a logic class practice in using the commutative and associative laws for conjunction, using the examples

(v)   Miriam is given that $((\alpha \wedge \beta) \wedge \gamma)$

and

(vi)   Miriam concludes that $((\gamma \wedge \beta) \wedge \alpha)$.

We can suppose α, β, and γ to be whatever example sentences we choose. In this case the sentence (v′) Miriam is given that $((\gamma \wedge \beta) \wedge \alpha)$

is false. This is what she concludes as a result of applying certain laws of logic. Yet it is not difficult to see that the semantics for $\wedge$ that Barwise and Perry offer on p. 303 (or p. 316) of (1983) produces

(vii) $u[[(\alpha \wedge \beta) \wedge \gamma]]e$ iff $u[[(\gamma \wedge \beta) \wedge \alpha]]e$.

Not difficult, but not trivial either. I am still not sure, for instance, whether the distributive laws, which combine conjunction and disjunction, are valid in Barwise and Perry's logic.

Actually, though, it is not necessary to have an α and a β that are completely situationally equivalent. The reason for this can be seen from the rule for $u[[\text{SEES THAT } \phi]]a,e$. To evaluate this, we look at $u[[\phi]]e'$, where e' is related to u, a, and e in certain ways. But we do not change u. Thus, if we take ϕ and ψ to be sentences, all of whose context-dependent features have been supplied by u, we require that $u[[\phi]]e$ and $u[[\psi]]e$ coincide on every e, but only with respect to that fixed u. In particular, this will mean that laws like the distributive laws will preserve equivalence. Also, in certain cases, even negation will be available, and, provided our choice of sentences is appropriately restricted, we will get the whole classical propositional calculus.

In this discussion I have considered it vital to use equivalences licensed by situation semantics itself. Obviously, it is no use using equivalences licensed by some other logic—say, classical logic—if the symbols in them are being interpreted differently. This would be like an intuitionist saying that 'it is true that' does not preserve logical equivalence, on the ground that, by his semantics, it does not preserve the classical equivalence of p and $\sim\sim p$. The point is that an intuitionist's $\sim$ is not classical $\sim$.

Why then do Barwise and Perry claim, as they do claim both on p. 175f. of (1983) and on p. 676f. of (1981b), that situation semantics does not allow substitution of logically equivalent sentences? I believe the answer can be seen from the examples they use to support their claim. Consider the following sentences ((9) and (10) from (1981b, 676)):

(viii) Fred sees Betty enter.

(ix) Fred sees Betty enter and (Sally smoke or not smoke).

(A similar example is given on p. 175 of (1983).) Barwise and Perry rightly point out that one cannot move from (viii) to (ix); in other words, (viii) can be true but (ix) false. They then take this to be an instance of substitution of logically equivalent sentences. However, the complements of (viii) and (ix) are not sentences at all but are what are called *naked infinitives.* Barwise and Perry know this, of course, and Barwise (1981) is devoted to examining the role of naked infinitives in perception sentences. Further, as Barwise and Perry take pains to stress, naked infinitive complements behave in very different ways from that-clauses. One difference in particular is relevant to (viii) and (ix): in the cases of naked infinitival complements of a verb of perception (e.g., 'sees') we can move from '*a* sees ϕ or ψ' to '*a* sees ϕ or *a* sees ψ' (1983, 182). I am not myself absolutely sure that this rule is valid, but, if it is, there seems to me a very simple explanation: it is that '*a* sees ϕ or ψ' is simply a reduced form of '*a* sees ϕ or *a* sees ψ'. If this is so, then (ix) is simply

(ix')   Fred sees Betty enter and Fred sees Sally smoke or Fred sees Sally not smoke.

There is a problem in (ix') about

(x)   Fred sees Sally not smoke.

I find it a difficult sentence to interpret at all, but in any case Barwise is right (1981, 378) to point out that $\sim$(*a* sees ϕ) does not entail (*a* sees $\sim\phi$). Now if (ix) really has the form (ix'), then there is no constituent logically equivalent to 'Betty enter' to be substituted for it.

Is (ix') really the form of (ix)? To prove that it is not, one would have to find an operator (say, a quantifier) that is inside the scope of 'sees' but outside the scope of 'or' or 'and'. However, as Barwise also shows, quantifiers seem to take wide scope with respect to naked infinitival complements. In fact, the very semantics Barwise and Perry provide for naked infinitives suggests why (ix') ought to be the correct form of (ix). On Barwise and Perry's semantics (see (1981b, 670) or (1983, 183–187)) a naked infinitive has as its semantic value, not a proposition, as a tensed sentence does, but rather a situation type. In more traditional theories a naked infinitive refers to an event. In either case we have a plausible explanation for (ix') as the form of (ix). Consider the analysis in terms of events. One can say simply that there are no such things as disjunctive events. There is the event of Betty entering and there is the event of Betty leaving. Fred may have seen either one of these, but there is no event of Betty-either-entering-or-leaving that he could have seen. This being so, then (ix') is the only way in which (ix) can be understood. (This also explains why 'Fred sees Sally not smoke' is so odd. There just is no such thing as an event of not smoking. We can only interpret this sentence by thinking of some event that is in some way contrary to smoking, which involved Sally and which Fred saw.)

The suggestion that events play a crucial role in the analysis of at least action sentences was made as long ago as Davidson (1967b), and it has more recently been argued (Higginbotham (1983), Vlach (1983)) that events give a more adequate account of naked infinitives than Barwise and Perry's "situations." One thing does seem to be clear. Events, if needed at all, are needed because certain phrases do *not* behave like sentences or other inflected clauses. To be sure, the question then arises whether events should be taken as unanalyzed particulars or should, as I would prefer to do, be themselves analyzed in terms of, say, possible worlds, times, individuals, and the like, but there is no reason to suppose that admitting the need for events in the analysis of *these* sentences has any relevance to the problem of explaining a difference in truth value between the earlier sentences (i) and (ii).

As far as propositional attitudes are concerned, my discussion of situation semantics could stop. However, I would like to make one or two comments on the ontology. Barwise and Perry try to give their ontology a very homely air. Situations are all around us, they say. That may be, but the point is whether situations, as they appear in Barwise and Perry's theory, are the best way of accounting for the commonsense world we live in. I want to show that there is one respect, in my opinion a vital one, in which possible-worlds semantics is explanatory in a way in which situation semantics is not. Barwise and Perry note (1981b, 679) that you cannot kiss someone without touching them. They rightly point out that this has nothing to do with facts about the English meaning of 'kiss' and 'touch': take any word you like for kissing, and any word you like for touching, you still cannot kiss without touching. In other words, the constraint has nothing to do with "meaning postulates" or other linguistic facts. Barwise and Perry impose the constraint by brute force. On p. 97 of (1983) they describe it as a *necessary constraint*. Necessary constraints are just one kind of constraint to be imposed on the structure of solutions. Possible-worlds semantics gives an explanation of why the constraint obtains. In possible-worlds semantics, the property of kissing will be a function from pairs of individuals to sets of worlds (or rather to sets of world-time pairs). The same will be true of the property of touching. But for any pair of individuals $\langle a,b \rangle$, the set of worlds in which a kisses b (at time t) will be a subset of the set of worlds in which a touches b (at time t). The constraint is automatically predicted from the nature of the functions that are the meanings of 'kiss' and 'touch'. It does not need to be imposed either by meaning postulates or by brute force.

In (1983) Barwise and Perry refer to possible-worlds semantics as a rival to situation semantics (p. 4), but they do not discuss it in any detail. The only extended discussion is on pp. 51–55 of (1980), in which their principal complaint is that it does not make use of partial functions. It is true that Montague Grammar can be more complicated than it need be because it uses only total functions, but that is certainly not essential to possible-worlds semantics; and, in fact, both the present book and Cresswell (1973a) make extensive use of partial functions.

In confining my remarks to issues relevant to the present book, I do not want to give the impression that there is nothing of value in Barwise and Perry's work. Much of what they say can and should be (and indeed frequently is) incorporated into any adequate semantic theory, whether based on situations or, as here, on possible worlds.

Chapter 9: Structured Meanings Again

Examples like those given in this chapter seem to me to show that no logical equivalence can be taken for granted. That is one of the reasons why the use of a nonstandard logic (intuitionistic, relevance, urn logic) will not help here. My example involves a law of classical logic. Those who do not like classical logic are welcome to use an example involving an equivalence from a logic they do like. Some authors want to adopt principles that assume that at least some equivalences cannot logically be doubted. Thus, Hill (1976, 214) suggests that 'Mary laughed and Sherry laughed' is always interchangeable in belief contexts with 'Sherry laughed and Mary laughed'. Possibly this may be so in belief contexts, but it is doubtful to me that they are interchangeable in the kind of contexts considered in this chapter. I have, however, argued that that-clauses are ambiguous in being sensitive to various levels of structure. Possibly there is a 'that' which is sensitive to the fact that 'Mary laughed and Sherry laughed' is a conjunction of 'Mary laughed' and 'Sherry laughed', though it is not sensitive to the order of the conjuncts.

Enç (1982) contains descriptions of devices that respond to complexes of properties. One could imagine a device (similar to the ones Enç discusses) of which it might be true to say that it registers that the disk is blue, but it might not be true to say that it *directly* registers that the disk is blue, but only that it directly registers that the disk is either blue and larger than 10cm in diameter or blue and not larger than 10cm in diameter. This would be so if the way the device tested for blueness, and the way it indicated the result of the test, was different depending on the size of the disk.

Lexical decomposition, in the guise of semantic feature theory, plays a prominent part in the semantic theory advocated by Jerrold Katz (1972). It was also much used by the generative semanticists (McCawley (1968 and (1971) and Lakoff (1971)) and by David Dowty (1979), though, to be fair, these authors argued that it was required to deal with phenomena involved with things like the scope of quantifiers. Fodor (1975, 124–156) argues strongly against decomposition. Fodor also observes that adequate definitions are very hard to come by in natural language ((1975, 148–154), (1981, 213)). If I am right, this is because we learn most words ostensively, and only in technical language as a rule do we learn them by definition. Emmon Bach has mentioned to me words like 'beekeeper' and 'unfalsifiable' as nontechnical, definitionally introduced words. I think I would prefer to treat these words not as simple, but as words with a compositionally determined meaning, though I suspect that there is little or no real content to the question whether they are treated in this way or definitionally.

I have been told that the proof of the equivalence of 'finite' and 'inductive' requires the axiom of choice and therefore that these words are not logically equivalent. My own view is that all the truths of set theory, including the axiom of choice, are true in all possible worlds and therefore are logically necessary in the only sense of that word that I admit. Perhaps some feel that the axiom of choice, being independent of the other axioms of set theory, is something that one can take or leave as one pleases. To feel this way is, I think, misguided. Consider an independence proof in an axiomatic formulation of the propositional calculus—say, the independence of $(p \lor q) \supset (q \lor p)$. Such a proof shows that one can give a semantical definition of an operator that satisfies all the *other* axioms involving disjunction, but that is not commutative. But this does nothing to show that *disjunction* is not commutative, and nothing to show that $(p \lor q) \supset (q \lor p)$ is not a logical truth about classical disjunction.

Chapter 10: Iterated Attitudes

The problem about iterated belief operators seems to have been first noticed in Cresswell (1975), though some of the points made there are repeated in Cresswell (1982). A hierarchy of **believe** operators might not be as objectionable as it first appears. In Cresswell (1973a, 103) I defended the hierarchy of truth predicates required for a levels-of-language solution to the semantic paradoxes. Presumably any approach to the semantic paradoxes that dispenses with a hierarchy of truth predicates (as for instance the one in Kripke (1975)) would have a parallel in a theory that allowed iterated attitudes. In Bigelow (1978) the meaning of the attitude verb in iterated contexts operates on a sort of surrogate of itself. Bigelow's theory is in many ways similar to the one defended in this book except that he does not use the ambiguity of that-clauses. Aldo Bressan and his colleagues have also worked on the problem of iterated attitudes; see Bonotto and Bressan (1983). Turner (1983) applies to Montague Grammar work done in Scott (1972) and (1975) on models of the λ-calculus in which functions do appear to apply to themselves. Levin (1982, 128) also makes this suggestion, and possibly it will prove to be an illuminating way of dealing with the problem.

Chapter 11: λ-Categorial Languages

The syntax and semantics of categorial languages is set out in a manner very close to that of the present chapter in chapters 5 and 6 of my *Logics and Languages* (Cresswell (1973a)). In Cresswell (1977) I tried to suggest some connections between categorial languages and phrase structure grammars, and between λ-categorial languages and transformational grammars. Ruttenberg (1976) shows that any sequence of symbols from the lexicon of a λ-categorial language that can be generated as a well-formed expression can also be generated in any order whatsoever with exactly the same value. Obviously, this means that if, as I suggested in Cresswell (1973a), a λ-categorial language is actually thought of as the deep structure of a natural language, there will be required all sorts of what I called *acceptability principles* (p. 224) to make sure that only acceptable surface sentences are generated. One of the suggestions of Lewis (1972) is that a categorial base language is transformationally related to the surface structures. Chapters 7 and 8 of Montague (1974) show how Montague conceived the relation between surface syntax and intensional logic.

Parts III and IV of Cresswell (1973a) were devoted to presenting the underlying structure of English as a λ-categorial language. Other authors who have worked with λ-categorial languages include Boër (1978a) and (1978b), Bigelow (1978), Edmonson (1978), and Boër and Edelstein (1979). In Cresswell (1973a) I thought of a proposition as simply a set of worlds, and I dealt with tense in a rather more complicated way. I became convinced of the utility of using intervals to deal with tense by Taylor's (1977) analysis of the progressive— though I prefer the analysis in Dowty (1977). I have since used time intervals in a number of studies of adverbial modification, perhaps the most interesting of which is the study of prepositions in Cresswell (1978a).

Humberstone (1981) suggests using what he calls *possibilities* as an analogue, in the case of worlds, to what intervals are in the case of moments. My reason for liking time intervals is that sometimes a sentence can be true at an interval without being true at any subinterval. If I build a house in 1983, there might be an interval *t* such that 'build a house' is true of me at that interval, without its being true at any subinterval (see Taylor (1977) and Dowty (1977)). So one would need evidence that a sentence could be true at a possibility, without being true at the worlds "in" that possibility. Humberstone does not have a notion of worlds "in" a possibility, but he does (p. 318) speak of one possibility as being a "refinement" of another, and one could presumably think of a world as a maximal refinement. Humberstone does not bring evidence that a sentence could be true at a possibility without being true at all its refinements. In fact, he adopts a principle that this is never so (p. 318). This enables him to hold on to classical logic. It may be that Humberstone's semantics can help with problems in the analysis of vagueness, but I am not convinced that the kinds of reasons that make plausible the use of intervals in place of moments can be used to justify possibilities in place of worlds.

The present book may be thought of as in the tradition of Montague Grammar, if that is loosely construed. Montague Grammar in a stricter sense refers to work based on the style of linguistic analysis found in chapters 6 through 8 of Montague (1974). In this work a fragment of a natural language is explicitly presented by means of a set of formal rules, each of which is interpreted via a translation rule into the language of intensional logic. It is the latter language that is given an interpretation in terms of possible worlds (strictly world-time pairs; see p. 228) and contextual indices. An introduction to Montague Grammar is found in Dowty, Wall, and Peters (1981), and a collection of articles occurs in Partee (1976). More recent work may be consulted by looking at issues of *Linguistics and Philosophy* and following up the references listed there. Among the more substantial and semantically interesting works are Dowty (1979) and Carlson (1978). I trust that these references will give the reader some idea of what has been done. The fullest treatment of propositional attitude sentences in Montague Grammar is probably Klein (1978). Klein does not however study logical or mathematical attitudes and does not use structured meanings.

I regard it as absolutely vital to point out the amount of genuine and detailed semantic study that has been done in this tradition. This should make it clear that I am proposing an account of propositional attitudes that fits in with a whole body of other work. Possible-worlds semantics seems to me to get down to work and get its hands dirty. This, to me, contrasts it with most other approaches. Though it is true that some specific semantical analysis has been done in the Davidson framework (e.g., Wheeler (1972) or Taylor (1977), as well as Davidson's own (1967b) or (1969)), yet it seems to me that most work within this tradition is excessively metatheoretical and is concerned either with asking what form a theory of meaning should have or with trying to show why alternative approaches are wrong (on the former, see for example the essays in Evans and McDowell (1976); on the latter, see Wallace (1972, 242f.)). The same comments seem by and large to be true of work in the Katz tradition, though it is more difficult to substantiate this when the criteria for success are so different. Though I have certainly tried to justify the use of possible worlds in semantics, and though I have on occasion alluded to the difficulties faced by alternative treatments of propositional attitudes, yet I regard the very vitality of possible-worlds semantics as the strongest reply to its critics.

I cannot emphasize too highly the importance of accommodating the semantics of propositional attitudes within the work already done in possible-worlds semantics. To repeat a point made earlier, but now with special reference to λ-categorial languages, it ought to be the case that any semantical analysis given within a λ-categorial language outside the area of propositional attitude sentences will automatically carry over without change to a fragment in which such sentences occur and will be an already adequate semantics in the extended fragment to the extent that it was already adequate. No reworking should be necessary. This is in marked contrast with the solutions discussed in the commentary on chapter 9, in which completely new entities are postulated for the meanings of sentences and the whole semantics has to be done over again.

I have followed Montague (1974) in allowing only abstracts in which one variable at a time is bound. The effect of multiple binding can always be obtained by iterated abstractions. Alternatively, it is obvious how the syntax and semantics of abstraction would go for abstracts like $\langle \lambda, x_1, \ldots, x_n, \alpha \rangle$. Another point about abstraction is that it allows the formulation of a constituent of the kind Prior used to call a *connecticate*, that is, a functor one of whose arguments is a name and the other a sentence. An example is 'believes that', and I have already noted that Prior advocated treating this phrase as a syntactic unit. If the 'that' involved is just *that*$_0$, and if $x \in X_1$ and $y \in X_0$ (i.e., if x is an individual variable and y is a propositional variable), then, using a two-place abstract, the expression $\langle \lambda, x, y, \langle \textbf{\textit{believes}}, x, \langle \textbf{\textit{that}}_0, y \rangle \rangle \rangle$ would be in category (0/10); that is, it would be one of

Prior's connecticates. In fact, Prior's argument for treating 'believes that' as a unit seems to amount to no more than this fact.

It is possible, despite what is said in the text, to treat nominals as names. Lewis (1972, 203f.) shows how. Nevertheless, it seems to me that the *natural* way of explaining the phenomena is to treat names as nominals. That all names can be treated as nominals is shown, not only by Lewis (p. 201f.), but also in Cresswell (1973a, 131f.). In this chapter 'name' means 'symbol in category 1', whose meaning is just the thing of which it is a name. If names are really descriptions, as suggested in chapter 5 and its commentary, then they would have to be put into catgegory (0(0/1)). In a categorial language the difference in interpretation of that-clauses has to be effected by a lexical ambiguity in *that*. In a Montague Grammar it would be possible for it to be realized in the syntactic rules that generate that-clauses. I do not regard the nature of the precise mechanism for realizing the ambiguity as part of my claim, provided only that it is realized somehow.

The analysis of quotation offered in this chapter is discussed on pp. 104–108 of Cresswell (1973a). (See also Bigelow (1975).) In neither of these works, however, was any account given of the use of an operator like qu^* to represent mixed quotation.

Chapter 12: Indirect Discourse (I)

The most explicit discussion of the relation between a language abstractly specified, as in this book, and the language spoken by a population is found in Lewis (1975). Those wishing to analyze language use via speakers' intentions are the followers of Grice (1957), (1968), and (1969). These include Schiffer (1972) and Bennett (1976).

The official title of the collection of articles I have referred to as "What I am now saying is false" is *The Paradox of the Liar* (Martin (1970)). But "What I am now saying is false" is repeated many times on the dust jacket.

The Prior/Cohen exchange is in Cohen (1957) and Prior (1961). Cohen (p. 225) produces the following example:

> If the policeman testifies that anything, which the prisoner deposes, is false, and the prisoner deposes that something, which the policeman testifies, is true, then something, which the policeman testifies is false and something, which the prisoner deposes, is true.

Cohen claims that this sentence is a logical truth (in other words, the argument it expresses is intuitively valid), but that its validity cannot be captured in a formal system since any paradox-free formalization will involve a hierarchy of levels. Cohen (p. 232) comments on the fact that most studies of the liar paradox have neglected the indirect discourse version. As far as I can tell, the situation has changed little since 1957. Cohen's article deserves to be better known.

Prior refers to Cohen's article on p. 20 of Prior (1961) and discusses it informally. Although he does not formalize Cohen's argument or demonstrate its validity, he does formalize some related arguments, and I shall show later how to formalize Cohen's. Prior's logic contains the classical propositional calculus, and quantification over propositions, with analogues of the standard principles of quantification theory. As well as individual variables, there are variables for one-place proposition-forming operators.

Prior uses Łukasiewicz's notation, but I shall use the more familiar Russellian symbols. I shall follow Prior, however, in using d as a one-place propositional operator, not necessarily a truth-functional operator or even one that respects logical equivalence. In such a logic Prior is easily able to prove

(i) $d\forall p(dp \supset \sim p) \supset (\exists p(dp \wedge p) \wedge \exists p(dp \wedge \sim p))$

(see Prior (1961, 17)). Assuming that p and $\sim p$ are never identical propositions, we therefore have

(ii) $d\forall p(dp \supset \sim p) \supset \exists p \exists q(p \neq q \wedge dp \wedge dq)$

If d means 'it is said by a Cretan that', then this last formula means that, if a Cretan says that everything said by a Cretan is false, then there are at least two things said by a Cretan. Cohen's argument turns into the following if d_1 means 'the policeman testifies that' and d_2 means 'the prisoner deposes that':

(iii) $(d_1\forall p(d_2 p \supset \sim p) \wedge d_2 \exists p(d_1 p \wedge p)) \supset$
          $(\exists p(d_1 p \wedge \sim p) \wedge \exists p(d_2 p \wedge p))$

This formula can also be proved in Prior's logic.

Now Prior's logic, as he stresses on p. 18, contains *no* principles involving the meaning of d. The proofs are completely general and show that there is no possibility of a functor that fails to give these results. As far as I am concerned, this shows that the troubles involved in the meaning of *say* are not due to an inadequate description of its meaning but are inherent in the nature of semantics itself. It is the same point that I made in chapter 4 in discussing Thomason's work on truth operators.

The separation of quantifying in from the analysis of *de re* sentences, discussed in the latter part of the chapter, would, I think, be supported by Lewis (1979a). Certainly he claims (p. 540) that knowledge of essence is too strong a requirement for *de re* reference. (Of course, if the "attitude" were a logical modality, the correct account of the *de re* use probably would be a simple quantification into a purely intensional context.) A fuller discussion of quantifying in to that-clauses with structured meanings is given in Cresswell and von Stechow (1982, 520–522). Quantifying in is not possible for quotational complements, but it is possible for structured meanings. This seems to me as it should be.

One of the best accounts of tense and aspect in possible-worlds semantics is Dowty (1979), which contains a substantial bibliography. Other works include Bäuerle (1979) and Tichý (1980).

Chapter 13: Indirect Discourse (II)

In giving the semantics for *say* when it is used in a *de re* sentence, we do actually have to incorporate data from the theory of the referential *use* of language into the semantics. For we need to say when a person is using a name, description, or other mechanism to pick out something. The kind of work that would be relevant to fixing the precise meaning of *say* in these contexts would include the work of Donnellan (1966) and (1972) on the use of descriptions and the work of Kripke (1972), Devitt (1974) and (1981), and others on the use of names. It is not my intention to discuss any of this work. A useful explicit discussion of when a speaker has succeeded in picking out something occurs in McGinn (1981).

Chapter 14: Discourse De Se

The phenomenon discussed in this chapter was noticed as early as Geach (1957) and has been discussed by Castañeda in (1968) and elsewhere. Castañeda introduces a pronoun he* (he calls it a *quasi-indicator*) that he regards as unanalyzable: strictly, some occurrences of he* are reducible to others, but these others "constitute a peculiar and irreducible mechanism of reference to persons" (p. 447). Castañeda has in mind (p. 448) incorporating he* into Hintikka's system of epistemic logic, as expounded in Hintikka (1962). (He feels that Hintikka's own treatment of the problem (see Hintikka (1966)) is inadequate.)

Lewis's view (1979a) is that, in believing, the subject self-ascribes a property, a property being construed in possible-worlds terms. Such a view seems also to be held by Chisholm (1981), except for the possible-worlds analysis of properties.

The story of Kaplan's pants has not yet (December 1983) appeared in print, although his manuscript, *Demonstratives*, has been widely circulated. Some of the material is available in Kaplan (1979), but not what is relevant to this chapter. Other examples are given in Perry (1979). Perry recalls following a trail of spilled sugar around a supermarket and wanting to warn the shopper that he was making a mess. Then he realized that he was the shopper.

Perry considers (pp. 12–15) the solution to the problem defended in this chapter but thinks he has an argument against it. His argument is unfortunately rather cryptic and confused, and to see what is wrong with it requires some care. Perhaps it is best to point out first that a proposition, construed as a set of world-time-person triples, may alternatively be seen as a function from people and times to sets of worlds. And such a function could be thought of as a property. This is the view of Lewis (1979a, 518), who analyzes the objects of belief as properties and claims that all believing is the self-ascription of properties. Actually, Lewis's notion of property is simply a function from things to sets of worlds. He deals with temporal dependence via time slices. I prefer not to, but this difference is not material here.

Now we can state Perry's argument: For a sentence of the form 'I believe that I am making a mess' to be true for person p at time t in world w is just for p at t to believe the proposition that is the value of the function that is the meaning of the sentence 'I am making a mess', for the index $\langle p,t \rangle$. And this proposition is the proposition that p is making a mess at t, as it might be the proposition that Perry is making a mess at noon. And belief in *this* proposition does not explain stopping the cart. Agreed. But on Lewis's view, this proposition is not the object of Perry's belief. No proposition is the object of Perry's belief. The objects of belief are properties. In this case, Perry's belief sentence would be true at $\langle w,t,p \rangle$ iff p self-ascribes the property that is the meaning of 'I am making a mess'. To be sure, Boër and Lycan point out (1980, 445), the idea of self-ascription of properties is by no means a clear and lucid one, but that is an objection of a quite different sort.

Boër and Lycan in fact argue strongly that all *de se* attitudes are just *de re* attitudes. Stalnaker (1981) can, I think, also be construed as making the same point. This is a conclusion that I would not resist, if it is true. A formal account of *de se* attitudes, using structured propositions, is given in von Stechow (1982). A particularly intriguing application of Lewis's idea is von Stechow's analysis of the famous sentence in Lakoff (1972, 639), "I dreamt that I was Brigitte Bardot and that I kissed me" (von Stechow (1982, 43–45)).

My criticisms of the potentially infinite list of contextual indices are found in Cresswell (1973a, 110f.), and the theory of contexts as properties of utterances developed there on pp. 111–119 was in response to these criticisms. It now seems to me that a world-time-person triple gives information as specific as that provided by any context property, and it may even be that the rather complex notion of context family defined there on p. 115 is formally equivalent to a $\langle w,t,p \rangle$ triple. Von Stechow (1981a, 159) in fact treats a context as a $\langle w,t,p \rangle$ triple.

There are, of course, contextual phenomena that seem best treated by thinking of an expression as containing a "hidden" argument place, which is sometimes filled by a bound variable, and sometimes contextually. In Cresswell (1978a) (see especially pp. 18–23) I used some ideas from Bigelow (1975) in the study of certain spatial uses of prepositions.

The question of whether *I* and *you* behave in an importantly different manner is discussed by Heidelberger (1982). On the analysis suggested in the text, the difference is that whereas *I* is tied directly to *p*, *you* is defined via the idea of the person *p* is addressing. This seems to me to locate the difference correctly.

If Harman (1975) is right in supposing that we think in natural (public) language, then at least some of our beliefs will be in that language. In speaking about representational systems appropriate to various attitudes, I should be taken neither to deny nor to endorse the view that the systems are distinct. Of course, in analyzing a word like *say*, we will be interested in the question of whether a sentence is *uttered*, that is, publicly produced. In analyzing *believe*, if Harman is right, we would still be interested in a sentence of the same language, but we would be interested not in whether it was publicly uttered but in whether it was in the subject's belief "store," however that is analyzed.

The notion of store must of course be metaphorical. And the metaphorical nature must be remembered. For instance, Field (1978, 16) claims that "there is no way that infinitely many sentences can be explicitly stored in a finite head." He does not say what is meant here by 'explicitly'. Consider the Turing machine that represents addition. Does it or does it not store the infinite set of triples $\langle n,m,n+m \rangle$? I would say it does. Of course, at any given time it has only *computed* a finite portion of what it stores. But it seems unreasonable to say that people only believe what they are at any moment expressing. And in any case, if *that* is what explicit beliefs are, then we *do* only have a finite number of them.

Field in the passage cited refers to p. 410 of Dennett (1975). Dennett writes, "My beliefs are apparently infinite, which means their storage, however miniaturized, will take up more room than there is in the brain." In this article, however, Dennett is working with a very severely constrained form of representation that he calls *brain writing*. To be sure, there is a problem about what a representation system might look like, and I have tried to put as few constraints as possible on such a system, not even requiring it to be, in any meaningful sense, "in" the head. It is a task for cognitive scientists, not for me, to investigate its nature.

Chapter 15: Semantics in the Picture

The work by Jeff Ross occurs in an unpublished thesis in philosophy and linguistics at La Trobe University. The original work in Dretske (1972) on contrastive stress was expanded in Dretske (1977) and commented on in Boër (1979). The work on passives in Keenan (1980) might be capable of an alternative interpretation, *viz* one in which the by-phrase is added to the transitive verb phrase before passivization. That at any rate seems how an analogous treatment of passive in Bach (1980) would go. If so, it would not precisely be an example of a structure-sensitive operator, unless one were to argue that such operators arise during the transformational history. A similar point involving 'buy' and 'sell' was made by Emmon Bach, who observed to me that although '*x* is bought' and '*x* is sold' are logically equivalent, yet '*x* is bought by *y*' and '*x* is sold by *y*' are not.

A more detailed account of the semantics of pictorial representation, using possible worlds, is found in Howell (1974). Howell draws on the work of Hintikka on the logic of perceptual statements. Howell notes a point also made in Cresswell (1983, 67f.), *viz* that one cannot simply speak of what a picture represents, but must rather speak of what a subject at a time takes it to represent. Howell (p. 101) actually suggests using a five-place operator reading "at time *t*, to a person *a* under conditions of observation *c*, *p* represents that." Howell does not undertake an analysis of impossible pictures, but he suggests that the work in Hintikka (1970) might help. Hintikka has himself of course written on pictorial representation in chapter 11 of Hintikka (1975a). Sober (1976) contains a long discussion on representation, including some remarks about the devil's tuning fork (or pitchfork). What he says on pp. 133–136, and indeed most of what he says in his article, seems compatible with the account I favor. Sober is concerned to claim that pictorial representation is not as different from linguistic representation as many theorists have supposed. Howell (1976) comments on his article.

Some discussion of wh-clauses in a λ-categorial language is found in Boër (1978b). Although Boër does not go into questions of hyper-intensionality, it does not seem any more difficult to deal with wh-clauses than with that-clauses.

The suggested analysis of (13) will not work quite so well with an example suggested to me by Bill Lycan:

(i) If what Gödel seems to have proved is true, then a lot of people have necessarily false beliefs.

It should be obvious that the having of these beliefs would *not* follow merely from Gödel's having done something observationally indistinguishable from what he has proved.

Why might (i) be considered true? Presumably because the necessarily false beliefs are the propositions that Gödel has proved. This means that the validity of (i) applies to the equally general

(ii) If p then, what x believes is true,

given that p is a proposition that x believes. If (ii) is valid (though I am not *absolutely* convinced that it is, or that (i) is either), its validity is quite independent of the precise meaning attached to 'if'. It might be interpreted as the conditional connective in some classical logic or a possible-worlds counterfactual logic, or even as the connective of a nonstandard logic, such as one of the "relevance" logics found in Anderson and Belnap (1975) or some even more bizarre logic still. Whatever the logic—since it is *always* a matter of fact whether a person realizes a logical connection—we can imagine a proposition q that is equivalent, in the favored logic, to the p in (ii) but that x does not believe, thus turning (ii) into a falsehood.

Bibliography

Anderson, A. R., and N. D. Belnap, Jr. (1975). *Entailment: The Logic of Relevance and Necessity.* Princeton, N.J., Princeton University Press.

Anderson, C. A. (1983). The paradox of the knower. *The Journal of Philosophy* 80, 338–355.

Åqvist, L. E. G. son (1973). Modal logic with subjunctive conditionals and dispositional predicates. *Journal of Philosophical Logic* 2, 1–76.

Arnaud, R. B. (1976). Sentence, utterance and samesayer. *Noûs* 10, 283–304.

Bach, E. W. (1980). In defense of passive. *Linguistics and Philosophy* 3, 297–341.

Bach, E. W. (1983). The metaphysics of natural language. In *Abstracts of the 7th International Congress of Logic, Methodology and Philosophy of Science,* vol. 2. Salzburg, University of Salzburg.

Bach, K. (1981). What's in a name. *Australasian Journal of Philosophy* 59, 371–386.

Bach, K. (1982). *De re* belief and methodological solipsism. In *Thought and Object: Essays on Intentionality,* ed. A. Woodfield, 121–151. Oxford, Clarendon Press.

Bach, K. (1983). Russell was right (almost). *Synthese* 54, 189–207.

Baker, L. R. (1982). *De re* belief in action. *The Philosophical Review* 91, 363–387.

Baldwin, T. (1982). Prior and Davidson on indirect speech. *Philosophical Studies* 42, 255–282.

Barcan Marcus, R. C. (1983). Rationality and believing the impossible. *The Journal of Philosophy* 80, 321–338.

Barwise, J. (1981). Scenes and other situations. *The Journal of Philosophy* 78, 369–397.

Barwise, J., and J. Perry (1980). The situation underground. In *Stanford Working Papers in Semantics,* vol. 1. Stanford, Stanford Cognitive Science Group, Stanford University.

Barwise, J., and J. Perry (1981a). Semantic innocence and uncompromising situations. In *Midwest Studies in Philosophy,* vol. 6, ed. P. A. French et al., 387–404. Minneapolis, University of Minnesota.

Barwise, J., and J. Perry (1981b). Situations and attitudes. *The Journal of Philosophy* 78, 668–691.

Barwise, J., and J. Perry (1983). *Situations and Attitudes.* Cambridge, Mass., Bradford/MIT Press.

Bauer, L. J. (1983). *English Word-formation.* Cambridge, Cambridge University Press.

Bäuerle, R. (1979). Tense logics and natural language. *Synthese* 40, 225–230.

Bäuerle, R. (1983). Pragmatisch-semantisch Aspekte der NP-Interpretation. In *Allgemeine Sprachwissenschaft, Sprachtypologie und Textlinguistik,* ed. M. Faust et al., 121–131. Tübingen, Gunter Narr.

Bealer, G. (1982). *Quality and Concept.* Oxford, Clarendon Press.

Bennett, J. F. (1976). *Linguistic Behaviour.* Cambridge, Cambridge University Press.

Bigelow, J. C. (1975). Contexts and quotation I and II. *Linguistische Berichte* 38, 1–21, and 39, 1–21.

Bigelow, J. C. (1978). Believing in semantics. *Linguistics and Philosophy* 2, 101–144.

Bigelow, J. C. (1981). Semantic nominalism. *Australasian Journal of Philosophy* 59, 403–421.

Boër, S. E. (1975). Proper names as predicates. *Philosophical Studies* 27, 389–400.

Boër, S. E. (1978a). Proper names and formal semiotic. *Synthese* 38, 73–112.

Boër, S. E. (1978b). 'Who' and 'whether': Towards a theory of indirect question clauses. *Linguistics and Philosophy* 2, 307–345.

Boër, S. E. (1979). Meaning and contrastive stress. *The Philosophical Review* 88, 263–298.

Boër, S. E. (forthcoming). Names and attitudes. In *Essays in Honor of Arthur Burks*, ed. M. Salmon. Dordrecht, Reidel.

Boër, S. E., and R. Edelstein (1979). Some numerical constructions in English. *Journal of Philosophical Logic* 8, 261–288.

Boër, S. E., and W. G. Lycan (1980). Who me? *The Philosophical Review* 89, 427–466.

Bonotto, C., and A. Bressan (1983). On generalized synonymy notions and corresponding quasi-senses. *Atti Acad. Naz. de Lincei* (VIII).

Bradley, R. D., and N. Swartz (1979). *Possible Worlds*. Oxford, Basil Blackwell.

Bresnan, J. W. (1970). On complementizers: Towards a syntactic theory of complement types. *Foundations of Language* 6, 297–321.

Burdick, H. R. (1982). A logical form for the propositional attitudes. *Synthese* 52, 185–230.

Burge, T. (1973). Reference and proper names. *The Journal of Philosophy* 70, 425–439.

Burge, T. (1978). Belief and synonymy. *The Journal of Philosophy* 75, 119–138.

Burge, T. (1979). Sinning against Frege. *The Philosophical Review* 88, 398–432.

Burge, T. (1982). Other bodies. In *Thought and Object: Essays on Intentionality*, ed. A. Woodfield, 97–120. Oxford, Clarendon Press.

Carlson, G. N. (1978). *Reference to Kinds in English*. Bloomington, Ind., Indiana University Linguistics Club.

Carnap, R. (1947). *Meaning and Necessity*. Chicago, University of Chicago Press.

Castañeda, H.-N. (1968). On the logic of attributions of self-knowledge to others. *The Journal of Philosophy* 65, 439–456.

Chisholm, R. M. (1981). *The First Person: An Essay on Reference and Intentionality*. Minneapolis, University of Minnesota Press.

Church, A. (1950). On Carnap's analysis of statements of assertion and belief. *Analysis* 10, 97–99.

Church, A. (1951). A formulation of the logic of sense and denotation. In *Structure, Method and Meaning*, ed. P. Henle, H. M. Kallen, and S. K. Langer, 3–24. New York, Liberal Arts Press.

Churchland, P. M. (1981). Eliminative materialism and the propositional attitudes. *The Journal of Philosophy* 78, 67–90.

Churchland, P. S. (1980). Language, thought and information. *Noûs* 14, 147–170.

Cohen, L. J. (1957). Can the logic of indirect discourse be formalized? *The Journal of Symbolic Logic* 22, 225–232.

Collins, A. W. (1979). Could our beliefs be representations in our brains? *The Journal of Philosophy* 76, 225–243.

Cresswell, M. J. (1973a). *Logics and Languages*. London, Methuen.

Cresswell, M. J. (1973b). Physical theories and possible worlds. *Logique et Analyse* 63/64, 495–511.

Cresswell, M. J. (1975). Hyperintensional logic. *Studia Logica* 34, 25–38.

Cresswell, M. J. (1977). Categorial languages. *Studia Logica* 36, 257–269.

Cresswell, M. J. (1978a). Prepositions and points of view. *Linguistics and Philosophy* 2, 1–41.

Cresswell, M. J. (1978b). Semantic competence. In *Meaning and Translation*, ed. F. Guenthner and M. Guenthner-Reutter, 9–43. London, Duckworth.

Cresswell, M. J. (1978c). Semantics and logic. *Theoretical Linguistics* 5, 19–30.

Cresswell, M. J. (1980). Quotational theories of propositional attitudes. *Journal of Philosophical Logic* 9, 17–40.

Cresswell, M. J. (1982). The autonomy of semantics. In Peters and Saarinen, eds. (1982), 69–86.

Cresswell, M. J. (1983). A highly impossible scene. In *Meaning, Use and Interpretation of Language*, ed. R. Bäuerle, Ch. Schwarze, and A. von Stechow, 62–78. Berlin, de Gruyter.

Cresswell, M. J., and A. von Stechow (1982). *De re* belief generalized. *Linguistics and Philosophy* 5, 503–535.

Davidson, D. (1967a). Truth and meaning. *Synthese* 17, 304–323.

Davidson, D. (1967b). The logical form of action sentences. In *The Logic of Decision and Action*, ed. N. Rescher, 81–95. Pittsburgh, University of Pittsburgh Press.

Davidson, D. (1969). On saying that. In *Words and Objections: Essays on the Work of W. V. Quine*, ed. D. Davidson and K. J. J. Hintikka, 158–174. Dordrecht, Reidel.

Dennett, D. C. (1975). Brain writing and mind reading. In *Language, Mind, and Knowledge*, ed. K. Gunderson, 403–415. Minneapolis, University of Minnesota Press. (Reprinted in Dennett (1978), 39–50.)

Dennett, D. C. (1978). *Brainstorms*. Cambridge, Mass., MIT Press. A Bradford book.

Devitt, M. (1974). Singular terms. *The Journal of Philosophy* 71, 183–205.

Devitt, M. (1976). Suspension of judgement: A response to Heidelberger on Kaplan. *Journal of Philosophical Logic* 5, 17–24.

Devitt, M. (1981). *Designation*. New York, Columbia University Press.

Donnellan, K. S. (1966). Reference and definite descriptions. *The Philosophical Review* 75, 281–304.

Donnellan, K. S. (1972). Proper names and identifying descriptions. In *Semantics of Natural Language*, ed. D. Davidson and G. Harman, 356–379. Dordrecht, Reidel.

Dowty, D. R. (1977). Toward a semantic analysis of verb aspect and the English "imperfective" progressive. *Linguistics and Philosophy* 1, 45–77.

Dowty, D. R. (1979). *Word Meaning and Montague Grammar: The Semantics of Verbs and Times in Generative Semantics and in Montague's PTQ*. Dordrecht, Reidel.

Dowty, D. R., R. E. Wall, and P. S. Peters (1981). *Introduction to Montague Semantics*. Dordrecht, Reidel.

Dretske, F. I. (1972). Contrastive stress. *The Philosophical Review* 81, 411–437.

Dretske, F. I. (1977). Referring to events. In *Midwest Studies in Philosophy*, vol. 2, ed. P. A. French et al., 90–99. Morris, Minn., University of Minnesota.

Dretske, F. I. (1981). *Knowledge and the Flow of Information*. Cambridge, Mass., The MIT Press. A Bradford book.

Dretske, F. I. (1983). The epistemology of belief. *Synthese* 55, 3–19.

Dummett, M. A. E. (1976). What is a theory of Meaning II. In Evans and McDowell, eds. (1976), 67–137.

Edmonson, J. A. (1978). How to get *both* in a categorial grammar. *Studies in Language* 2, 295–312.

Enç, B. (1982). Intentional states of mechanical devices. *Mind* 91, 161–182.

Escher, M. C. (1967). *The Graphic Work of M. C. Escher*, new revised and expanded edition. London, Oldbourne.

Evans, G., and J. McDowell, eds. (1976). *Truth and Meaning*. Oxford, Clarendon Press.

Field, H. H. (1978). Mental representation. *Erkenntnis* 13, 9–61.

Fodor, J. A. (1975). *The Language of Thought*. Hassocks, Harvester Press.

Fodor, J. A. (1981). *RePresentations*. Cambridge, Mass., MIT Press. A Bradford book.

Fodor, J. A. (1982). Cognitive science and the twin-earth problem. *Notre Dame Journal of Formal Logic* 23, 98–118.

Fraassen, B. C. van (1979). Propositional attitudes in weak pragmatics. *Studia Logica* 38, 365–374.

Frege, G. (1892). Über Sinn und Bedeutung. *Zeitschrift für Philosophie und Philosophische Kritik* (n.s.) 100, 25–50. (Translated as "On sense and reference" in Frege (1952), 56–78.)

Frege, G. (1918). Der Gedanke. Eine logische Untersuchung. *Beiträge zur Philosophie des deutschen Idealismus* 1, 143–157. (Translated by A. M. and M. Quinton as "The thought: A logical enquiry." *Mind* 65 (1956), 289–311.)

Frege, G. (1952). *Translations from the Philosophical Writings of Gottlob Frege*, trans. P. T. Geach and M. Black. Oxford, Basil Blackwell.

Geach, P. T. (1957). On beliefs about oneself. *Analysis* 18, 23f. (Reprinted in Geach (1972), 128–129.)

Geach, P. T. (1962). *Reference and Generality*. Ithaca, N.Y., Cornell University Press.

Geach, P. T. (1967). Intentional identity. *The Journal of Philosophy* 64, 627–632. (Reprinted in Geach (1972), 146–153.)

Geach, P. T. (1972). *Logic Matters*. Oxford, Basil Blackwell.

Geach, P. T. (1976). Two kinds of intentionality. *The Monist* 59, 306–320.

Grabski, M. (1978). Some operators cancelling hyperintensionality. *Amsterdam Papers in Formal Grammar*, vol. 2, 141–153. Amsterdam, Centrale Interfaculteit, Universiteit van Amsterdam.

Grice, H. P. (1957). Meaning. *The Philosophical Review* 66, 377–388.

Grice, H. P. (1968). Utterer's meaning, sentence meaning, and word meanings. *Foundations of Language* 4, 225–242.

Grice, H. P. (1969). Utterer's meaning and intentions. *The Philosophical Review* 78, 147–177.

Grover, D. L., J. L. Camp, and N. D. Belnap, Jr. (1975). A prosentential theory of truth. *Philosophical Studies* 27, 73–125.

Halmos, P. R. (1960). *Naive Set Theory*. Princeton, N.J., Van Nostrand.

Harman, G. (1975). Language, thought and communication. In *Language, Mind, and Knowledge*, ed. K. Gunderson, 270–298. Minneapolis, University of Minnesota Press.

Harman, G. (1982). Conceptual role semantics. *Notre Dame Journal of Formal Logic* 23, 242–256.

Heidelberger, H. (1974). Kaplan on Quine and suspension of judgment. *Journal of Philosophical Logic* 3, 441–443.

Heidelberger, H. (1982). What is it to understand a sentence that contains an indexical? *Philosophy and Phenomenological Research* 43, 21–34.

Heijenoort, J. van (1977a). Sense in Frege. *Journal of Philosophical Logic* 6, 93–102.

Heijenoort, J. van (1977b). Frege on sense identity. *Journal of Philosophical Logic* 6, 103–108.

Heny, F., ed. (1981). *Ambiguities in Intensional Contexts*. Dordrecht, Reidel.

Hermes, H. (1969). *Enumerability, Decidability, Computability*. Berlin, Springer.

Higginbotham, J. (1983). The logic of perceptual reports: An alternative to situation semantics. *The Journal of Philosophy* 80, 100–127.

Hill, C. S. (1976). Toward a theory of meaning for belief sentences. *Philosophical Studies* 30, 209–226.

Hintikka, K. J. J. (1962). *Knowledge and Belief*. Ithaca, N.Y., Cornell University Press.

Hintikka, K. J. J. (1966). 'Knowing oneself' and other problems in epistemic logic. *Theoria* 32, 1–13.

Hintikka, K. J. J. (1969). *Models for Modalities*. Dordrecht, Reidel.

Hintikka, K. J. J. (1970). Knowledge, belief and logical consequence. *Ajatus* 32, 32–47. (Reprinted in Hintikka (1975a), 179–191.)

Hintikka, K. J. J. (1975a). *The Intentions of Intentionality and Other New Models for Modalities*. Dordrecht, Reidel.

Hintikka, K. J. J. (1975b). Impossible possible worlds vindicated. *Journal of Philosophical Logic* 4, 475–484.

Hintikka, K. J. J. (1982). Game-theoretical semantics: Insights and prospects. *Notre Dame Journal of Formal Logic* 23, 219–241.

Hornsby, J. (1976). Proper names: A defence of Burge. *Philosophical Studies* 30, 227–234.

Howell, R. (1974). The logical structure of pictorial representation. *Theoria* 40, 76–109.

Howell, R. (1976). Ordinary pictures, mental representations and logical forms. *Synthese* 33, 149–174.

Humberstone, I. L. (1981). From worlds to possibilities. *Journal of Philosophical Logic* 10, 313–339.

Johnson-Laird, P. N. (1982). Formal semantics and the psychology of meaning. In Peters and Saarinen, eds. (1982), 1–68.

Kamp, J. A. W. (1971). Formal properties of 'now'. *Theoria* 37, 227–273.

Kaplan, D. (1969). Quantifying in. In *Words and Objections: Essays on the Work of W. V. Quine*, ed. D. Davidson and K. J. J. Hintikka, 206–242. Dordrecht, Reidel.

Kaplan, D. (1978). Dthat. In *Pragmatics*, ed. P. Cole, 221–243. Syntax and Semantics, vol. 9. New York, Academic Press.

Kaplan, D. (1979). On the logic of demonstratives. *Journal of Philosophical Logic* 8, 81–98.

Katz, F. M., and J. J. Katz (1977). Is necessity the mother of intension? *The Philosophical Review* 86, 70–96.

Katz, J. J. (1972). *Semantic Theory*. New York, Harper and Row.

Katz, J. J. (1982). Common sense in semantics. *Notre Dame Journal of Formal Logic* 23, 174–218.

Keenan, E. L. (1980). Passive is phrasal (not sentential or lexical). In *Lexical Grammar*, ed. T. Hoekstra, H. van der Hulst, and M. Moortgat, 181–213. Dordrecht, Foris Publications.

Klein, E. (1978). *On Sentences Which Report Beliefs, Desires and Other Mental Attitudes*. Ph.D. thesis, University of Cambridge.

Kneale, W. C., and M. Kneale (1962). *The Development of Logic*. Oxford, Clarendon Press.

Kraut, R. (1983). There are no *de dicto* attitudes. *Synthese* 54, 275–294.

Kripke, S. A. (1959). A completeness theorem in modal logic. *The Journal of Symbolic Logic* 24, 1–19.

Kripke, S. A. (1972). Naming and necessity. In *Semantics of Natural Language*, ed. D. Davidson and G. Harman, 253–355. Dordrecht, Reidel.

Kripke, S. A. (1975). Outline of a theory of truth. *The Journal of Philosophy* 72, 690–716.

Kripke, S. A. (1977). Speakers reference and semantic reference. In *Midwest Studies in Philosophy*, vol. 2, ed. P. A. French et al., 255–276. Morris, Minn., University of Minnesota.

Kripke, S. A. (1979). A puzzle about belief. In *Meaning and Use*, ed. A. Margalit, 239–283. Dordrecht, Reidel.

Kroon, F. W. (1982). Contingency and the *a posteriori*. *Australasian Journal of Philosophy* 60, 40–54.

Lakoff, G. (1971). On generative semantics. In *Semantics: An Interdisciplinary Reader in Philosophy, Linguistics and Psychology*, ed. D. D. Steinberg and L. A. Jakobovits, 329–340. Cambridge, Cambridge University Press.

Lakoff, G. (1972). Linguistics and natural logic. In *Semantics of Natural Language*, ed. D. Davidson and G. Harman, 545–665. Dordrecht, Reidel.

Levin, H. D. (1982). *Categorial Grammar and the Logical Form of Quantification*. Naples, Bibliopolis.

Lewis, D. K. (1970). Anselm and actuality. *Noûs* 4, 175–188.

Lewis, D. K. (1972). General semantics. In *Semantics of Natural Language*, ed. D. Davidson and G. Harman, 169–218. Dordrecht, Reidel.

Lewis, D. K. (1973). *Counterfactuals*. Oxford, Basil Blackwell.

Lewis, D. K. (1975). Languages and language. *Language, Mind, and Knowledge*, ed. K. Gunderson, 3–35. Minneapolis, University of Minnesota Press.

Lewis, D. K. (1979a). Attitudes *de dicto* and *de se*. *The Philosophical Review* 88, 513–543.

Lewis, D. K. (1979b). Scorekeeping in a language game. *Journal of Philosophical Logic* 8, 340–359.

Lewis, D. K. (1980). Veridical hallucination and prosthetic vision. *Australasian Journal of Philosophy* 58, 239–249.

Lewis, D. K. (1981). What puzzling Pierre does not believe. *Australasian Journal of Philosophy* 59, 283–289.

Lewis, D. K. (1983). Individuation by acquaintance and by stipulation. *The Philosophical Review* 92, 3–32.

Loar, B. (1976). The semantics of singular terms. *Philosophical Studies* 30, 353–377.

Loux, M. J., ed. (1979). *The Possible and the Actual*. Ithaca, N.Y., Cornell University Press.

Lycan, W. G. (1979). The trouble with possible worlds. In Loux, ed. (1979), 274–316.

Lycan, W. G. (1981). Toward a homuncular theory of believing. *Cognition and Brain Theory* 4, 139–159.

McCawley, J. D. (1968). Lexical insertion in a transformational grammar without deep structure. In *Papers from the 4th Regional Meeting: Chicago Linguistic Society*, 71–80. Chicago, University of Chicago.

McCawley, J. D. (1971). Prelexical syntax. *Georgetown University Monographs on Languages and Linguistics*, no. 20, 19–33.

McGinn, C. (1981). The mechanism of reference. *Synthese* 49, 157–186.

McGinn, C. (1982). The structure of content. In *Thought and Object: Essays on Intentionality*, ed. A. Woodfield, 207–258. Oxford, Clarendon Press.

Machina, K. F. (1976). Truth, belief and vagueness. *Journal of Philosophical Logic* 5, 47–78.

Martin, R. L. (1970). *The Paradox of the Liar*. New Haven, Conn., Yale University Press.

Montague, R. M. (1974). *Formal Philosophy*, ed. R. H. Thomason. New Haven, Conn., Yale University Press.

Moore, R. C., and G. G. Hendrix (1982). Computational models of belief and the semantics of belief sentences. In Peters and Saarinen, eds. (1982), 107–127.

Nute, D. (1978). Proper names: How to become a causal theorist while remaining a sense theorist. *Philosophia* 8, 43–57.

Over, D. E. (1983). On Kripke's puzzle. *Mind* 92, 253–256.

Parsons, T. (1980). *Nonexistent Objects*. New Haven, Conn., Yale University Press.

Partee, B. H. (1973). The semantics of belief sentences. In *Approaches to Natural Language*, ed. K. J. J. Hintikka et al., 309–336. Dordrecht, Reidel.

Partee, B. H., ed. (1976). *Montague Grammar*. New York, Academic Press.

Partee, B. H. (1979). Semantics—mathematics or psychology? In *Semantics from Different Points of View*, ed. R. Bäuerle et al., 1–14. Berlin, Springer.

Partee, B. H. (1982). Belief sentences and the limits of semantics. In Peters and Saarinen, eds. (1982), 87–106.

Partee, B. H. (1983). Compositionality. Unpublished manuscript. Amherst, University of Massachusetts.

Pelletier, F. J. (1982). (X). *Notre Dame Journal of Formal Logic* 23, 316–326.

Pendlebury, M. (1982). Hob, Nob, and Hecate: The problem of quantifying out. *Australasian Journal of Philosophy* 60, 346–354.

Perry, J. (1979). The problem of the essential indexical. *Noûs* 13, 3–21.

Peters, P. S., and E. Saarinen, eds. (1982). *Processes, Beliefs and Questions*. Dordrecht, Reidel.

Plantinga, A. (1974). *The Nature of Necessity*. Oxford, Clarendon Press.

Prior, A. N. (1961). On a family of paradoxes. *Notre Dame Journal of Formal Logic* 2, 16–32.

Prior, A. N. (1963). Oratio obliqua. *Aristotelian Society Supplementary Volume* 37, 115–126.

Prior, A. N. (1971). *Objects of Thought*. Oxford, Clarendon Press.

Putnam, H. (1960). Minds and machines. In *Dimensions of Mind*, ed. S. Hook, 138–164. New York, New York University Press.

Putnam, H. (1975). The meaning of Meaning. In *Language, Mind, and Knowledge*, ed. K. Gunderson, 131–193. Minneapolis, University of Minnesota Press.

Quine, W. V. O. (1953). *From a Logical Point of View*. 2nd edition 1961. Cambridge, Mass., Harvard University Press.

Quine, W. V. O. (1956). Quantifiers and propositional attitudes. *The Journal of Philosophy* 53, 177–187.

Quine, W. V. O. (1960). *Word and Object*. Cambridge, Mass., MIT Press.

Quine, W. V. O. (1969). *Ontological Relativity and Other Essays*. New York, Columbia University Press.

Rantala, V. (1975). Urn models: A new kind of non-standard model for first-order logic. *Journal of Philosophical Logic* 4, 455–474.

Reddam, J. P. (1982). Van Fraassen on propositional attitudes. *Philosophical Studies* 42, 101–110.

Reeves, A. L. (1973). In defence of a simple solution. *Australasian Journal of Philosophy* 51, 17–38.

Rescher, N. (1975). *A Theory of Possibility*. Pittsburgh, University of Pittsburgh Press.

Routley, F. R. (1980). *Exploring Meinong's Jungle and Beyond*. Canberra, Australian National University.

Russell, B. A. W. (1905). On denoting. *Mind* (n.s.) 14, 479–493.

Ruttenburg, J. (1976). Some difficulties with Cresswell's semantics and the method of shallow structure. *U/Mass Occasional Papers* II, ed. J. T. Stillings. Amherst, University of Massachusetts.

Ryle, G. (1938). Categories. *Proceedings of the Aristotelian Society* 28, 189–206.

Saarinen, E. (1978). Intentional identity interpreted: A case study of the relations among quantifiers, pronouns, and propositional attitudes. In *Game Theoretical Semantics*, ed. E. Saarinen, 245–327. Dordrecht, Reidel.

Saarinen, E. (1982). Linguistic intuition and reductionism: Comments on Katz's paper. *Notre Dame Journal of Formal Logic* 23, 296–304.

Schiffer, S. (1972). *Meaning*. Oxford, Oxford University Press.
Schiffer, S. (1977). Naming and knowing. In *Midwest Studies in Philosophy*, vol. 2, ed. P. A. French et al., 28–41. Morris, Minn., University of Minnesota.
Schiffer, S. (1982). Intention-based semantics. *Notre Dame Journal of Formal Logic* 23, 119–156.
Scott, D. S. (1972). Continuous lattices. In *Toposes, Algebraic Geometry and Logic*, ed. F. W. Lawvere, 97–136. Berlin, Springer.
Scott, D. S. (1975). Lambda calculus and recursion theory. In *Proceedings of the Third Scandinavian Logic Symposium*, ed. S. Kanger, 154–193. Amsterdam, North Holland.
Searle, J. R. (1969). *Speech Acts: An Essay in the Philosophy of Language*. Cambridge, Cambridge University Press.
Segerberg, K. (1973). Two dimensional modal logic. *Journal of Philosophical Logic* 2, 77–96.
Sharvy, R. (1969). Things. *The Monist* 53, 488–504.
Skyrms, B. (1978). An immaculate conception of modality. *The Journal of Philosophy* 75, 368–387.
Sober, E. (1976). Mental representation. *Synthese* 33, 101–148.
Stalnaker, R. C. (1976). Propositions. In *Issues in the Philosophy of Language*, ed. A. F. Mackay and D. D. Merrill, 79–91. New Haven, Conn., Yale University Press.
Stalnaker, R. C. (1978). Assertion. In *Pragmatics*, ed. P. Cole, 315–332. Syntax and Semantics, vol. 9. New York, Academic Press.
Stalnaker, R. C. (1981). Indexical belief. *Synthese* 49, 129–151.
von Stechow, A. (1981a). Presupposition and context. In *Aspects of Philosophical Logic*, ed. U. Mönnich, 157–224. Dordrecht, Reidel.
von Stechow, A. (1981b). Topic, focus and local relevance. In *Crossing the Boundaries in Linguistics*, ed. W. Klein and W. Levelt, 95–130. Dordrecht, Reidel.
von Stechow, A. (1982). Structured propositions. *Arbeitspapiere SFB 99*, Universität Konstanz.
Taylor, B. (1977). Tense and continuity. Linguistics and Philosophy 1, 199–220.
Thomason, R. H. (1976). Some extensions of Montague grammar. In Partee, ed. (1976), 77–117.
Thomason, R. H. (1977). Indirect discourse is not quotational. *The Monist* 60, 340–354.
Thomason, R. H. (1980a). A note on syntactical treatments of modality. *Synthese* 44, 391–395.
Thomason, R. H. (1980b). A model theory for propositional attitudes. *Linguistics and Philosophy* 4, 47–70.
Tichý, P. (1980). The logic of temporal discourse. *Linguistics and Philosophy* 3, 343–369.
Turner, R. (1983). Montague semantics, nominalization and Scott's domains. *Linguistics and Philosophy* 6, 259–288.
Tye, M. (1978). The puzzle of Hesperus and Phosphorus. *Australasian Journal of Philosophy* 56, 219–224.
Vendler, Z. (1975). On what we know. *Language, Mind, and Knowledge*, ed. K. Gunderson, 370–390. Minneapolis, University of Minnesota Press.
Vlach, F. (1983). On situation semantics for perception. *Synthese* 54, 129–152.
Wallace, J. (1972). On the frame of reference. *Semantics of Natural Language*, ed. D. Davidson and G. Harman, 219–252. Dordrecht, Reidel.
Wheeler, S. C. III (1972). Attributives and their modifiers. *Noûs* 6, 310–334.
Winograd, T. (1972). *Understanding Natural Language*. New York, Academic Press.
Wittgenstein, L. (1921). *Tractatus Logico Philosophicus*. (Translated by D. F. Pears and B. F. McGinness.) 2nd printing 1963. London, Routledge and Kegan Paul.

Wittgenstein, L. (1953). *Philosophical Investigations.* (Translated by G. E. M. Anscombe.) Oxford, Basil Blackwell.

Zalta, E. N. (1983). *Abstract Objects: An Introduction to Axiomatic Metaphysics.* Dordrecht, Reidel.

Ziff, P. (1977). About proper names. *Mind* 86, 319–332.

Index

(*Separate works have not been listed where there are fewer than six page references under an author's name.*)

Abstraction operator, 97, 101, 179
Acceptability principles, 177
Addition, 10–19, 26–27
Adjectives, 98
Adverbs, 98, 136
Ambiguity in propositional attitude
  sentences, 12, 34–36, 87–88, 147–148,
  167
  in sentences with names, 48–49,
  156
'and', 72
Anderson, A. R., 168, 186
Anderson, C. A., 148
Åqvist, L. E. G. son, 154
Argument, of a function, 61
Arnaud, R. B., 161
Autonomy of semantics, 129
Axiom of choice, 176

Bach, E. W., 139, 164, 176, 185
Bach, K., 140, 141, 150, 156
Baker, L. R., 158
Baldwin, T., 147
Barcan Marcus, R. C., 142
Barwise, J., 168–175
Basic particular situations, 162, 167
Bauer, L. J., 139
Bäuerle, R., 154, 182
Bealer, G., 167
'beekeeper', 139, 176
Belief
  computational model of, 57
  de re, 17–23, 141–144
  hierarchy of belief predicates, 91–92
  under a mode of presentation, 143–144
  special problems about, 57, 89

Belief/desire explanation of behavior,
  54–56, 158–160
'Believes that' as a syntactic unit, 147,
  179–180
Belnap, N. D., Jr., 147, 168, 186
Bennett, J. F., 158, 180
Bigelow, J. C., 4
  (1975), 152, 180, 184
  (1978), 137, 177
  (1981), 164
Binding of variables, 100–101
Boër, S. E.
  (1975), 153
  (1978a), 153, 177
  (1978b), 177, 186
  (1979), 185
  (forthcoming), 143, 149, 155, 161
  and Edelstein (1979), 139, 177
  and Lycan (1980), 183
Bonotto, C., 177
Bradley, R. D., 167
Bresnan, J. W., 146
Bressan, A., 177
Burdick, H. R., 143–144
Burge, T., 150, 151, 153, 156, 159
'by mistake', 134
By-phrases, 80, 134–135, 185

Camp, J. L., 147
Carlson, G. N., 122, 178
Carnap, R., 70, 77, 165
Castañeda, H.-N., 124, 182
Categorial language, 96–97
Category
  semantic, 69
  syntactic, 95–96

Causal theory of reference, 149
Character, 155, 165–166
Characteristic function, 63
Chisholm, R. M., 182
Church, A., 91, 148
Churchland, P. M., 55
Churchland, P. S., 55
Cognitive science, 129
Cohen, L. J., 108, 180–181
Collins, A. W., 157, 159
Common nouns, 98
Complement (of a set of worlds), 72
Complement sentence, 14
Compositionality, 10, 138–139
  functional, 25–28
Computable function, 62
Computational models of the mental
  life, 17, 55, 57, 157
Computational sciences, 58
Connecticate, 179
Content of an attitude, 55, 157–160
  and character, 155, 165–166
  and content*, 141–142
Context of use, 100, 124–128, 169, 184
Contradictory *de re* beliefs, 21–22,
  143–144
Contrastive stress, 134, 185
Conventionality of language, 9, 138
Cresswell, M. J.
  (1973a), 29, 98, 126, 146, 162, 164, 167,
    168, 175, 176, 177, 180, 184
  (1973b), 162
  (1975), 90, 176
  (1977), 177
  (1978a), 177
  (1978b), 145, 158, 164
  (1978c), 164
  (1980), 148
  (1982), 57, 58, 129, 157, 176
  (1983), 132, 185
  and von Stechow (1982), 18, 140, 144

D_σ, 69, 99
D_0, 69, 100, 125
D_1, 69, 99
Davidson, D.
  (1967a), 137
  (1967b), 174, 179
  (1969), 5, 137–139, 147, 161, 179
De dicto attitudes, 19–20, 46

Deducing, 78–79, 171–172
"Deep" structure, 98, 105
De expressione attitudes, 46–50, 149, 151,
  156
Defined function, for a given argument,
  61
Definite descriptions, 140
  in a categorical language, 98
  and *de dicto* attitudes, 19–20, 149
  names as, 47–48, 150–154
  rigidization, 154–155
Definitions, 81, 176
Dennett, D. C., 185
Denotation, 165
De nunc attitudes, 124
De re attitudes, 18, 25, 110
  belief, 21–23, 140–141, 158–159
Description theory of names, 47–48,
  149–153. *See also* Definite
  descriptions
De se attitudes, 121–126, 182–183
Devil's tuning fork, 133
Devitt, M., 143, 144, 152–153, 182
Direct discourse, 41, 115–117
Domain of a function, 61
Donnellan, K. S., 149, 182
Double indexing, 154, 165–166
Dowty, D. R., 176, 177, 178, 182
Dretske, F. I., 134, 163, 185
Dummett, M. A. E., 163

Edelstein, R., 139, 177
Edmonson, J. A., 177
Empirical predicates, 64–67
Enç, B., 175
Entailment, 163–164
Escher, M. C., 132–134
Evans, G., 179
Events, 173–174
Extension, 70, 165

F_σ, 100
false, 109
Fictional entities, 142–143
Field, H. H., 139, 158, 163, 167, 184–185
Finite set, 82, 176
Focus, 80, 134
Fodor, J. A.
  (1975), 17, 128, 140, 157, 160, 163, 176
  (1981), 53–56, 157–160, 162
  (1982), 157, 165, 166

Fraassen, B. C. van, 141, 148, 155
Frege, G., 26, 70, 72, 91, 151
  (1892), 147
  (1918), 157
Frege's principle, 138
Function, 61–62
  arithmetical, 11
  computable, 62
  functional compositionality, 25–28
Functor, 85, 96, 98

Geach, P. T., 42, 119, 143, 182
Gödel's theorem, 39
Grabski, M., 148
Grice, H. P., 158, 180
Grover, D. L., 147

Halmos, P. R., 161
Harman, G., 145, 160, 184
*he**, 125, 182
Heavens, 167
Heidelberger, H., 144
Heijenoort, J. van, 147
Hendrix, G. G., 57–59, 129
Heny, F., 144
Hermes, H., 162
Hesperus, 20, 44–49, 149–151
Higginbotham, J., 174
Hill, C. S., 143, 147, 175
Hintikka, K. J. J., 40
  (1962), 148, 182
  (1966), 182
  (1969), 148, 168, 170
  (1970), 185
  (1975a), 146, 148, 185
  (1975b), 168
  (1982), 138
Historical theory of reference, 149
Hornsby, J., 153
Howell, R., 185, 186
Humberstone, I. L., 178
Hyperintensional propositions, 72–74,
  166–167

'I' (personal pronoun), 123, 125–126
Identity, 18, 19, 28
if, 135, 186
Impossible pictures, 131–134
Impossible worlds, 74–75
Indirect discourse, 41–45, 53–55, 73–74,
  105–127

Inductive set, 82, 176
Intension, 69–70, 72, 73, 101, 165
Intensional isomorphism, 77
Intensional logic, 98, 177
Intention-based semantics, 145, 159
Internal representations, 12, 53–57,
  128–129, 160, 184–185
Intersection, 72–73
Intervals, 100, 177–178
Intransitive verbs, 98
I(*p*), 73
*it**, 124
Iterated attitudes, 85, 176–177

Johnson-Laird, P. N., 138

Kamp, J. A. W., 154
Kant, I., 10
Kaplan, D., 123
  (1969), 141, 144
  (1978), 40, 154
  (1979), 155, 183
Kaplan's pants, 123, 127, 183
Katz, F. M., 146
Katz, J. J., 27–28, 160, 179
  (1972), 145, 164, 176
  (1982), 145, 146
  Katz and Katz (1977), 146
Keenan, E. L., 135, 185
Klein, E., 39, 144, 146, 178
Kneale, M., 147, 165
Kneale, W. C., 147, 165
Knowledge of truth conditions, 27, 145
Kraut, R., 143
Kripke, S. A., 28, 70
  (1959), 167
  (1972), 149–152, 165, 182
  (1975), 176
  (1977), 154
  (1979), 141–142, 150–152, 155–156
Kroon, F. W., 140

ℒ (language), 42–43, 59, 100, 106
Lakoff, G., 176, 183
λ-abstraction, 97, 101, 179
λ-categorial language, 95–97, 177
  meaning assignment for, 100–101
Language of thought, 53, 160
Learning by ostension, 63
Levin, H. D., 177

Lewis, D. K.
  (1970), 154
  (1972), 58, 77, 100, 146, 158, 166, 169, 177, 180
  (1973), 167
  (1975), 158, 180
  (1979a), 121, 182
  (1979b), 127, 152
  (1981), 142
  (1983), 143
Lexical decomposition, 81–82, 146, 176
Liar paradox, 108–110, 180–181
Loar, B., 150
Lycan, W. G., 66, 155, 162, 183, 186

McCawley, J. D., 176
McDowell, J., 179
McGinn, C., 150, 159, 160, 182
Machina, K. F., 138
Macrostructure constraint, 80, 83, 87, 91
Martin, R. L., 108, 180
Mathematics, 81–83, 139
Meaning assignment, V, 42–43, 100
Meaning postulates, 163
Media prepositions, 131
Methodological solipsism, 159, 165–166
Modal objection to the description
  theory of proper names, 47, 150, 155
Mode of presentation, 143–144
Montague, R. M., 40, 70, 72, 98, 146, 147, 148, 155, 165, 169, 177, 178, 179
Montague Grammar, 72, 95, 146, 166, 175, 177–178, 180
Moore, R. C., 57–59, 129

Naked infinitives, 172–174
Names, 29–30, 86
  and descriptions, 44–49, 149–153
  in λ-categorial languages, 96, 99
  and nominals, 98, 180
  vivid names, 141, 144
Narrow scope of a description, 140
Negation, 72–75, 85–89
Nominal, 29, 98, 113–114
Nominal description theory of names, 150
not, 86, 96, 98
Noun phrase, (NP), 29, 98, 146
Nute, D., 152

Object of an attitude, 53–54
  distinguished from content, 55, 157–160
$\omega(a)$, 67, 69–70, 101
$\omega(a_1,\ldots,a_n)$, 99
ω_{not}, 86
ω_{sings}, 86
One-place function, 62
One-to-one function, 62
Ontology, 9, 65, 72, 99, 164
Ortcutt, B. J., 21–23, 144, 160
Ostension, 63
Over, D. E., 152

Pants on fire, 123
Paradoxes, 36–40, 108–110, 176–177, 180–181
Parsons, T., 164
Partee, B. H.
  (1973), 43, 137
  (1976), 178
  (1979), 57
  (1982), 115, 145, 153
  (1983), 138
Passives, 80, 134–135, 185
Pelletier, F. J., 145
Pendlebury, M., 143
Perceptual predicates, 64–65
Perry, J., 168–175, 183
Peters, P. S., 157, 178
Phosphorus, 20, 44–49, 149–151, 153
Physicalism, 163
Physical theory, 66, 162
Pictures, 131–134, 185
Pierre, 141–143, 151, 155
Plantinga, A., 167, 168
Platonism, 164
Possibilities, 178
Possible worlds, 64, 100, 162, 167, 174
Possible-worlds semantics, 3–4
  vitality of, 179
Predicates, 63, 67
  names as, 153
Prepositions, 98, 131–134
Prior, A. N., 108, 110, 146–147
Pronouns of laziness, 119
Properties, 67, 167, 182–183
Propositional attitudes
  general recipe for, 128–129
  problem of, 4
  sentences of, 14, 139

Propositional calculus, 95–96
Propositions
  hyperintensional propositions, 72–74
  sets of worlds, 67
  sets of world-time pairs, 100
Putnam, H., 70–71, 159, 160, 162, 165–166

$\langle qu, \alpha \rangle$, 103, 116–117
$\langle qu^*, \alpha \rangle$, 103, 117–118
Quantifying in, 110–111, 181–182
Quine, W. V. O., 21, 118, 161, 162, 163
Quotation, 103–104, 115–119, 180
Quotational theories of propositional attitudes, 41–45, 148–149

Range of a function, 61
Rantala, V., 168
Recursive function theory, 162
Reddam, J. P., 141
Reeves, A. L., 140
Reference of an expression, 26–31, 70, 86–87, 165
'Relevance' logic, 168, 175, 186
Representations, 12, 53–57, 128–129, 157–160, 184–185
  semantic representation, 98
Rescher, N., 166–167
Rigid descriptions, 48, 154–155
Ross, J., 131, 185
Routley, F. R., 164, 168
Russell, B. A. W., 20, 47, 140, 151
Ruttenberg, J., 177
Ryle, G., 67

Saarinen, E., 143, 145, 157
Salience, 152
says. *See* indirect discourse; V(*says*)
Schiffer, S., 143, 145, 159, 180
Scope (of a description), 140
Scott, D. S., 177
Searle, J. R., 145
Segerberg, K., 154
Semantic category, 69, 164
Semantic paradoxes, 36–40, 108–110, 176–177, 180–181
Semantic prepositions, 131–134
Semantic representation, language of, 98
Semantics, autonomy of, 129
Semantic syntax, 139

Sense of an expression, 26, 28, 30, 70, 86–90, 165
Sentence, as a syntactic category, 95
Set theory, 72, 161–162, 164, 176
Sharvy, R., 140
Signal, railway, 80–81
Simple predicates, 64–65
Situations, 162, 167–169
  situation semantics, 168–175
Skyrms, B., 148
Sober, E., 185
Stalnaker, R. C., 139, 154, 155, 183
Stechow, A. von, 46, 149
  (1981a), 169, 184
  (1981b), 80, 134
  (1982), 140, 183
  Cresswell and von Stechow (1982), 18, 140, 144, 182
Surface realization, 115
Suspension of judgment, 144
Swatz, N., 167
Synonymy, 42–43, 59, 106, 148, 161, 163

Taski, A., 40, 137
$(\tau/\sigma_1,...,\sigma_n)$, 69, 96
Taylor, B., 177, 178, 179
Technical discourse, 81–83
'that', 29–31
  ambiguity of, 35–36
  that-clause, 14, 30, 87–91, 101–102, 111, 146–147
  $that_0$, 37–38, 40, 87–91, 102, 105, 111–112, 121, 124
  $that_s$, 37–38
  $that_{((0/0),0)}$, 88
  $that_{((0/0),(0/1),1)}$, 88
  $that_{((0/1,1),1,1)}$, 90
  $that_{((0/1)1)}$, 102, 113–114
  $that_{((0/\sigma_1,...,\sigma_n)\sigma_1,...,\sigma_n)}$, 102
Things, 69, 99, 164
Thomason, R. H., 39–40, 73, 146, 148, 166
Tichý, P., 182
Time interval, 100, 177–178
Token physicalism, 163
Topic and focus, 80, 134
Transitive verbs, 98
Translation argument, 148
'true', 36–40
  true in a world, 72
Truth conditions, 3, 27, 145

Turing machines, 12–13, 162, 184
Turner, R., 177
Twin-Earth, 71, 165–166
Tye, M., 150

Undefined function, for a given
  argument, 61
Urn models, 168, 175

V, meaning assignment, 42–43, 59, 100,
  106
Vagueness, 5, 138
Value of a function, 61
Value assignment to variables, 101
Variable, 100–101
Vendler, Z., 146
Verbs, 98
Verificationism, 67, 162
Vivid name, 141, 144
Vlach, F., 154, 174
V(*says*), 106, 113, 116
V(*that$_0$*), 105
V$_{v}$, 101, 111

$\langle w,t \rangle$, 100
$\langle w,t,p \rangle$, 125
Wall, R. E., 178
Wallace, J., 179
Water, 71, 165–166
what, 109, 135
Wheeler, S. C., III, 179
whether, 135
wide scope of a description, 45, 140
Winograd, T., 157
witches, 143
Wittgenstein, L., 3, 63, 137, 162, 167
World. *See also* Possible worlds
  impossible worlds, 74–75

X$_{\sigma}$, 100
XYZ, 71, 165–166

you, 127

Zalta, E. N., 164
0,1,(0/1),... etc.
  as semantic categories, 69
  as syntactic categories, 95–100
Ziff, P., 150